From Death to Rebirth

Ritual and Conversion in Antiquity

Thomas M. Finn

Paulist Press ◆ New York ◆ Mahwah, N.J.

The Publisher gratefully acknowledges the use of the following. Excerpts from *Augustine: Confessions,* edited by James J. O'Donnell. Copyright 1992. Reprinted by permission of Oxford University Press. Excerpts from *The Babylonian Talmud: Seder Nashim, Yebamot I,* edited by I. Epstein. Copyright 1936. Reprinted by permission of The Soncino Press. Reprinted by permission of the publishers and the Loeb Classical Library, excerpts from *Apuleius: The Metamorphoses* (vols. 1 & 2), edited and translated by J. Arthur Hanson, Cambridge, Mass.: Harvard University Press, 1989.

Cover design by Stuart Simons

Book design by Theresa M. Sparacio

Library of Congress Cataloging-in-Publication Data

Finn, Thomas M. (Thomas Macy), 1927–
    From death to rebirth : ritual and conversion in antiquity / Thomas M. Finn.
        p.   cm.
    Includes bibliographical references and index.
    ISBN 0-8091-3689-9 (alk. paper)
    1. Conversion—Comparative studies. 2. Conversion—History of doctrines—Early church, ca. 30–600. 3. Proselytes and proselytizing, Jewish. 4. Rome—Religion. I. Title.
BL805.F56 1997
291.4′2—dc21   97-1341
                                                                                        CIP

Published by Paulist Press
997 Macarthur Boulevard
Mahwah, New Jersey 07430

Printed and bound in the
United States of America

CONTENTS

PREFACE

Every book has a personal history. This book started out in winter 1991 as a history of the catechumenate. The inspiration came from my colleague, Professor Thomas Halton of Catholic University. I had just finished two volumes on early Christian baptism and the catechumenate for a series that he edits, The Message of the Fathers of the Church (Liturgical Press, a Michael Glazier book, vols. 5, 6). He remarked that students of the history, literature, and thought of the early church—a discipline called patristics—needed a documentary history of the catechumenate as it developed in the East and West.

I had hardly left port for the ancient Mediterranean world to start the project before I realized that my real interest was the process of conversion in antiquity, which I suspected was a ritual process for religions other than Christianity. My first task, based on the conviction that modernity and antiquity had light to shed on conversion, was to acquaint myself with modern research on conversion. My next task was to study conversion in postexilic Judaism; it was followed by a study of the Pagan religions of the Greco-Roman world. Only then was I in a position to understand and present conversion in early Christianity.

That was five years ago. Without the help of four institutions and a number of colleagues, I would still be wandering, a new Odysseus, across the dark blue sea of the Mediterranean for another five years. Perhaps I might never have made landfall.

The first institution is the College of William and Mary. I have been privileged to teach for more than two decades in a college whose highest priority is effective, scholarly teaching. To match its insistence that effective undergraduate teaching requires continuing scholarship, the College encourages its faculty to compete for generous research assignments and summer grants. Two College research leaves and a summer research grant made this book possible, and the holdings of the Earl Gregg Swem Library, its library carrels, and its uniformly competent library staff facilitated its completion. That it is a book rather than an aggregation of chapters, that the chapters are written in clear, expository English, and that the chapters on Judaism are well informed is due to my William and Mary colleague in the Religion Department, Professor Dvora Weisberg, whose scholarly field is rabbinics. Without her perceptive editorial eye, steady editorial hand, and fine critical sense, this book would be much less of a book. That I was able to produce a manuscript for publication at all is due to the long-standing, generous, and unfailingly good-humored computer expertise of the department's assistant, Mrs. Tamara Cooper.

The second institution is the Woodstock Theological Center, with its rich biblical and patristic collection and accomplished staff. The first drafts of the chapters on conversion in antiquity and modernity (1) and on second-temple and rabbinic Judaism (4 and 5) were written there while I was on research leave in 1990–1991.

The third institution to which I have a long-standing debt is the National Endowment for the Humanities, particularly to its summer research and seminar grant programs. The NEH grants prompted me to think in new ways about material with which I was in danger of becoming all too familiar. A seminar on the social world of early Christianity at Yale University (1977) directed by Professor Wayne Meeks inspired me to approach conversion from the perspective of social history. Grants that brought me to the Jewish Theological Seminary in New York to study the foundations of postbiblical Judaism (1980) and to Yeshiva University to explore the Jewish encounter with Hellenism (1981) under the direction of Professor Louis Feldman gave me the impetus I needed for the research reflected in the chapters on Judaism (4 and 5). A third summer seminar on the ancient Roman family at the American Academy at Rome (1991) directed by Professors Richard Saller and John Bodel enabled me to do the basic research for the chapters on conversion in Greco-Roman paganism (2 and 3).

The fourth institution to which I am indebted is the Institute for Ecumenical and Cultural Research at Saint John's Abbey and University, Collegeville, Minnesota. The institute offered me a position as scholar in residence (fall 1995), an exciting place to live, and easy access to the Alcuin Library, with its uniquely rich patristic and liturgical holdings. The chapters on early Christianity (6–9) could not have been written (and rewritten) elsewhere, and certainly not without the interest, patristic background, and unfailing editorial help of its director, Dr. Patrick Henry. The Institute's president, Dr. Kilian McDonnell, O.S.B, whose mastery of the ancient and modern literature on early Christian initiation proved consistently invaluable, read and commented on the chapter on conversion and catechumenate in the first and second Christian centuries (6). In addition, two members of the faculty of Saint John's School of Theology proved generous friends to me and my enterprise. Professor Charles Bobertz and I spent many an hour discussing the applicability of a ritual approach to earliest Christianity and the New Testament. Professor Maxwell E. Johnson kept me from shipwreck on the shoals of the third century with his critique of Chapter 7. His cutting-edge research on third-century Alexandrian liturgical history, coupled with his firsthand knowledge of the most recent research on documents central to my work, made the chapter state of the art.

Two other colleagues have had a hand in the history of this book. The first is Professor Gary Porton of the Program for the Study of Religion at the University of Illinois. His acclaimed work on proselytes and careful reading of the chapters on conversion in ancient Judaism (3 and 4) proved both timely and invaluable for my understanding of conversion and the issues surrounding it.

The second colleague I wish to mention is Rev. Lawrence Boadt, C.S.P., professor of biblical studies at the Washington Theological Union and senior editor of the Paulist Press. The fact that this study has seen the light of published day is due particularly to his patience, expertise in biblical studies, encouragement, and unflustered good sense.

Finally, to the Paulist Fathers, among whom I developed my interest in conversion and studied patristics, I dedicate *From Death to Rebirth: Ritual and Conversion in Antiquity,* especially to the members of the ordination class of 1959.

TMF
College of William and Mary
Williamsburg, Virginia
March 29, 1996

ABBREVIATIONS

AB   *Anchor Bible.* Garden City, New York. Doubleday, 1964–.

ABD   *Anchor Bible Dictionary,* ed. David Noel Freedman et al. New York. Doubleday, 1992.

ACW   Ancient Christian Writers. New York. Westminster, 1946–.

ANF   Ante-Nicene Fathers. Buffalo and New York, 1885–1899.

ANRW   Aufstieg und Niedergang der Römischen Welt, ed. Wolfgang Hess et al. Berlin/New York. Walter de Gruyter, 1970–.

CBQ   *Catholic Biblical Quarterly.* Washington, 1915–.

CCL   Corpus christianorum. Series latina. Turnhout and Paris, 1953–.

CSCO   Corpus scriptorum christianorum orientalium. Paris/Louvain, 1903–.

CSEL   Corpus scriptorum ecclesiasticorum latinorum. Vienna, 1866–.

ECBC 5 T. M. Finn, *Early Christian Baptism and the Catechumenate: West and East Syria.* Collegeville. Liturgical Press (A Michael Glazier Book, Message of the Fathers 5), 1992.

ECBC 6 T. M. Finn, *Early Christian Baptism and the Catechumenate: Italy, North Africa, and Egypt.* Collegeville. Liturgical Press (A Michael Glazier Book, Message of the Fathers 6), 1992.

ER   *Encyclopedia of Religion,* ed. Mircea Eliade. New York. Macmillan Publishing Company, 1987.

FC	Fathers of the Church. Washington, D.C. Catholic University of America Press, 1947–.
FP	Florilegium patristicum, ed. Berhardus Geyer et al. Bonn, 1904–.
GLS	Globe Liturgy Studies. Bramcote, Nottingham, England. Grove Books Limited,1975–.
HTR	*Harvard Theological Review.* Cambridge. Harvard Divinity School, 1907–.
JAAR	*Journal of the American Academy of Religion.* Atlanta, 1932–.
JBL	*Journal of Biblical Literature.* Decatur, 1882–.
JJS	*Journal of Jewish Studies.* 1949–.
JRS	*Journal of Religious Studies.* Sir Wilfrid Laurier University, 1986–.
LNPF	A Select Library of Nicene and Post-Nicene Fathers of the Christian Church. Buffalo and New York, 1886–1900; reprinted: Grand Rapids, 1952–.
Loeb	Loeb Classical Library. London/New York/Cambridge. William Heinemann Ltd./ G. P. Putnam's Sons/ Harvard University Press, 1900–.
LQF	Liturgiewissenschaftliche Quellen und Forschungen, ed. P. Mohlberg et al. Münster, 1939–.
NTS	*New Testament Studies.* Cambridge University Press, 1954–.
PG	J. Migne, Patrologia graeca. Paris, 1886–.
PL	J. Migne, Patrologia latina. Paris, 1844–.
RSR	*Religious Studies Review.* Atlanta. Scholars Press, 1974–.
SC	Sources chrétiennes. Paris. Editions du Cerf, 1941–.
SCA	Studies in Christian Antiquity, ed. Johannes Quasten. Washington, D.C. Catholic University of American Press, 1941–.
SL	*Studia Liturgica.* 1970–.
SP	*Studia Patristica.* Papers Presented to the International Conferences on Patristic Studies. Berlin, 1957–.
SPCK	Society for Promoting Christian Knowledge. London.
ST	*Studia Theologica.* Oslo. Scandinavian University Press, 1946–.
TDNT	*Theological Dictionary of the New Testament,* ed. Gerhard Kittel. Grand Rapids. Eerdmans, 1968.
VC	*Vigiliae Christianae.* Leiden. E. J. Brill, 1946–.

INTRODUCTION

This book is about religious conversion in the Greco-Roman world, the same world that gave the West the terms conversion and religion. Politically, it was a world constructed by conquest. The conquests of Alexander the Great (336–323 B.C.E.) made it a Greek world, and the conquests of Rome (212 B.C.E.–356 C.E.), a Roman world, one that stretched from Britain to the Euphrates. Geographically, this Greek and Roman world centered on the Mediterranean, which the Greeks scoured in sleek black ships and the Romans called "our lake" *(mare nostrum).*

I. A Greco-Roman World

What made this Mediterranean world Greco-Roman, however, was culture.[1] With the foundation of Cumae (near Naples) in 750 B.C.E.,[2] Greek culture was in a position gradually to transform Roman culture, particularly in southern Italy and Sicily. Indeed, the region was soon known as *Magna Graecia,* because of its numerous and famous Greek colonies. The transformation accelerated when Alexander and his successors aggressively implemented a policy of Hellenizing the eastern Mediterranean world. The transformation was completed when Rome, once it was established as the power in the western Mediterranean (201 B.C.E.), looked east. Within thirty-five years, she dominated Greece, and, eventually, the entire Mediterranean world.

Although conqueror of the Greek heartland, Rome was herself conquered by Hellenic culture. Romans had never been out of touch with the Greek world, and few of the well-off could resist the attractions of civilized Greek life. Roman gods and goddesses were identified with

7

Greek deities. Greek comedy and tragedy, bilingual education, and Greek art and architecture transformed upper-class life and soon trickled down to the lower classes. The exchange, of course, was two-way; Roman law, statecraft, and administration had their own transforming effect on Greek urban life. Indeed, by the first century C.E. the Mediterranean world had two capitals, Alexandria, the cultural capital, and Rome, the administrative.

Thus, a "Greco-Roman" world. It would last intact (relatively) until the Lombards settled in Northern Italy in 568 C.E., and Islam tore away North Africa, Egypt, Palestine, and East Syria in the next century. But our immediate concern is with conversion in Greco-Roman religions.

II. Culture, Religion, and Conversion in the Greco-Roman World

In Greco-Roman antiquity, culture and religion were inseparable, so much so that worship and culture were interchangeable. Indeed, the word *culture* derives from the word *colere* ("to labor at" or "cultivate") and denotes a worshiper *(cultor)*; similarly, *worship* derives from *cultus* ("tending" or "caring for"). How people tended divinity was the wellspring of ancient culture. The appurtenances of culture—art, architecture, dance, drama, literature, music—were works of worship. Like religion and culture, art and the sacred were inseparable.

Religion and worship were also interchangeable. Classical Hebrew, Greek, and Latin have no word for religion; the closest they come is "piety" or "dutiful reverence" (*eusebia,* Greek; *pietas,* Latin) or the "observance" of the Torah (*dat,* Hebrew). The emphasis is on doing. According to Cicero, the religious person is one who dutifully follows inherited ritual.[3] Late Latin acquired a term for religion—*religio,* a word of uncertain derivation—and Augustine attempted a definition: "Religion offers concern and veneration to a certain higher nature, which people call divine."[4] Cicero and Augustine are both faithful witnesses to the religions of their world; religion is the traditional way of offering dutiful reverence to divinity.

The heart of the matter was ritual: the kind and content of religious observances properly performed *(ritus)*. The culture of the Greco-Roman world was a ritual culture, one that knew, understood, performed, and even abused its rites. Thanks to our Western Enlightenment heritage and some contemporary religious attitudes, "cult" is a term of opprobrium. But that was not always the case. As will be clear, one can speak beneficently about the cults of the Greco-Roman world, yet I prefer to speak of its religions, that is, its three ways of worship: Pagan, Jewish, and Christian.

Conversion was part and parcel of religion, because, like moderns, the ancients changed their ways of worshiping. Sometimes the change referred to conversion within a religion. A person might change the degree of care with which he or she worshiped, a change from lax and formal to intense and personal. From nominal Paganism, for instance, a Pagan might become a devotee of a goddess like Isis and a member of her community. A Jew might become more observant by joining the Jewish sectaries at Qumran, or like Josephus, the Jewish historian (37–100 C.E.), by joining the Pharisees. A Christian might become more devout and dedicated by joining an ascetic or a Gnostic community. Sometimes the change might involve crossing religious boundaries. A pagan might become a Jew, or a Jew, a Christian, or a Christian, a devotee of Mithra. The evidence of conversion in ancient Paganism, Judaism, and Christianity is extensive.

III. Method and Procedure

In exploring conversion in Greco-Roman antiquity, this book attempts to answer two questions: What constituted conversion? and what was the process? Despite the persistent image of conversion as a sudden and dramatic change, the ancient evidence, as will be clear, confirms what modern social scientific research indicates, namely, that it was an extended social, psychological, and religious process that led to personal transformation.

Beyond confirmation, the evidence reveals a dimension of conversion not well understood in our day, a dimension that constitutes the thesis of this book: Conversion in Greco-Roman religion, whether Pagan, Jewish, or Christian, was an extended ritual process that combined teaching and symbolic enactment—the cognitive and the performative—and yielded commitment and transformation.

To give an account of the what and how of conversion in the Mediterranean world is an adventure in history. Although the task is largely textual and archaeological, it is neither archival nor dull. Where the evidence permits—and it often does—I have adopted direct narrative, using the historical present and real people. Where analysis is called for, I have availed myself of modern and contemporary studies in ancient history, ritual, sociology, psychology, and anthropology. To understand and interpret the conversion process in antiquity requires that one see the process in its social setting, which calls for social analysis. I am all too aware, however, of the chasm of time, space, culture, and language that yawns between modernity and antiquity. In an enterprise like this, the danger always lurks of imposing Western and late-twentieth-century perspectives on conversion in Greco-Roman antiquity. Let the reader beware. Nonetheless, the risk is worth taking, for ancient and contemporary men and women are not species alien to each other. In my attempt to reconstruct and interpret conversion in ancient Paganism, Judaism, and Christianity for myself and for the reader, I have found the work of social psychologists of religion, like Peter Berger, and symbolic anthropologists, like Victor Turner, helpful in understanding how people build worlds of transcendent meaning and perform in them.

Religion and Conversion

The first chapter—Conversion: The Lineage of a Word—is devoted to a study of the terminology of conversion in its classical and biblical settings. I describe what the term meant in the Greco-Roman Pagan and biblical religions. I also consider what current historical and social scientific research has to say about conversion, about which I would like to give a word of explanation.

The modern research with which I am concerned was launched by William James at the turn of the century (1902) in the wake of the Second Great Awakening. Several decades later (1933), his Harvard colleague, Arthur Darby Nock, published his classical study of conversion from Alexander the Great (d. 323 B.C.E.) to Augustine of Hippo (d. 430 C.E.).[5]

Contemporary research in the social sciences, ancient history, and ancient religions came to the fore after the Second World War and continues to provide much new and fruitful information and discoveries for students of conversion. Like Nock, who availed himself of the analytic work of James and others, the later chapters of this book bring to bear the perspectives of many scholars and disciplines on the study of conversion in antiquity.

There are, as I have suggested, problems with reading the past through lenses ground by modern research. Let one example suffice. Since religion and conversion are inextricably bound together, how one views religion affects how one views conversion. Arthur Darby Nock, for instance, saw two kinds of religion in the Greco-Roman world. The first is traditional, part of an inherited scheme of life. It has for the traditionalist, he writes,

> the emotional value attaching to a thing in which he has grown up, often intensified by the solemnity of the puberty ceremonies in which he has heard the weightier matters of the law.[6]

Traditional religion is a system of observances characteristic of a self-enclosed social unit, conditioned by elementary needs, and without interest in, or important contacts with, superior religions. The essential element, for Nock, is practice, without any pervasive ideal of holiness other than that sanctioned by custom. As a result, there is no religious frontier to cross in traditional religion, no crisis of identity, no choice between two different views and ways of life, nor any sense that one is right and the other wrong. He found no evidence for conversion in traditional Pagan religions.

The second type is prophetic religion, in which, according to Nock, a person

> experiences a sudden and profound dissatisfaction with things as they are, is fired with a new idea, and launches out on a new path in a sincere conviction that he has been led by something external and objective.[7]

In prophetic religion the individual is faced with a choice that means the renunciation of her or his past and entry into a religious world wholly other than the one she or he has known. True religion is prophetic, and only the person who embraces it can be a true convert. In such a view, conversion to and within inherited religions is ruled out; only conversion to or within Judaism and Christianity, the two prophetic religions of the Mediterranean world, counts.

Although there is much in the ancient data to support Nock's concept of traditional religion, the academic study of religion of the past several decades commends a different understanding of what constitutes religion. As William James saw long ago, religion is universal among humans, diverse rather than uniform, and points to a transcendent world unlike the world perceived by the senses. His view accords with Augustine's view that religion offers concern and veneration to a higher nature that people call divine. It also accords with the following contemporary working definition that informs my study of Greco-Roman religion: "Religion is that system of activities and beliefs directed toward that which is perceived to be of sacred value and transforming power."[8] The advantage of religion defined according to James, Augustine, and academic study is that it allows for the possibility of conversion both to and within Paganism as well as to and within Judaism and Christianity.

Paganism

The second and third chapters concentrate on Paganism. The second identifies characteristics of Paganism that modern and contemporary studies of the religions of the Mediterranean world have brought to light. I found such a chapter necessary because, like cult, Pagan has become a word of opprobrium. The reason can be found in antiquity, namely, in the unremitting Jewish and Christian attacks on Paganism as idolatry and, therefore, false religion. The chapter is devoted to understanding Pagans as religious people quite capable of conversion.

The third chapter studies two religious communities that exemplify religion as a system of activities and beliefs directed toward that which is seen to be of sacred value and transforming power. The first community is the mystery religion of Isis, and the subject for direct narration, Lucius. The source is the celebrated *Metamorphoses* of Apuleius of Madauros, a work known to Augustine of Hippo. The second is a community of Neopythagoreans described by the philosopher Iamblichus in his *Pythagorean Way of Life*. Both religious communities exhibit an exacting process for entry that combines theological instruction with the performance of a complex symbolic enactment that results in the transforming union with the sacred. They function as living models of both religion and conversion in Greco-Roman antiquity.

Judaism

Early Judaism, usually called second-temple Judaism, is the subject of the fourth chapter (539 B.C.E.–70 C.E.). Conversion to Israel before the Babylonian exile (597/587 B.C.E.) was not possible; entry into the covenanted people of God was only by birth. When the exiles returned from Babylonia (beginning in 539 B.C.E.) and built the second temple, a shift in Israelite identity from ethnicity to religion occurred; a Gentile could become a Jew. The story of Izates in the Book of Judith records how. But a number of issues arise and must be considered, among them, whether circumcision was a uniform requirement for male proselytes, who was attracted to Judaism and why, the status of the proselyte in Israel, and whether there was a theology of mission and a mission program.

The return from exile also gave rise to sectarianism, disclosing many forms of early Judaism and the possibility of conversion within Judaism. Two sectarian groups stand out as representative of conversion to the true Judaism, the sectaries of Qumran and the disciples of John the Baptist. The *Community Rule* and the *Damascus Document* of the Dead Sea Scrolls recount conversion at Qumran, and the New Testament gospels, conversion to the Johannites.

Conversion in the rabbinic period (70–500 C.E.) is the subject of the fifth chapter. Set against the background of sectarians, the rise of the Pharisees, the succession of the rabbis, and the development of Mishnah and Talmud, two processes occupy center stage. The first was normative for Palestine and the diaspora: the conversion process detailed in the Babylonian Talmud. Attending the account are discussions of the attraction of Judaism, the criteria for conversion, the screening of candidates, and the ritual process. The second was an alternative process, suggesting that there was some diversity in the way one became a Jew, at least in the diaspora. The subject is the conversion of a remarkable Gentile Egyptian woman, Asenath, recounted in the celebrated romance, *Joseph and Asenath.*

Christianity

From its beginnings in the Johannite movement, Christianity was a missionary movement; Christian communities were communities of converts from the start. In the course of the first four centuries they developed diverse processes of conversion.

A. THE FIRST TWO CENTURIES

The sixth chapter studies the chronological development of how one became a Christian in the apostolic and postapostolic period. The first section explores a series of problems in Christian origins, among them, (1) John the Baptist and conversion, (2) John, Jesus and the

Johannites, (3) the origin of Christian baptism, (4) baptism in the name of Jesus and in the Spirit, and (5) preaching, teaching, and conversion.

The second section traces the development of the Christian process of conversion—the catechumenate—through the end of the second century. Conversion literature and central figures permit direct narrative: the *Didache,* the Pseudo-Clementine *Recognitions,* Justin Martyr and the *Dialogue with Trypho* and *First Apology,* and Clement and the School of Alexandria.

B. THE THIRD CENTURY

Chapter 7 studies the century critical to the form and shape of the catechumenate in its diversity across the Mediterranean world from Rome to East Syria. Several documents and figures permit direct narration of third-century Christian conversion, among them *Apostolic Tradition* (conversion in Rome), Origen's homilies on the Gospel of Luke and Exodus, Gregory the Wonderworker's *Panegyric to Origen* (Alexandria and Caesarea), Tertullian's treatise *On Baptism* (North Africa), and the *Teaching of the Twelve Holy Apostles and Disciples of Our Savior* (*Didascalia;* West Syria). Two documents only recently recovered permit a description of conversion in East Syria, *Gospel of Philip* and the *Acts of Judas Thomas,* a romance that recounts the conversion of the South Indian royal household.

C. FOURTH-CENTURY JERUSALEM

As an extended, complex, and dramatic ritual process, conversion is nowhere better documented than in fourth-century Jerusalem. An eyewitness account, the *Diary of Egeria,* and the creedal and baptismal homilies of the city's bishop, Cyril, permit the reader to enter into the drama. The background against which conversion in Jerusalem is set contains discussions about (1) the problems of dating and attribution of both documents, (2) the origin and development of the church at Jerusalem, (3) the impact of the Constantinian settlement, (4) the emperor's building program and the holy places, (5) the size and structure of the Jerusalem church, (6) Lent and the catechumenate, (7) the creedal curriculum for instruction, (8) exorcism and the rites of confiding the creed, (9) Holy Week, (10) the Easter Vigil and the rites of baptism, including a theology of ritual, and (11) Easter Week mystagogy and the eucharist.

D. FOURTH-CENTURY MILAN: AMBROSE AND AUGUSTINE

Besides the New Testament, no work has shaped Western thinking about conversion more than the *Confessions* of Augustine of Hippo. Prompted by Augustine himself, people customarily identify the moment of his conversion as the drama in the garden at Milan recounted in the eighth book (8:29). This final chapter, however, locates the moment in the baptismal drama at Milan in April 387 C.E., a drama that begins with Augustine's inscription in the catechumenate as an infant. The last act opens with his enrollment as a catechumen accepted for baptism at the beginning of Lent 387. The chapter sets Augustine's conversion in the context of his life and against the catechumenate and baptismal rites in Milan, as commented on by Ambrose.

Augustine's autobiography of a convert and Ambrose's Lenten and baptismal homilies lead the reader through the process of conversion from beginning to end, establishing conversion in late Western antiquity as a liturgical event, the counterpart of conversion in the Jerusalem of Cyril and Egeria.

Conclusion

The conclusion draws together the findings in each of the chapters to document an extended definition of conversion that at once reflects and modifies the characteristics identified in contemporary social scientific research. Conversion in Greco-Roman antiquity is a complex social, psychological, and religious process that exhibits the following characteristics: (1) a crisis of social and personal identity, (2) a quest for order, purpose, and meaning in life, (3) a stable encounter with the divine within a sacred community, (4) continual cognitive and performative interaction with the community, especially through homiletic instruction and ritual, (5) a clear-cut personal commitment facilitated by cognitive and performative interaction, and (6) transformation of spirit and conduct described in metaphors of rebirth, resurrection, and enlightenment.

Perhaps it is not good strategy to give away the ending at the beginning. In some ways I have written a detective story, more accurately, a mystery. But what happens between the introduction and the conclusion is the thing. The words of children playing recorded by antiquity's quintessential convert suggest the next step: "Pick up and read. Pick up and read" (*Confessions* 8:29).

NOTES

1. For an account the spread of Hellenism, see James D. Newsome, *Greeks, Romans, Jews: Contents of Culture and Belief in the New Testament World* (Philadelphia: Trinity International Press, 1992) 1–32.

2. Through out this study I use B.C.E. to mean "before the common era," which is the common scholarly equivalent of B.C. (before Christ). I use C.E. to mean the "common era," the equivalent of A.D. (in the year of the Lord).

3. Cicero, *De natura deorum academica* 2:28.72 (H. Rackham, ed., *Cicero: De natura deorum academica,* Loeb [1933] 192–93).

4. Augustine, *De diversis questionibus LXXXIII* 31:1 (PL 40:19): *Religio est quae superioris cuiusdam naturae, quam divinam, curam cerimoniamquae affert.* For further references, see the Conclusion, n. 12.

5. See Chapter 1, "VII. A Contemporary Look," and nn. 45–50.

6. Arthur Darby Nock, *Conversion: The Old and the New in Religion from Alexander the Great to Augustine of Hippo* (London: Oxford University Press, 1933) 2.

7. Ibid.

8. The definition captures well the work of Gerardus van der Leeuw, Rudolf Otto, and Mircea Eliade, for whom the contrast between the sacred and the profane is the defining characteristic of religion as it is historically and phenomenologically studied. I owe the definition to my colleague, James C. Livingston, *The Anatomy of the Sacred: An Introduction to Religion,* 2nd ed. (New York: Macmillan, 1993) 11; for a discussion of the academic study of religion, see 3–23.

Chapter 1

CONVERSION: THE LINEAGE OF A WORD

Amazing Grace! How sweet the sound
That saved a wretch like me!
I once was lost, but now am found,
Was blind, but now I see.

This celebrated hymn of John Newton (1725–1807) characterizes conversion for most of the English-speaking world. Newton's lines express a pietism that broke the mold of dogmatic Protestantism in the seventeenth century, underlay the Great Awakening in the United States in the eighteenth, fired the evangelical revival in the nineteenth, and continues to inspire evangelical Christians today. But the experience the hymn evokes is far older than the Reformation tradition of the West.

I. An Overview

Persistence

The persistence of religions—Paganism, Judaism, and Christianity—in Greco-Roman antiquity is astonishing. Pagans struggled first to survive the Christian attack on them as impious and their religion as pernicious, and then to entrench themselves when the Emperor Theodosius made Catholic Christianity the religion of the empire (381 C.E.). Jews, who spread across the entire Mediterranean world, had an even longer history of survival. They had to swim against the powerful currents of Hellenism following the conquests of Alexander the Great (d. 323 B.C.E.), grapple with mounting Roman hostility toward them in the early empire, and surmount the same Theodosian

17

establishment, one that outlawed both Judaism and Paganism. Early Christians remain a persistent puzzle, particularly because of their survival and spread from an obscure Palestinian Jewish sect to the established religion of the Roman Empire in the face of determined imperial attempts to stamp them out.

Were you to ask Christians, Pagans, and Jews how they persisted, they would quite frankly answer that their survival and spread was miraculous proof of God's power and the authenticating mark of their religion's divine origin.[1] In short, they had found and assembled the theological pieces of the historical puzzle. But the puzzle was far from complete.

Late last century other pieces began to turn up, largely through the digging of social scientists and cultural historians.[2] What they found about the survival and spread of Christianity can also be said of both Judaism and Paganism. Prominent among the pieces were Christianity's capacity to adapt to its surroundings, its strong appeal to society's "little people," its ability to secure people against loneliness, and its thorough-going ritual life.

Pieces from the social and cultural setting have been unearthed as well, especially the Roman Empire's precipitous decline, coupled with a growing ferment of new religious feelings; the pervasive sense of uprootedness that engulfed late Roman antiquity; the clash between the Christian sense of community and Roman social and imperial hostility; and careers in civil service, in the army, and in education that gave many Christians access to avenues of geographical and social mobility.

For the word *Christian,* substitute *Jew* or *Pagan* and you will have a fairly complete and reasonably accurate picture of the persistence of ancient Greco-Roman religions.

To sense the fit of these pieces in the Jewish puzzle, one need only think of the way in which the Jews who returned from exile in Babylon began to understand their identity as springing more from religious convictions and practices and less from ethnic origins. Among them was born the Judaism that we must consider in the fourth and fifth chapters. About the fit of the Pagan pieces, one need only think of distinctive forms of personal religion that sprang up under the umbrella of Roman civic religion, especially in the philosophical schools, in the mystery cults, and in devotion to Asclepius—all to be discussed in the second and third chapters.

Conversion

The key piece of the puzzle for ancient Christians, Jews, and Pagans, however, was conversion. All three survived, spread, and flourished because people either intensified their piety or left one religion for another. Many Pagans who were nominally pious became deeply pious. The second-century satirist, Lucian of Samosata (120–180 C.E.), for instance, commented to an interlocutor: "Don't you think it wonderful, in the name of Zeus, that once a slave, I am now free! . . . once witless and befogged, now saner?"[3] This same movement was also reflected in Jewish experience: many intensified their piety, especially in sects like the community at Qumran that produced the Dead Sea Scrolls. That Christians, too, went from nominal to devout was strikingly dramatized by the ascetics of the Egyptian desert.

Some pagans became Jews; even royalty, like the king of Adiabene, converted.[4] Still others became Christians, as the Book of Acts, with its almost two dozen conversion stories, dramatizes, not to mention the apocryphal *Acts* of the apostles.[5]

Traffic went the other way as well. Jews became Pagans, like the assimilationists in Alexandria who started out in the front seat at the synagogue, moved back to the last seat, and finally ended up singing in the Pagan religious processions on the street outside.[6] Others, like Paul of Tarsus, became Christians.

Conversely, Christians became Jews and Pagans.[7] Throughout the first four centuries, Christians found Judaism attractive—sometimes irresistibly so. Community solidarity, synagogue liturgy and the festivals, and obedience to a Torah that illuminated clearly the path to follow were the major attractions.

The lure of Paganism was more complex. Roman religion rooted one in an ancient and venerable tradition. Pagan myth, ritual, and festivals permeated the culture that enveloped the people of the empire. And observance of the rites, customs, and traditions often proved to be a litmus test for proper allegiance to the state, whose welfare depended on the benevolence of the gods.

Unfortunately, the ancients, with their penchant for narration and description, never attempted to define systematically what they meant by conversion. But we are not altogether at sea, for in antiquity a set of Hebrew, Greek, and Latin terms meaning "motion" and "change" appear frequently in ancient texts to designate conversion.[8] They denote a "turning towards, from, away, return. . . . " The Hebrew root is *shub;* the Greek, *[s]trephein;* the Latin, *[con]vertere.* All three point directly to a physical or material move or change, yet indirectly to a change of spirit or mind, specifically to a change of conviction and way of life.

II. A Greek View

Among classical Greeks (500–300 B.C.E.) it was almost second nature to turn one's gaze, fixed on a material object—a tree, for example—to a consideration of what makes an object what is. A shift or turning from the outer to the inner, from the matter at hand to the heart of the matter, a new way of seeing: such was the indirect or metaphorical change *(trephein)* for the Greeks.

But turning was not only an act of mind and attention, for it could have a deep impact on one's life. Plato left his followers in the academy a classic example. In his *Republic,* the philosopher envisions humankind born and raised in a cave. The cave mouth is open toward the sunlight, but people have their necks chained and cannot turn their heads to see outside. For light, they have behind and above them a blazing fire; before them is a wall that serves as a screen. Figures, like marionettes, pass between the fire and the wall, some talking, some silent; the fire casts their shadows on the screen, and shadows are all the prisoners can see.

From the shadows comes a voice, the source of which is hard to find. Eventually, one prisoner is unshackled, told to stand, then to turn, to walk toward the light, and to struggle up and out into the sunlight. Plato concludes his metaphor:

> When he approaches the light his eyes will be dazzled, and he will not be able to see anything at all of what are now called realities. . . . He will need to grow accustomed to the sight of the upper world. And first he will see the shadows best, next the reflections of humans and other objects in the water, and then the objects themselves, then he will gaze upon the light of the moon and the stars and the spangled heaven; and he will see the sky and the stars by night better than the moon or the light of the sun by day. . . . Last of all he will be able to see the sun, and not mere reflections of [the sun] . . . , but he will see him in his own proper place, and not in another; and he will contemplate him as he is. . . . Then if he

recalled his fellow prisoners and what passed for wisdom in his
former dwelling-place, he would surely think himself happy in the
change and be sorry for them. . . . (*Repub.* 7:515–16)[9]

Throughout the passage, Plato makes much use of forms of the
Greek *[s]trephein*. He plants in the idea of conversion a personal
process of turning away from an old mode of seeing and existing to
a new way, a turning from what people evaluate as shadows to what
they understand to be reality. Implicit in the idea is contemplation of
reality itself, an emphasis Plato's distant heir at Rome, Plotinus
(205–270 C.E.), underscores.

For Plotinus, conversion requires a turn from lethargy of the spirit
to the "eye" at the depths of the soul, followed by emergence through
its opening to contemplate the things of the mind, and thus to ascend to
the mind of God. Conversion as a philosophical quest whose goal is
contemplation of real and lasting truth—the divine—left its deep mark
on the meaning of the term *conversion.*[10]

III. A Biblical View

In the Bible, the context is quite different: personal and ethical
rather than philosophical and contemplative. The image is return, reconciliation, and rededication.

A Hebrew View

In its metaphorical sense, the Hebrew term—primarily forms of
shub—addresses the relationship between God and his people, in particular, the people's fidelity and infidelity.[11] As the prophets were accustomed
to put the matter, "From the days of your forefathers you have been way-
ward and have not kept my laws. If you will return to me, I will return to
you, says the Lord of Hosts" (Mal 3:7). The turning here is mutual, and
for Israel, the return to God and to the terms of his covenant is corporate
rather than individual; when "I" is used, it is the collective "I."

At the root of the idea is covenant: first and foremost, Israel was a
people formed by the covenant, which, in turn, grounded and shaped
the people's personal relations with God. The constant prophetic
lament is that Israel is unfaithful to God and to the terms of the
covenant. As a result, infidelity and reconciliation—turning away from
God and turning back—molded the biblical sense of conversion. This

gave rise to a penitential practice of fasting, to prayer, and, eventually, to the rites of the Day of Atonement *(Yom Kippur),* in short, to a rich and well-articulated liturgy that prompted God, who had once freed Israel from Egypt and shepherded the people through the wilderness of Sinai into the Promised Land, to liberate them once again by reconciling them to himself and turning their feet back to the proper path. Conversion in the traditions of Israel was repentance *[teshubah],* which involved the "three r's" of the covenant: return, reconciliation, and rededication. The penitential psalms capture the tradition best, and among them the classic is Psalm 50 (51). Supposedly rooted in David's adultery with Bathsheba (2 Sm 11–12), the text reads:

> Have mercy on me, O God, in your kindness,
>> in your immense compassion delete my rebellious acts.
> Again and again, wash me of my guilt,
>> and of my sin clean me. . . .
> Indeed, I was brought forth in iniquity,
>> and in sin my mother conceived me.
> Since you indeed prefer truth
>> to both cleverness and secret lore,
> Teach me wisdom!
> Unsin me, I'll indeed be purer than gushing water,
> Wash me, and I'll be much whiter than snow.
> Let me hear songs of joy and gladness,
>> the bones you cursed rejoice.
> Turn your face from my sins,
>> and delete all my crimes.
> A clean heart, O God, create in me,
>> and re-create within me a resolute spirit.
> Do not banish me from your presence,
>> nor deprive me of your holy spirit.
> Give me again your saving joy,
>> and by your generous spirit sustain me,
> That I may teach rebels your ways,
>> and sinners to return to you. . . . (Ps 51 [50])[12]

A Greek and Latin View

Greek-speaking Jews translated the Hebrew Bible into their language about 200 B.C.E. (the Septuagint—LXX—a version that they and Christians later adopted as their own and regarded as inspired). The translators chose forms of *[s]trephein,* already stamped with conversion as a philosophical quest, to render the Hebrew *shub.* For instance, in Psalm 51 above, both turnings (vv. 11, 15) are rendered by forms of the Greek verb *(epistrephein).* Subsequently, the early Latin (second century, Christian) versions petition God not to "turn away" *(avertere,* v. 11) and sinners "to convert" *(convertere,* v. 15).[13] In short, translation from Hebrew into Greek and Latin blended the biblical with the Greek and Latin linguistic and cultural traditions about the meaning of conversion. Conversion involved a new way of seeing and living coupled with the repentance, reconciliation, and rededication to God characteristic of biblical penitence. Both aspects, however, emphasized conversion as quest for what is ultimately real and true—the quest for the divine—with this difference: in biblical tradition God takes the initiative.

A Sectarian Jewish View

Encounters between cultures, however, are never neat and complete. When Greek and Hebrew (and, subsequently, Latin) met, another brace of Greek terms, *metanoein/metanoia* (Latin, *paenitere/paenitentia),* appeared that emphasized conversion as repentance. In the Greek and Latin world the terms were rare and meant a change of mind and feelings, remorse for an error or a bad choice, regret for a mistake, but nothing deeper or more permanent. Nonetheless, the translators of the Greek Bible used these terms to emphasize a change that affects the direction, conduct, and shape of one's life—a deep moral and spiritual change. Their full status as synonyms for *[s]trephein,* however, awaited the authors of the inter-testamental literature known as the "apocrypha" and "pseudepigrapha" (200 B.C.E.–200 C.E.).

The author of the intertestamental *Testament of Abraham,* a document that exists in two versions, uses the terms *strephein* and *metanoia* synonymously. In both versions, the archangel Michael, sent by God, comes to notify Abraham that his time to die and to make a will or testament (thus the title) has arrived. Michael escorts the patriarch on a chariot tour of the world. The tour discloses sinners in the act of sinning. Indignant, the righteous Abraham calls for their destruction, which is accomplished immediately. God orders the chariot turned around lest Abraham destroy the whole inhabited world busily sinning! The trouble is that Abraham, as a man without sin, has no empathy for sinners. The moral is that God wants Abraham to see the results of his merciless judgments and repent for the souls he has destroyed. Abraham understands and prays that his victims be returned to life. The longer of the two versions is the more succinct on this point and reads:

> Then the Lord God spoke with Michael saying, "Turn Abraham around *[apostrepson]* to his house and do not let him go around all creation which I made, for he has no mercy upon the sinners, but I have mercy upon the sinners that they may turn *[epistrepsousin]* and live *[zesosin]* and repent *[metanoesosin]* of their sins and be saved *[sothesontai]*.[14]

The turning here is a complex process—to turn toward God, to live, to repent, and to be saved. Such is the process of conversion or *metanoia/teshubah,* at least according to some of the sects in early Judaism. This process is strikingly reflected among the sectaries of Qumran: the members spoke of their community as bearers of the "Covenant of Repentance" *(berith teshuvah).* To turn toward God, to live, to repent, and to be saved describes the conversion of both the candidate entering the covenant and the members of the covenant community from the youngest to the oldest. It is both a process of initial commitment and the renewal of commitment to the community.[15]

IV. A Christian View

Among these Jewish sectarian communities was an obscure group—often called Nazarenes and eventually Christians—who had a distinctive view of the covenant which proved unacceptable to most Jews: it was a new covenant or testament, established in the blood of Jesus of Nazareth. To understand what conversion meant among them one needs to turn in some detail to their principal writings.

The Synoptic Gospels

In the synoptic gospels the language and dynamics of conversion are penitential and prefer the Greek term used among other sects, *metanoia.* From the moment that John the Baptist appears, *metanoia* is the essential condition of entry into the kingdom; the Baptist proclaims a "baptism of repentance" *(baptisma metanoias,* Mk 1:4; also Mt 3:11; Lk 3:3–4). Although John's baptism requires reformation of life and yields forgiveness and readiness for the imminent kingdom of God, the synoptic authors see his baptismal call as anticipatory, preparing the way for Jesus, who actually brings the kingdom. Indeed, Jesus inaugurates the kingdom by receiving John's baptism of repentance, which he later links with his own death (Mk 10:38–39). Paul and his heirs fashioned around this link an influential theology of baptism:

> Have you not forgotten that when we were baptized into union with Christ Jesus we were baptized into his death? By baptism we were buried with him, and lay dead, in order that, as Christ was raised from the dead in the splendor of the Father, so also we might set our feet upon the new path of life. (Rom 6:3–4)[16]

In proclaiming the kingdom, however, the synoptic Jesus joined conversion and belief—belief in the good news that the kingdom has come: "The time has come; the kingdom of God is upon you; repent *[metanoeite]* and believe *[pisteuete]* the gospel" (Mk 1:14; Mt 4:17). This fusion proved important for later generations because faith both as response and as the intellectual content of the response soon entered the world of conversion. Indeed, early Christians, as we will see, eventually fashioned an interrogatory creedal baptismal formula ("Do you believe in God the Father Almighty . . . ? And in his Son . . . ? And in the Holy Spirit . . . ?") and established twin rituals: confiding the baptismal creed to those about to be baptized *(traditio symboli)* and professing it *(redditio symboli)* in the ritual process of conversion.[17] Repentance and faith as response and belief, signified by *metanoia,* entered the cultural and linguistic tradition of conversion.

A Pauline View

In Paul's indisputably authentic letters the conventional terms for conversion seldom appear: sometimes he uses them about others, but never about himself.[18] Indeed, he can even use the conventional *epistrepho* for "backsliding" (Gal 4:9)—turning back. Paul understood conversion primarily as transformation *(metamorphosis)* from one way of being and living to another. To make his understanding clear, he uses some bold images.

One is movement from darkness into light: "For the same God who said, 'Out of darkness let light shine' [Gn 1:3], has caused this light to shine within us, to give the light of revelation—the revelation of the glory of God in the face of Jesus Christ" (2 Cor 4:6). Similarly, for Paul's immediate disciples conversion is delivery from the domain of darkness into "the realm of light" (Col 1:12–13). Conditioned by a

Greco-Roman world in which philosophers and mystery religions held out the promise of enlightenment, and prompted by Paul, other early Christians were persuaded to call baptism "enlightenment": to baptize *(baptizein)* was to enlighten *(photizein),* for baptism was the hinge upon which conversion turned.[19]

A second bold image in Paul is "new creation." He thinks the key to transformation is revelation *(apocalypsis),* specifically, God's revelation in Christ, a revelation that wholly disrupts a person's life.[20] For Paul, the whole of his previous life is the darkness from which he was delivered. Although it was a life in which he faithfully maintained all that pertained to Judaism, he now considers it rubbish (Phil 3:8). For his "converts" it is a life circumscribed by "flesh" *(kata sarka)* and idolatry. For both apostle and disciples the revelation means transformation from death to life "in Christ," that is, to a living bond with the risen Savior rooted in sharing life with him *(koinonia)* in the here and now. Thus, for Paul and his heirs, conversion is an act of God, the heart of which is an organic union with the Christ who had died and is risen. The result is transformation in Christ—one is a new creation:

> So whoever is in Christ is a new creation; old things have passed away; behold, new things have come. And all this is from God, who has reconciled us to himself through Christ and given us the ministry of reconciliation, namely, God was reconciling the world to himself in Christ. (2 Cor 5:17–19)

Whether being led from darkness to light or made into a new creation, conversion in the Pauline view is transformation. Baptism is the "turning point": "Have you forgotten . . . ? By baptism we were buried with him and lay dead, in order that, as Christ was raised from the dead . . . , so we also might set our feet upon the new path of life" (Rom 6:34–35).

A Johannine View

It was not only Paul who emphasized conversion as transformation. In John's gospel, Jesus promises that no follower of his shall wander in the dark but shall have the "light of life" (Jn 8:52)—a transformation that involves the trauma of new birth. To the potential convert Nicodemus, Jesus makes the point unmistakable in a passage that would become the charter for "born again" Christians:

In truth, in very truth I tell you, unless a man be born over again *(gennethe anothen)* he cannot see the kingdom of God . . . no one can enter the kingdom of God without being born from water and the spirit. Flesh can give birth only to flesh; it is spirit that gives birth to spirit." (Jn 3:3–6)

The issue is not simply the renewal or even the reformation of the subject, but a new origin, a birth from "above" that breaks one's ties with "this world" and its evil ways.[21] In 1 Peter, which has much affinity with John, transformation is also rebirth. At the outset the author sets the letter's new-birth theme by linking it with resurrection: "God . . . who according to his great mercy caused us to be born anew *(ana-gennesas)* into a living hope through the resurrection of Jesus Christ from the dead . . . " (1 Pt 1:3).[22] He addresses his audience as "newborn infants," who must crave pure milk to thrive (1 Pt 2:2–3).

Within a hundred years, as we will see, along with the eucharistic wine, the newly baptized are given a cup of milk and honey mixed (normal baby food in antiquity).[23] Nonetheless, other than being passive subjects, their conversion, according to the author, owes nothing to them, for it is God "who has called [them] out of darkness into his marvelous light" (1 Pt 2:9). Again, in neither John nor 1 Peter does one find the traditional terminology about conversion. People are reborn.

Luke's View

The bridge between repentance and transformation is provided by Luke. He prefers repentance terminology, especially *metanoia,* which he expands in his gospel to include joyful reconciliation and forgiveness. The model conversion story in his gospel is the parable of a lost sheep (Lk 15:4–7), in which astonishing, even drastic, measures are taken.[24] The shepherd leaves the ninety-nine in the desert and embarks on a search for one who did not exactly stray but got lost. The shepherd mounts the lost one on his shoulders, then gathers his friends and neighbors to rejoice with him because "I have found my lost sheep" (Lk 15:6). Discovery and joy lighten the somber hues of repentance.

Conversion is the major theme in Luke's second volume, the Acts of the Apostles. Luke weaves twenty-one conversion accounts into his work.[25] He continues to use the language of repentance. The Lucan Paul can sum up his entire apostolic career: "I turned first to the inhabitants of Damascus, and then to Jerusalem and all the country of Judaea, and to the Gentiles, and sounded the call to repent *[metanoein]* and turn to God *[epistrephein]*"—a call that, as we have seen, initiated the process of conversion.[26]

But it is a *process:* one that begins with faith. Indeed, the author has a marked preference for the phrase "to become a believer *[to gegenos episteusen]*," and frequently calls converts believers, whom he had already characterized in his version of the gospel parable of the sower as "those who listen to the word and hold on to it with a noble and generous mind: these yield a crop through their persistence" (Lk 8:15).[27] Although conversion necessarily engages faith both as an act and as content (*the* faith), repentance is indispensable, and forgiveness, which he sometimes equates with salvation, is its first effect. In the conversion of Cornelius, Luke has Peter sum up what appears to be the evangelist's own outlook: "Everyone who believes in him [Jesus] receives forgiveness through his name" (Acts 10:43); and he alters it only slightly in his account of Paul's words to his Philippian jailer: "Believe in the Lord Jesus and you and your household will be saved" (Acts 16:31).

To faith and forgiveness, we must add a third phase of the process, namely, discipleship. Where appropriate, Luke equates convert, believer, and disciple *(mathetês),* clearly portraying the true convert as the believer who has both accepted Jesus' teaching and followed Jesus' way of life and destiny in an intimate and personal way—so much so that, among all the evangelists, Luke alone speaks of Christianity as "the Way."[28]

His persistent appeal is to the imitation of heroic virtue, especially with Christ and Paul as models. Subsequent early Christian writers continued the tradition by insisting that conduct is the mirror of conviction; indeed, from the very earliest catechetical literature on, moral reformation is the litmus test for true conversion.[29]

Luke, however, replaces "to be converted" with "to be baptized" so often that the phrases seem like two sides of the same coin, leading to the fourth phase of conversion, baptism. When Peter's Pentecost audience feels cut to the heart and asks him what they are to do, Peter immediately answers: "Repent and be baptized *[metanoesante kai baptistheto]*" (Acts 2:38). Examples abound, including the account of Philip's converts in Samaria and his Ethiopian convert and the account of Paul's conversion in Ananias' house.[30] Other than repeated insistence on baptism, however, the evangelist tells us almost nothing about the rite, and barely even mentions that Jesus "had been baptized" (Lk 3:22). He simply takes baptism for granted in conversion.

There remains one final part of the process. Full conversion is linked to the gift of the Holy Spirit. It is here especially that Luke builds the bridge between repentance and transformation. To be sure, the relationship between the Spirit and baptism is at best ambiguous in Acts: sometimes the gift comes before the rite, sometimes afterward, even with a considerable lapse of time.[31] Whatever the reason for the ambiguity, the striking effect of the Spirit's descent on the candidate is transformation. As in Luke's gospel, there is a model conversion story—Paul's. On a mission to harass the Christians in Damascus, Paul encounters the risen Jesus and is blinded. When Paul, following instructions, comes to Ananias' house in the city, the prophet assures him that his sight will return and that he will be filled with the Holy Spirit. The scales fall from his eyes, he receives his sight, is baptized, and, full of the Spirit, he inaugurates his mission—a wholly new man (Acts 9:17–19).[32] In the midst of blindness, according to Luke, Paul finally sees.

Transformation from blindness to sight is the Holy Spirit's work. Indeed, the prominence of sudden transformation through the Spirit strongly suggests that the "Spirit encounter" is Luke's preferred model for conversion.[33] But his canvas is far broader than an individual or even a group portrait: Luke depicts conversion as the effect of God's initiative intended as a work of communal witness rather than a work of individual solace.[34]

An Apocryphal View

To this point we have concentrated on conversion in the biblical canon. But just outside the canon stand a series of what might be called romances, the apocryphal *Acts* of the apostles. The *Acts of John, of Peter, of Paul, of Andrew,* and *of Judas Thomas,* the oldest, are particularly interesting because, like Luke's Acts, their narrative thread is conversion. Miracle stories dominate. In the *Acts of Judas Thomas,* for instance, the apostle's allotted mission is India, which he attempts to make Christian by converting its leaders. The work contains thirteen stories, the last recounting the martyrdom of Thomas and the conversion of the king, whose son was healed by "dust of that spot where the bones of the Apostle had laid."[35] Although miracle is central, it is only part of the *Acts'* structure, as is the case with all the apocryphal *Acts:* (1) the preaching of the gospel, (2) the acts and teachings of an apostle, and (3) the apostle's martyrdom. *The Acts of Judas Thomas* emphasizes the liturgy of baptism and the eucharist, as if to say that these rituals are the storehouses of Jesus' and the apostles' miracles. Underlying all the *Acts,* nonetheless, is the conviction that conversion is primarily transformation: death to an old way of living and thinking, and resurrection to a new way centered in a community of believers.[36]

V. Lineage in Review

Change stands at the center of conversion's lineage. In Greek and Latin history the change is from an old way of seeing to a new way— seeing things as they really are and living accordingly. Normally, the shadows are gradually dispersed and the eyes of the mind are opened. Sometimes conversion turned out to be a philosophical quest for the divine, at other times, an encounter with deity shrouded in a religion of mystery.

In its biblical history the change is marked by penitence, repentance from infidelity to God, and reconciliation with him, coupled with rededication to following his will.

Sometimes the change involved changing religions: Jews became Pagans; Pagans, Jews; Pagans and Jews became Christians; and Christians, Pagans or Jews. Sometimes conversion meant becoming more engaged in the values inherent in the religion of one's birth. The sectaries at Qumran went to their desert fastness to find a purer Judaism; the convert to philosophy often sought a more devout and committed Paganism; the Jew who embraced Christianity, like the Essene at Qumran, often acted to achieve faithful observance of the Torah.

Classical and biblical conversion met when the Greek translators of the Bible used the conventional Greek terms for conversion to render the usual Hebrew terms. The encounter was deepened with the rise of Jewish sects like the one at Qumran, which emphasized repentance as a change of mind, thinking, and understanding *(metanoia).* Among the sects, first-century Christians gave conversion a shape that became definitive. Shaped by both the classical and the biblical tradition of conversion as a new way of seeing and as repentance, most Christian writers emphasized conversion as a process of transformation with baptism as the hinge upon which it turned. For them it meant a transforming change of religion, but not something over and done with. Conversion was intended to be ongoing.

VI. Continuing Conversion

This lifelong characteristic of conversion found insistent voice in two Alexandrians. The first, Clement, who taught in the city during the late second century, saw conversion as a lifelong journey of the spirit from the world of too solid flesh to God. From the first stirrings of faith, he argued, the aim of Christian life is to "become God, who divinizes [human beings] by a gradual process of ascent first to faith, then to knowledge, and finally to love."[37] No ordinary undertaking, the journey is an odyssey of transformation that includes liberation from slavery to Satan, passage from darkness to light, the outpouring of God's mercy, baptismal rebirth, membership in God's people, exemption from judgment, and, finally, the transforming acquisition of full knowledge and love.[38]

Clement's image of conversion blended the philosophical quest with the biblical goal of transformation. Origen, his younger contemporary, portrays conversion as a reliving of the Exodus journey, which begins with God's "philanthropy":

> He made one special descent in order to convert *[epistrepsai]* those whom the divine scripture calls the "lost sheep of the house of Israel" [Mt 15:24]; in certain parables [Mt 17:12–13; Lk 15:4–7], the shepherd is said to have come down to them, leaving on the mountains those who had not gone astray.[39]

The strays (viz., all human beings) have so strong a natural tendency to sin that they do so by habit; nevertheless, if they entrust themselves to God and act accordingly, they will, he says, "have undergone so thorough a change *[tes pantalous metaboles]*" that their lives will become "a model of the perfect life."[40] As for the journey itself, it turns on the Exodus from Egypt: the convert abandons Egypt through the Red Sea of baptism, across the Sinai wilderness of life and its testing, passes over the Jordan at life's end, and enters into the celestial Promised Land of Paradise.[41] For those who have not made the journey without straying, there awaits a second baptism, the "baptism of fire" in the Jordan, which will burn away their failures, allowing entry to the ancient garden.[42]

Clement and Origen gathered up all the nuances with which the classical, biblical, and apocryphal traditions invested conversion. To convert means to repent, to believe, to be baptized, to be transformed in spirit, and to make a lifelong journey of ascent to God. The conversion road would bifurcate toward the end of the third century, with one fork coursing through the desert filled with monks and nuns, the other, through what came to be called the catechumenate, the subject of the last three chapters of this study.

VII. A Contemporary Look

Although neither the ancients nor their medieval heirs attempted a systematic definition of conversion, modern religious studies have.[43] William James and fellow psychologists initiated the attempt a hundred years ago in the afterglow of America's Second Great Awakening, led by revivalist Charles Grandison Finney (d. 1875).[44] In his Gifford Lectures of 1902 (subsequently published as a celebrated volume, *The Varieties of Religious Experience*), James devoted two lectures to conversion, which he defined as the process "gradual or sudden, by which a self hitherto divided or consciously wrong, inferior and unhappy becomes unified and consciously right, superior and happy, by consequence of its firmer hold on religious realities."[45] He identified the fundamental psychological characteristics of the process as (1) a severe crisis of conflict, guilt, and other trials ultimately resolved by (2) an intense and sudden transformation. Conversion represented a prime example of the unification of the divided self.[46]

Although James acknowledged the existence of conversion as a gradual process, religion for him was first and foremost an individual experience prior to any rational, intellectual understanding of it—what individuals experience in their "solitude" as they stand in relation to "whatever they consider divine."[47] So also, conversion: it is what individuals experience in their solitude as they encounter the divine in a new way prior to any rational apprehension of it.

A generation later (1933), the historian of religions Arthur Darby Nock studied conversion in Greco-Roman antiquity, using lenses prescribed by James and colleagues.[48] Save for Judaism and Christianity, he found no clear crossing of religious boundaries. The people of antiquity, he concluded, normally did not leave their old spiritual homes for new ones. To be sure, they might readily accept (and sometimes eagerly seek) new forms of worship as supplements, but such acceptance involved neither a crisis nor a new set of convictions nor self-surrender. They continued to adhere to their old gods, even if under new names, with different dress, and in new ways.

As a result, Nock was prompted to distinguish between adhesion, which characterized participation in the traditional religions of Greece and Rome, and what he considered conversion. For him, ancient Judaism and Christianity involved true conversion; both were, in his words, "prophetic" religions that demand a "deliberate turning from indifference or from an earlier form of piety to another, a turning which implies a consciousness that a great change was involved." This was not a conviction that the old was right and is still right or that both old and new are right. Conversion demanded a decision to reject the old as wrong and accept the new as right.[49] The nub was that conversion required a reorientation of "soul," as Nock puts it, or of "personal center of energy," as James puts it.

For several decades the systematic study of conversion stayed largely where James and Nock left it. With the rise of new religious movements, the resurgence of "born again" evangelical Christianity coupled with the spread of the charismatic movement and the arrival of the new religious "cults," the years since 1950 have seen a quickened interest in the study of conversion, especially among social scientists. The current research literature is at once diverse and daunting—well beyond the capacity of this volume or a shelf of volumes to analyze.[50]

Nonetheless, social scientists have developed a model of conversion that can be especially useful in organizing the more settled findings applicable to a study of conversion in early Christianity.[51] The model's principal characteristics include a convert's (1) situation in her or his social, cultural, and religious worlds—in short, as situated in the total context or setting; (2) experience of an identity crisis;[52] (3) active search for a new identity, meaning, and purpose in life; (4) encounter with a new religious reality that engages her or his emotional, intellectual, and cognitive needs; (5) continual and mutual interaction with the community that embodies the new religious reality; (6) clear-cut choice between her or his previous way of living and a new way that yields commitment; and, finally, (7) gradual transformation, resulting in a reorientation of attitudes and values mirrored in conduct.[53]

VIII. A Ritual View

Until recently one characteristic has been all but absent from social scientific research on conversion, one upon which the ancients were quite insistent: ritual.[54] For them, conversion was embedded in complex and richly articulated ritual processes.

A casualty at first of the currents that produced the Protestant Reformation and then the Enlightenment—ritual equals magic and superstition—ritual studies have only recently seen the light of day in the work of researchers in anthropology and students of ritual,[55] especially in the pioneering work of Arnold van Gennep, a Belgian contemporary of James and Nock, whose work was apparently unknown to them.

A colleague of anthropologists Marcel Mauss and Emile Durkheim, van Gennep focused his study on the many rituals reported from preliterate societies and on the sacred texts of Hinduism, Judaism, and Christianity.[56] In search of a theory for interpreting critical changes of status in human societies, he found that critical changes of status— birth, adulthood, marriage, and death—exhibit three phases: separation, transition, and incorporation.

To explain, he likened society to a many-roomed house in which the family moves about from room to room through passages, down hallways, and across thresholds. In these three phases—he called them *les rites de passage*—he proposed that society takes its members by the hand and leads them from one social status to another, down corridors and across thresholds. In rites of separation, society severs them from a previous status, the asexual world of infancy/childhood, for instance, and conducts them to and through the rites of incorporation into the sexual adult status with its deep responsibilities.

The transitional condition between separation and incorporation is of particular interest for conversion.[57] Van Gennep called it *limen*, a Latin term meaning boundary (a shoreline, a threshold of a room, a plat of land); indeed, he described the phases of passage and their rites as preliminal, liminal, and postliminal.

The work of the British anthropologist, Victor Turner, on the transitional or liminal phase, has best illuminated the ritual dimension of conversion. The key is Turner's concept of liminality, about which he says:

> The attributes of liminality or liminal personae ("threshold people") are necessarily ambiguous, since this condition and these persons elude or slip through the network of classifications that normally locate states and positions in cultural space. Liminal entities are neither here nor there; they are betwixt and between the positions assigned and arrayed by law, convention and ceremonial.[58]

The condition of liminality, he discovered, is a fertile source of rituals and symbols, not to mention myths, philosophical systems, works of art, and the quality at the very heart of human community, a quality that he calls *communitas* and defines as an intense awareness of being bound together in a community of shared experience well articulated by Martin Buber's symbol, "I-Thou." Based on preliminary studies, the evidence from Greco-Roman antiquity persuades me that potential converts were (and are) just such "threshold people" and, further, that their passage from one religious status and identity was attended—some might say effected—by complex rites.[59]

Save for the liturgical renewal in churches of Catholic substance, ritual is missing in much contemporary work on conversion; I trust that the chapters that follow help fill in the gap.[60]

NOTES

1. For Jews it was God's power and fidelity to his covenant; for Pagans, the power of their divinities coupled with their own piety; for Christians it was God's providential plan: *oikonomia[s] tou theou* (Eusebius, *Ecclesiastical History* 1.1.2; G. Bardy, ed., *Eusèbe de Césarée: Histoire Ecclésiastique,* vol. 1, SC 31 [1978] 3 passim)—God's providence. According to ancient historian Ramsay MacMullen, power was the common denominator in Greco-Roman religions. Citing Tertullian that the gods "win faith [*fides*] through various signs, miracles, and oracles" (*Apology* 21:31), MacMullen comments that *fides* here (or *pistis* in Greek) means the sudden and irresistible conviction that some being of supernatural power had manifested himself or herself; "submissive reliance" then follows ("Conversion: A Historian's View," *The Second Century* 5 [1985/1986] 74—the entire issue is devoted to conversion in antiquity). He develops his thesis in his *Paganism in the Roman Empire* (New Haven: Yale University Press, 1981), 93–112, especially 96–97.

2. For what follows see my article, "Ritual Process and the Survival of Early Christianity: A Study of the *Apostolic Tradition* of Hippolytus," *JRS* 3 (1989) 69 and nn. 1–8, 80–81. Adolf von Harnack at the turn of the century initiated what can be considered the first "social history" of the early Christian movement. For a recent study of Harnack's work, critique, and discussion of subsequent "social world" research and conclusions, see Michael L. White, "Adolf von Harnack and the 'Expansion' of Early Christianity: A Reappraisal of Social History," *The Second Century* 5.2 (1985/1986) 97–127.

3. Lucian, *Wisdom of Nigrinus* 1, Loeb (1913), cited in Eugene V. Gallagher, *Expectation and Experience: Explaining Religious Conversion* (Atlanta: Scholars Press [Ventures in Religion 2, ed. W. Scott Green], 1990) 114.

4. The reference is in Josephus, *Antiquities of the Jews* 20:17–96, cited in Martin Goodman, *Mission and Conversion: Proselytizing in the Religious History of the Roman Empire* (Oxford: Clarendon Press, 1994) 64–65. See Chapter 4, "Izates of Adiabene."

5. For which, see Eugene V. Gallagher, "Conversion and Salvation in the Apocryphal Acts of the Apostles," *The Second Century* 8.1 (1991) 13–29. They are those of Thomas, Peter, and Paul. Gallagher takes exception to MacMullen's point that credence in miracles was the primary motive for conversion; he argues that the interpretive theme in the *Acts,* replete with miracle stories, is the conception of conversion as death and resurrection—an entrance into new life. In short, miracle is secondary to the expectation of new life (19).

6. For Jewish converts to Paganism, see Goodman, *Mission and Conversion,* 134–35; and Harry Austryn Wolfson, *Philo: Foundations of Religious Philosophy in Judaism, Christianity, and Islam,* vol. 1 (Cambridge: Harvard University Press, 1948) 73–78.

7. For the Theodosian code on the subject of Christians becoming Jews (*Codex Theodosianus* 16:8.19, 22, 26), see the account in Goodman, *Mission and Conversion,* 140. For the attraction of Judaism for Christians, see Robert L. Wilken, *John Chrysostom and the Jews: Rhetoric and Reality in the Late Fourth Century* (Berkeley: University of California Press, 1983). For Christians sacrificing to the gods and offering incense to the emperor, see Cyprian's *De lapsis* (Joseph Martin, ed., *Cyprian: De lapsis,* FP 21 [1930]). Jews and Christians crossing boundaries would be known to their coreligionists as apostates, and their motives and characters impugned, but such charges are not thereby proved by their making.

8. For a detailed analysis of the terms and their meanings, see Paul Aubin, *Le problème de la 'conversion': Étude sur un terme commun a l'hellenisme et au christianisme des trois premiers siècles* (Paris: Beauchesne, 1962); William L. Holladay, *The Root "Shub" in the Old Testament* (Leiden: E. J. Brill, 1958); *"Strepso"* in *TDNT* 7 (1971) 714–29; Christoph Barth,

"Notes on 'Return' in the Old Testament," *The Ecumenical Review* 19 (1967) 310–12; Aloys H. Dirksen, *The New Testament Concept of Metanoia* (Dissertation, Catholic University of America, 1932); "*Metanoeo*," *TDNT* 4 (1967) 975–1008; and J. W. Heikkinen, "Notes on 'Epistrepho' and 'Metanoeo,'" *The Ecumenical Review* 19 (1967) 313–16. The most accessible recent treatment is Ronald D. Witherup, *Conversion in the New Testament* (Collegeville: Liturgical Press [A Michael Glazier Book, Zacchaeus Studies: New Testament, ed. Mary Ann Getty], 1994)—114–19 contain a selected bibliography. For an additional recent and valuable New Testament study, see Beverly R. Gaventa, *From Darkness to Light: Conversion in the New Testament* (Philadelphia: Fortress Press, 1986).

9. Plato, *Politeias* 7, pars. 515–16 (John Burnet, ed., *Platonis Opera* IV [Oxford: Clarendon Press, 1902]).

10. The two philosophers to give the root term *[s]trephein* prominence were Epictetus (c. 50-c. 130 C.E.), the Stoic, and Plotinus, though, of course, others had used it, albeit seldom. Aubin writes: "Plotinus found this word particularly congenial for expressing the notion of 'concentration' which is so important in his system and which he may have derived from Indian philosophy" (*Le problème,* 185). Aubin finds pre-Constantinian Christians used *[s]trephein* nineteen times before the death of the philosopher and thirteen hundred times afterward (186).

11. The verb *nhm* ("to regret" or "to be sorry") is also used but never in the sense of "to repent," and almost always to mean God's change of intention. *Shuv* is the more important theologically. For discussion, see Witherup, *Conversion in the New Testament,* 8–16.

12. The translation is that of Mitchell Dahood, *The Anchor Bible: Psalms II, 51–100* (Garden City, N.Y.: Doubleday, 1968) vv. 1–2.

13. Thus, *La vetus latina hispana, El Salterio,* vol. V, sec. II (Madrid: Consejo superior de investigaciones cientificas instituto Francisco Suarez, 1962) 616–21. The text presents five Latin versions in parallel columns along with the Septuagint.

14. See *Testament of Abraham,* recension B, 12, ed. Michael Stone (Missoula: Society of Biblical Literature, 1972) 80–82, for text and translation. For other references, see Dirksen, *The New Testament Concept of Metanoia,* 153–64: Septuagint, Sibylline Oracles, Philo, and Josephus.

15. *Damascus Document* 9:15. For discussion about entry and renewal, see Matthew Black, *The Scrolls and Christian Origins: Studies in the Jewish Background of the New Testament* (New York: Charles Scribner's, 1961) 91–102. In his treatise *On Virtue,* Philo of Alexandria equates the content of the two terms, *metanoia* and *teshuvah* (Dirksen, *The New Testament Concept of Metanoia,* 161–62). See Chapter 5, Sectarian Judaism, Qumran.

16. Absent in the second century fathers, Paul's baptismal theology

appears first in Origen. See my *ECBC* 6:191–211 and the general introduction: symbolic participation; and my entry "Sacraments," in Everett Ferguson et al., eds., *Encyclopedia of Early Christianity* (New York: Garland, 1990) 811–15. One correction will be made in the second edition: on p. 812, the Origen citation is from his *Homilies on Exodus,* 5:2, not his *Commentary on John.*

  17. See Chapters 6 and 7. I have collected a variety of texts with their exposition in my *ECBC* 5, especially 14–15, 43–51.

  18. For discussion, see Alan Segal, *Paul the Convert: The Apostolate and Apostasy of Saul the Pharisee* (New Haven: Yale University Press, 1990) 18–20, 72–114; and Gaventa, *From Darkness to Light,* 17–51. Paul uses the verb *epistrephein,* but not the noun *epistrophe.* See 1 Thes 1:9–10; Gal 4:8–9; 2 Cor 3:15–16. He also uses *metanoein/metanoia,* but only about people who already have come to faith in Christ; he never characterizes coming to faith as an act of repentance. See 2 Cor 7:9–10, 12:21; Rom 2:4; and Gaventa, 40–43.

  19. Thus, Justin Martyr (d. c. 160 C.E.), *First Apology* 61 (PG:421.B): "Moreover, this washing [baptism] is called enlightenment *[photismos],* since those who learn these things [i.e., how one is consecrated to Christ] are enlightened *[photizomenon]* in understanding. Moreover, the enlightened one *[photizomenos]* is washed in the name of Jesus Christ." See Chapter 6, Justin Martyr, and Thomas Halton, "Baptism as Illumination," *Irish Theological Quarterly* 32 (1965) 28–41. From Clement of Alexandria on, enlightenment terminology becomes a usual way of speaking about conversion and baptism. In the course of time the baptismal candle and vesting in white, rituals symbolizing enlightenment, became an integral part of the baptismal liturgy.

  20. Thus, Gaventa, *From Darkness to Light,* 28, with which Segal, *Paul the Convert,* and Witherup, *Conversion in the New Testament,* 88–99 would agree. For Paul's conversion as based on a transforming mystical encounter with the risen and glorified Jesus in the form of an ascent into heaven, see James D. Tabor, *Things Unutterable: Paul's Ascent to Paradise in Its Greco–Roman, Judaic, and Early Christian Contexts* (Lanham, Md.: University Press of America [Studies in Judaism, ed. Jacob Neusner], 1986), especially 19–21.

  21. Thus, Gaventa, *From Darkness to Light,* 130–38, and Witherup, *Conversion in the New Testament,* 74–87.

  22. The translation is Gaventa's, *From Darkness to Light,* 138. There is good reason for thinking that 1 Peter reflects a number of baptismal themes contemporary with the author; some have suggested that it is based on a baptismal homily the author has adapted for his epistolary audience, a suggestion I find difficult to sustain.

  23. Tertullian, *Against Marcion* 1:14 (PL 2:287.A). Tertullian here calls it the "food which one feeds infants."

  24. Thus, Witherup, *Conversion in the New Testament,* 47–50. But see

also the prodigal son parable (15:11–32) and the Zacchaeus story (19:5–10). The joy of finding the lost is a strong current in Luke.

25. See the following: Acts 2:38–39 (the conclusion to Peter's sermon at Pentecost); 4:4 (Peter's sermon at the "Beautiful Gate"); 8:26–40 (Philip and the Ethiopian eunuch, which is a lead-in to the next two); 9:32–43 (the healing of Aeneas and the raising of Tabitha/Dorcas); 9:1–18 (the first account of Paul's conversion); 10:44–48 (the conversion of Cornelius and his household); 13:12 (the conversion of the governor of Cyprus, Sergius Paulus); 13:52 (the converts at Pisidian Antioch); 14:20 (the converts at Lystra); 15:3 (the story of the conversion of the Gentiles); 15:19 (the Council of Jerusalem and the Gentiles turning to God); 16:14 (the conversion of Lydia, the "purple fabric" merchant); 16:33 (the conversion of the jailer at Philippi); 17:4 (conversions in Thessalonika); 17:12 (many Beroeans become believers); 17:33–34 (Dionysius and some other Athenian converts); 18:9 (conversion of the Corinthians, including Crispus and household); 19:1–3 (Ephesian converts and John's baptism); 19:9–10 (Ephesian converts and Tyrannus' lecture hall); 22:6–16 (the second account of Paul's conversion); 26:12–23 (the third account of Paul's conversion); and 28:24 (some converts among the Roman Jews).

26. Acts 26:20. This is the terminology with which Acts starts as well. See Peter's Pentecost sermon (2:38). Nonetheless, when Luke speaks of the Gentile mission, the following phrase, albeit in a variety of forms, is frequent and may have been technical for the conversion of Gentiles, perhaps because of the Jerusalem council (Acts 15): "the Gentiles who are turning to God *(apo ton ethnon epistrepsousin epi ton theon)*": 14:15; 15:3, 20; 21:25. For a discussion of the process of conversion in Luke, see Joseph A. Fitzmyer, *The Gospel According to Luke (I–IX): Introduction, Translation, and Notes,* AB 28 (1981) 235–57. Where appropriate, the translations in Acts that follow are his. But see also Witherup, *Conversion in the New Testament,* 57–73.

27. See also Acts 4:3; 13:12; 17:12; 18:8, 9; and 18:29—9:2.

28. For the equivalency, see Acts 14:20, 22, 27; 18:23; and 19:1–2; the usual New English Bible translation is "convert," whereas the RSV and NRSV are literal: "disciple." The term *way* is used only by Luke: Acts 9:2; 19:9, 23; 22:4; 24:14, 22. For discussion of discipleship in Luke, see Fitzmyer, *The Gospel According to Luke,* 241–43.

29. For discussion, see Walter J. Burghardt, "Catechetics in the Early Church," *The Living Light* 1 (1964) 100–118. The earliest text to exemplify the moral-formation approach is the *Didache,* for which, see Chapter 6, and Jonathan Reed, "The Hebrew Epic and the *Didache,*" in Clayton N. Jefford, *The Didache in Context: Essays on Its Text, History, and Transmission* (Leiden and New York: E. J. Brill, 1995) 213–25.

30. Acts 2:38; 8:13, 38; 9:18; 10:48. Also 16:33; 18:9; 19:6.

31. See Chapter 6, baptism in the name of Jesus, and baptism in the Holy

Spirit. In the conversion of Cornelius and household, the Spirit "came upon all" before baptism (Acts 10:44); in Ephesus, however, Paul found a number of Apollos' converts who had not received the Spirit at all (19:1–6; see also the Samaritans, 8:16). Often Luke does not mention the gift of the Spirit when he speaks of the newly converted. For discussion of attempts to untangle the relationship, see Fitzmyer, *The Gospel According to Luke,* 227–31, 239–41.

32. But see also the following accounts: 8:26–40 (the Ethiopian eunuch); 10:1—11:18; 15:7–11 (Cornelius); 16:14–15 (Lydia); and 16:25–34 (the Philippian jailer) for other major accounts; for discussion, see Witherup, *Conversion in the New Testament,* 62–73. Some think that Paul experienced his encounter with the risen Jesus as a prophetic call. Segal notes, however, that his change was from Pharisaic Judaism, in which he had been reared, to a "particular kind of gentile community of God-fearers, living without the law, and the change was powered by Paul's absorption into the spirit" (*Paul the Convert,* 117).

33. Thus, Segal: " . . . in Luke's time the quickness of the conversion apparently emphasizes the miraculous power of the spirit. So Luke also portrays Paul's conversion as a sudden Damascus Road experience. Luke uses Paul's example doubly, both as a paradigm of a convert and as the model for Christian missionaries" (*Paul the Convert,* 18).

34. Thus, Gaventa, *From Darkness to Light,* 92. She contends that, although Paul is not a paradigmatic convert, these are the assumptions behind Luke's account, especially of Paul's conversion.

35. *The Acts of Thomas* 170 (A. F. J. Klijn, *The Acts of Thomas: Introduction, Text, Commentary* [Leiden: E. J. Brill (Supplements to the New Testament 5, ed. W. C. van Unnik), 1962] 154, 304).

36. For discussion, see Gallagher, "Conversion and Salvation in the Apocryphal Acts of the Apostles," 13–29, especially 18–21.

37. Clement, *Exhortation to the Greeks* 1:8, 4 (SC 2bis, 64).

38. For discussion, see Aubin, *Le problème de la conversion,* 114–36. For Clementine texts, see my *ECBC* 6:180–91. For further discussion, see Chapters 6 and 7.

39. Origen, *Against Celsus* 4:17 (SC 136, 222–24).

40. Origen, *Against Celsus* 3:66 (SC 136, 150); see also 1:9 (SC 132, 100): responding to Celsus' assertion that reason must always be followed as guide, or deception is bound to follow, Origen asks whether the majority of believers, who have renounced the "great flood" of vice in which they once lived and now live a reformed life through simple faith, ought to have deferred conversion *(epistrophen)* until they had the leisure to study the doctrines of faith. He observes that the grind of daily living, coupled with human weakness, renders rare those given to rational thought, especially when it comes to conversion and the reformation of life. For Origen's texts, see my *ECBC*

5:191–211, and also, John Clark Smith, "Conversion in Origen," *Scottish Journal of Theology* 32 (1979) 217–40.

41. For Origen's vision of conversion as exodus, see Chapter 7, and his texts in my *ECBC* 5:191–211.

42. Origen, *Homilies on St. Luke* 24 (SC 87, 324, 326; Finn, *ECBC 5,* 209–10).

43. Karl F. Morrison has studied conversion in the eleventh and twelfth centuries, with the following conclusion: "For them [eleventh and twelfth centuries], conversion was not formal [i.e., change of religion] but supernatural and empathetic. The heart turned not to Christianity of Church but to Christ; by mystic union, it turned into Christ" (*Understanding Conversion* [Charlottesville: University of Virginia Press, 1992] 186). His study is a metaphorical analysis, and the model against which he works is the one created by Arthur Darby Nock, for which see below, n. 48.

44. For bibliography and brief analysis of the current state of research from a variety of social science perspectives, see Lewis R. Rambo, "Current Research on Religious Conversion," *RSR* 8 (1982) 146–59, and his *Understanding Religious Conversion* (New Haven: Yale University Press, 1993), in which he develops a "process oriented" model as a way to organize the findings of modern research; see especially his bibliography, 209–34. Eugene V. Gallagher explores a series of individual cases to assess the current status of the study of conversion: *Expectation and Experience: Explaining Religious Conversion* (Atlanta: Scholars Press [Ventures in Religion 2, ed. W. Scott Green], 1990). For an account of Finney and the scholarship on him, see James Craig Holte, *The Conversion Experience in America: A Sourcebook on Religious Conversion Autobiography* (New York: Greenwood Press, 1992) 101–9.

45. William James, *Varieties of Religious Experience* (New York: Longmans, Green, 1902) 189; he elaborates on the definition in the balance of the lecture and the next (190–258), reviewing at some length the work of Professors Starbuck, Leuba, and Coe, fellow psychologists, who were also attempting empirically to characterize conversion. Gallagher, *Expectation and Experience,* 12–24.

46. Thus, Gallagher, *Expectation and Experience,* 18. For a valuable analysis and critique of James, see the entire section, 12–24.

47. James, *Varieties,* 42.

48. Arthur Darby Nock, *Conversion: The Old and the New in Religion from Alexander the Great to Augustine of Hippo* (Oxford: Clarendon Press, 1933), see especially 1–16; see also his "Conversion and Adolescence," in *Essays on Religion in the Ancient World,* ed. Zeph Stewart, vol. 2 (Oxford: Clarendon Press, 1972) 469–80. Gallagher explores Nock's and MacMullen's theories of conversion in late antiquity (*Expectation and Experience,* 109–33).

49. Nock, *Conversion,* 7. For James, the soul is "the habitual center of personal energy," and to say one is converted "means, in these terms, that religious ideas, previously peripheral in his consciousness, now take a central place, and the religious aims form the habitual center of [one's] personal energy" (*Varieties,* 196). Nock considers conversion to philosophy in antiquity a special case (164–86) and allows that the Orphic mystery-cult communities in Greece, approximating philosophical schools, knew conversion (15–16, 77–98).

50. For a survey of current work coupled with bibliography, see Rambo, already mentioned ("Current Research"); Larry D. Shinn, "Who Gets to Define Religion? The Conversion/Brainwashing Controversy," *RSR* 19 (1993) 195–207; and Segal, *Paul the Convert,* 285–300. For sustained attempts to integrate contemporary thinking about conversion and Christianity, see Walter Conn, *Christian Conversion: A Developmental Interpretation of Autonomy and Surrender* (Mahwah, N.J.: Paulist Press, 1986); Rambo, *Understanding Religious Conversion;* and Gallagher, *Expectation and Experience.*

51. They are detailed and explained in Rambo, "Conversion," *ER* 4:75–78. In his most recent work, *Understanding Religious Conversion,* Rambo offers a heuristic model that explores the stages of the "multilayered processes involved in conversion" (16): content, crisis, quest, encounter, interaction, commitment, and consequences. He uses this model as the strategy for organizing the complex data yielded by scientific research.

52. The term is Erik Erikson's, used to describe what he considers the major crisis of late adolescence and early adulthood, and employed in his analysis of Martin Luther's conversion; see his *Young Man Luther: A Study in Psychoanalysis and History* (New York: Norton, 1958). He originally planned the study of Luther's conversion as a chapter in a book on late adolescence and early adulthood, but, he remarks, "Luther proved too bulky [!] a man" (7).

53. These characteristics are those of Rambo, "Current Research"; but see Larry D. Shinn, "Who Gets to Define Religion," 204, who agrees with his "holistic" model but adds that he "would encourage the addition of a cross-cultural and global faiths perspective that can be found by looking at not merely traditional (mainline faiths) but nontraditional (sectarian and marginal groups) conversions in America and around the world."

54. Rambo reports and analyzes the research in *Understanding Religious Conversion,* especially, 113–18, 127–32. He observes that in the past many dismissed ritual as the empty repetition of religious words and actions. "It is my view that religious action—regularized, sustained, and intentional—is fundamental to the conversion experience. Ritual fosters the necessary orientation, the readiness of mind and soul to have a conversion experience, and it consolidates conversion after the initial experience" (114).

55. Ritual Studies is an emergent interdisciplinary field that began in earnest only in 1977. It stands in the middle ground between the anthropologist, who studies rituals with a critical normative eye, and the liturgical scholar, who is usually a participant-observer. See Ronald L. Grimes, *Beginnings in Ritual Studies,* rev. ed. (Columbia: University of South Carolina Press, 1995); and his overview, "Ritual Studies," in *ER* 12:422–25.

56. Arnold van Gennep, *The Rites of Passage,* trans. Monika B. Vizedom and Gabrielle L. Caffe (Chicago: University of Chicago Press, 1960). The original work, *Les Rites de passage,* was published in 1908. For a recent reprise, see Barbara G. Meyerhoff, Linda A. Camino, and Edith Turner, "Rites of Passage: An Overview," *ER* 12:380–87, and Douglas Davies, "Introduction: Raising the Issues," in Jean Holm and John Bowker, eds., *Rites of Passage* (London: Pinter Publishers, 1994): the subsequent chapters cover the major living religions.

57. Salon T. Kimball, in the introduction to the English translation of *The Rites of Passage,* traces the history of van Gennep's findings and their influence on sociology and anthropology, more accurately their curious lack of influence, from 1908 to the publication of the translation in 1960.

58. Victor Turner, *The Ritual Process: Structure and Antistructure* (Chicago: Aldine Press, 1969) 85.

59. Turner's work has proved invaluable for ritual studies, especially for those religious traditions that find liturgy at the center of religious life: see Lyndon I. Farwell, *Betwixt and Between: The Anthropological Contributions of Mary Douglas and Victor Turner toward a Renewal of Roman Catholic Ritual* (Dissertation, Claremont College, 1976). My preliminary studies are: "Ritual Process and the Survival of Early Christianity: A Study of the *Apostolic Tradition* of Hippolytus" *JRS* 3 (1989) 68–69; "It Happened One Saturday Night: Ritual and Conversion in Augustine's North Africa,"*JAAR* 58 (1990) 589–616; and "Ritual and Conversion: The Case of Augustine," *Festschrift in Honor of Thomas L. Halton,* ed. John Pettrucione (Washington, D.C.: Catholic University of America Press, forthcoming 1997). See also my two volumes, *ECBC* 5, 6, which collect and interpret the patristic evidence.

60. Rooted in the Romantic response to the Enlightenment, it started with the Tractarian Movement in England and the worship reform movement at the Abbey of Solesmes in France. Interest in ritual grew during the early decades of this century in Britain under the leadership of Dom Gregory Dix and in the United States under Dom Virgil Michel at Saint John's Abbey, Collegeville, Minn. Its vigor left its deep mark on the Second Vatican Council, and in the post–Vatican II world of Roman Catholicism a great deal of scholarly attention has been paid to conversion and the ritual process. For recent general study, see Cheslyn Jones, Geoffrey Wainwright, Edward J. Yarnold, and Paul F. Bradshaw, eds., *The Study of the Liturgy,* rev. ed. (London: SPCK; New York:

Oxford University Press, 1992), especially 3–84. Fine bibliographies introduce each essay.

Central to pastoral concern among Roman Catholics is the restored Rite of Christian Initiation of Adults (RCIA), for which, see *Ordinis baptismi adultorum* in *Acta Apostolicae Sedis* 64 (1972) 252; *The Rite of Christian Initiation of Adults,* 2nd. ed. (Vatican City: Vatican Polyglot Press, 1974); and *Documents of the Liturgy, 1963–1979: Conciliar, Papal, and Curial Texts,* the International Commission on English in the Liturgy (Collegeville: Liturgical Press, 1979) 2328–67. This rite is mandatory for Catholic dioceses in the United States, for which, see *The Rite of Christian Initiation of Adults: Approved for Use in the Dioceses of the United States of America by the National Conference of Catholic Bishops and Confirmed by the Apostolic See* (Washington D.C.: United States Catholic Conference, 1988).

Chapter 2

GRECO-ROMAN PAGANISM:
SOME CHARACTERISTICS

I. Introduction: Paganism

The Greco-Roman world spanned some seven centuries (333 B.C.E.–478 C.E.) and thousands of miles—from Britain east to Iran and from Germany south to the Sahara. Greek in culture because of the conquests of Alexander the Great (356–323 B.C.E.), it was administratively Roman even before the accession of the first Roman emperor, Augustus (27 B.C.E.–14 C.E.).

In the east (the Balkans through Iraq) this vast and complex world gave birth to the Byzantine Empire (324–1453 C.E.), which both watched and resisted the rise of Islam and the Arabs (632–1453 C.E.); in the west (the Balkans through the British Isles), it was home to the Middle Ages (500–1400 C.E.), nurtured the earliest years of modern Europe, and also both watched and resisted Islam and the Arabs.

Save for Judaism and Christianity, the religions of the Greco-Roman world are little known. As numerous as the geographical divisions of that ancient world, they exhibit certain characteristics that permit the use of an encompassing term like *Paganism,* and they provide the background necessary to discuss conversion in the Greco-Roman world.

Right off, a difficulty—the term *Pagan.* I highlight the difficulty by capitalizing the term. To the Romans, *pagani* meant the inhabitants of an Italian country district; eventually it came to denote their religions, and finally, at least among ancient Jews and early Christians, *Pagan* soon came to be a term of contempt for those inhabitants of the empire who were not Christians or Jews: Pagans were impious and immoral because they worshiped false gods. *Pagani* and immoral idolaters were synonymous for both Christians and Jews.

The apostle Paul recapitulates and reinforces attitudes ancient and modern: "God gave them up to a debased mind and to things that should not be done. They were filled with envy, covetousness, malice" (Rom 2:29). The trenchant early Christian writer Tertullian (c. 160–c. 240), in a ringing indictment of Pagans and their religion, captures the contempt when he says that the gods are names for men long dead and that their devotees treat them sacrilegiously: they go to the temple of the state gods [the Capitol] as if they were going to the vegetable market, and then treat the deities "as sources of income."[1] The Talmud records God's severe judgment of Pagan Persia and Rome at the end of days. Despite their accomplishments for the world, Rome will depart crushed in spirit because she acted only to satisfy her own selfish desires, and Persia, because she built marvels by warfare and forced labor.[2]

A steady stream of invective caused people, ancient and modern, to equate Paganism with false religion and immorality and to see it as a mixture of magic, superstition, and primitive depravity. As a result, it is hard to imagine sincere Pagans who lived devout, selfless, and reflective lives. Nor is it easy for people to concede vitality to the Pagan religions, in spite of the fact that ancient literature and inscriptions abound with testimonies to the devout Pagan in the Greco-Roman world.

The following inscription is representative. The words of an unknown worshiper inscribed long ago in the temple at ancient Talmis in Upper Egypt capture the piety of an ancient Greco-Roman Pagan:

> O rayshooting lord Mandulis, Titan, Makareus [all epithets for the Egyptian high god, Ra], having beheld some radiant signs of your power, I pondered on them, and, occupied with them, I wished to know for sure whether you are the sun god. I made myself a stranger to all vice and all godlessness, was chaste for a long period, and made the due incense-offering in holy piety. I had a vision and found rest. For you did bend to me . . . and show me yourself going through the heavenly vault . . . then after washing yourself in the holy water of immortality [sunset and night], you did again appear [the rising sun]. You did come at the due season of your rising, giving breath of life and great power to your image and to your shrine. Then I knew you, Mandulis.[3]

II. Divinity, Power, and Worship

Antiquity's Pagan religions were rooted in experiences of nature and its power. The ancients experienced the forces and vitality of nature as divine. Lifeless nature did not exist. As one scholar puts it, "Scratch a spring and find a naiad, scratch a river and find a god, scratch a tree and find a dyad, dive below the sea's surface and find the nereids."[4]

Against this backdrop of "lively divinity," with its continuous cycles of birth and rebirth and the endless fertility of the world, stood the great earth-mother goddesses like Isis (Egypt), Cybele (Asia Minor), Demeter and Artemis (Greece), Juno (Rome), and Caelestis (North Africa). And behind them stood the experience of nature's raw power—the sky-father gods like Greece's Zeus and Rome's Jupiter and North Africa's Saturn, who held in their hands the awesome power of the universe. Zeus' (or Jupiter's) thunderbolt is legendary.

What differentiated the gods from human beings was power: power was the essence of divinity. The gods had power in such amplitude that death could not overcome them. Thus, their customary name, "The Immortals." Not so, human beings: with their limp powers, death systematically could and did conquer them; they were "The Mortals."

Apotheosis

Nonetheless, an unbridgeable chasm did not divide the immortals from the mortals. In the breach stood the hero and the king. Both could achieve godlike honors and immortality. A hero could be a person of legendary strength and courage, like Heracles, or a sage, like Apollonius of Tyana, a contemporary of Jesus. An ascetic, mystic, and Neopythagorean sage, Apollonius made the circuit of the eastern Mediterranean world dispensing wisdom, reforming morals, and working miracles. A third-century C.E. account depicts his remarkable death in the temple of Dictyanna in Crete—the guards, thinking him a thief, shackled and imprisoned him. We read that he loosened the shackles and

> ran to the doors of the temple, which opened wide to receive him; and when he had passed within they closed afresh, as they had been shut, and there was heard a chorus of maidens singing from within the temple, and their song was this; "Hasten from earth, hasten to Heaven, Hasten." In other words, "Ascend from earth."[5]

Possessed of extraordinary power, Apollonius became an immortal. Similarly, from the time of Alexander the Great, the Greek world tended to look on the king as divine because of his power—a Zeus writ small, so to speak. By the mid-third century B.C.E. arresting divine titles were given kings, the most expressive being, "Savior and Benefactor."[6]

Given the Hellenistic tradition, it was merely a matter of time before the Roman emperor came to be worshiped as divine.[7] By the second century of our era the imperial cult was in full swing. A marvel of Greco-Roman art that stands in the courtyard of the Vatican Library illustrates the movement. The base of the column displays in relief an apotheosis of the highly respected and much-loved emperor Antoninus Pius (138–161 C.E.). His wife and lifelong companion, Faustina, accompanies him in the ascent.

Whether hero or king, a person of extraordinary power could traverse the gulf between human beings and the gods to join the immortals. They had what makes for divinity: power.

Worship: Response to Power

Faced with power both natural and regal, the ancients had a uniform reaction, especially the little people of Greece and Rome. The encounter with divine power caused terror, terror bred by the hardnosed realities of matter, nature, and happenstance. They knew firsthand that fires, plagues, and earthquakes could engulf entire cities. To be sure, the gods were felt to be ever present with people, but so was their anger, anger that could flash out at any act of omission that disturbed the right relation between them and human beings—especially a ritual act of omission. The welfare of individual and empire depended on maintaining the right relationship with the gods.

All of which takes us from power and anger to cult. Worship, especially the long-hallowed rituals of the past, had as its aim the restoration and maintenance of that fragile right relationship. Ritual and religion were the same thing in antiquity, for ritual held the divine and human in solution.

At the heart of worship was sacrifice to a god or goddess. Undergirding sacrifice, however, was the attempt to win (or to win back) the divine approval. The usual sacrifice had two stages: first, a solemn promise to offer sacrifice for favors received *(nuncupatio),* and second, the follow-through or fulfillment *(solutio),* granted, of course, that the deity responded.

Although self-giving and devotion were far from absent, baldly put the principle was "give to receive" *(do ut des),* giving the impression that Greco-Roman religion was based on bribery—a problem that bothered as many ancients as moderns. But the human context suggests that the practice was as complex as the motivations involved in friendship and love, two human experiences in which appeasement, propitiation, and expiation (giving and getting) all have their accustomed place.

Benign Divinity: Asclepius[8]

Frightening power and terror were not the whole story. For the power-gods gradually came to share their prominence with the sun-gods, who brought into the world benign power symbolized by life and light: Helios the Greek, Mithras the Persian, and Ra the Egyptian (also referred to as Re), who, as Ra-Mandulis, inspired the prayer cited at the outset of the chapter.

The sun was not the only life-force. Prominent for centuries was Asclepius, the healing hero-god who could mend the spirit as well as the body. His festivals included hymns, processions, sacrifices, and cures. Inscriptions hail him as "Savior," and the following words suggest why:

> Asclepius, child of Apollo, these words come from your devoted servant. Blessed one, God whom I yearn for, how shall I enter your golden house unless your heart incline towards me and you will to heal me and restore me to your shrine again, so that I may look on my God, who is brighter than earth in springtime? Divine, Blessed One, you alone have power. With your loving kindness you are a great gift from the supreme gods to mankind, a refuge from trouble.[9]

Asclepius was the model physician: "The one who gently takes pains with the sick, that is, considering them deserving of watchful care . . . administering to them gently"; and ancient testimonies visualize him as the protector from "the withering that comes from death."[10]

The very fact that these testimonies, containing an enchanting mixture of giving and getting, submission and dependence, and aspiration and hope, were preserved suggests that they offered hope to many a troubled person.

III. Syncretism and the Profusion of Gods

However single-mindedly the ancients might pursue divine Asclepius, they invoked many gods. They knew a divine profusion. Despite currents of belief in one deity as supreme, Paganism was polytheistic.

Part of the reason was geography. Just as the ancients were rooted in a profuse natural world, they were also rooted in a profusion of places. The religion of one locale differed from that of its neighbor. Conditioned by rough terrain, unpredictable floods, and foreign incursions, the religions of Mesopotamia (modern Iraq and Iran) exhibit the wish, but no hope, for life after death. The reverse is true of Egypt: with its annual Nile floods, fertility, and divine king, life after death eventually became every Egyptian's birthright, as the devotee of Re-Mandulis hints in his vision at Talmis' temple.

Toleration and Loyalty

Yet Paganism's very profusion invites one to consider two related characteristics of Greco-Roman religions: toleration and loyalty. The differences of face, form, and name among the gods did not make for sharp divisions. Rooted in shared experiences of their neighboring but differing worlds, the beliefs of one locale struck responsive chords far and near. Greek Zeus could bear the name, face, and form of Roman Jupiter. Both embodied the same natural omnipotence and stood at the top of the religious pyramid. Egypt's Isis reminded the Anatolians (modern Turkey) of their protectress and mother, Cybele, whom the Romans subsequently brought to Rome two hundred years before the birth of Christ as the Great Mother *(Magna Mater/Meter)*. Whether under the guise of Isis, Cybele, Artemis, or Juno, she was the great one who assured fertility, protection for women, and nurture for children. Indeed, Isis could identify herself to a devotee from a distant land and of a very different religious turn of mind: "I have come, I the mother of the universe . . . my one person manifests the aspect of all gods and goddesses. . . . "[11]

Called syncretism, this divine interchangeability was a characteristic that penetrated to the roots of ancient religion. In Rome's Campus Martius, it produced the Pantheon, the striking circular monument to all the gods, completed in 25 B.C.E. and twice rebuilt. In Carthage syncretism transformed the Phoenician Tanit into Caelestis and finally into Rome's Juno.

The ancients were not thereby promiscuous about divinity. When people emigrated, their gods came with them. As a result, the great cities of the empire sprouted many a temple dedicated to foreign deities. When the emperor Elagabalus (218–222 C.E.—a priest of the Syrian sun-god Elah-Gabal from whom he took his name) assumed the royal purple, he built his god two splendid temples in Rome. The cult of Isis, the national deity of Egypt, migrated from Philae in the south of Egypt to Alexandria, and from there all across the Mediterranean; she was, as we shall see in the next chapter, served by a professional Egyptian priesthood that employed sacred Nile water in the cult's rites.

People remained loyal to their local gods and goddesses, yet were quite able to see, as if their deities were transparencies, a wider horizon for divinity. Accommodation and assimilation proved to be the rule of their ancient days, but not apparently to loyalty's detriment, for intuitively they saw the affinities between native and foreign gods.

Nonetheless, it bears repeating: power was the essence of divinity. Under the empire, people directed belief more and more to divine power and less and less to individual deities. The power embodied in a god or goddess eclipsed the individual embodying it. From this interest in power developed the habit of investing one deity with the attributes of others in the art and inscriptions of the period: by so doing one invested the deity in question with an accumulation of divine powers.

Some have thought that this ascendancy was driven by currents of monotheism, but it was not necessarily so. A deity might well (and sometimes did) evoke the kind of devotion that held Isis, for instance, to be the one who is all, but such devotion did not necessarily betoken conversion to belief in the goddess as the one divinity, the source of all.

This apparent monotheism, called henotheism, resulted more from a rush of interest in divine power than in divine person—however clothed Isis might be in an accumulation of divine power. By thus invoking her, the devotee did not necessarily become her follower to the exclusion of other deities.

As a result of this mixture of toleration and loyalty, Arthur Darby Nock, whom we considered in the first chapter, observed, syncretism "led not to any definite crossing of religious frontiers, in which an old spiritual home was left for a new once and for all, but to men's having one foot on each side of a fence which was cultural and not creedal."[12] In his view, the new cult was supplementary; its adoption was not conversion but "adhesion."

As we shall see in our consideration of personal religion below, there were sporadic indications of conversion; in the mystery religions and philosophical schools, the subjects of the next chapter, the indications are far from sporadic.

IV. Civic Religion

State Religion

Although people desperately sought to be one with deity and to share in divine power, their desire was not centered only on themselves as individuals; the Greco-Roman self was a social self. As if by necessity, they sought unity with deity and a share in the power of the gods for the commonwealth as well, and, in Roman imperial times, also for the emperor. Like the Hellenistic king, he had come to embody the state. Indeed, Greco-Roman religion was primarily civic. That the emperor became the embodiment of the state in the imperial period reflected an ancient conviction, namely, that the welfare of the state depended ultimately on the good pleasure of the gods, specifically, on the beneficence with which they wielded their power. Religious acts, were, therefore, civic acts, nor was there any clear distinction between religion and politics.

Senate and Assembly

In republican Rome (509–31 B.C.E.) the central mediator between the gods and human beings was not the priesthood but the senate.[13] The priests were experts, technicians, and advisors, but the senators, as a body, had the ultimate control over human approaches to the divine; they were the state in its formal constitution.

Certain groups of priests *(collegia)* could and did mediate between the people and the gods, for instance the augurs, whose role was to discover by observation of signs (especially birds) whether the gods did or did not approve a proposed military or political action or sacred site.[14] From this derives our English phrase that a venture might (or might not) "augur well."

Although the focal point of divine communication, they were an advisory body to the senate, which had the principal power to mediate, even to the point of deciding what constituted a sign sent by the gods. Controlling peoples' responses to such signs was also a senatorial responsibility.

And what can be said about the religious role of the senate can be said of the emperor. After Augustus became, as emperor, the first among the senators *(princeps),* he assumed the high-priestly role and title *pontifex maximus* (12 B.C.E.). As *princeps,* he embodied the senate, the priesthoods, and the people; in short, he was the mediator, and to him in particular fell the responsibility of ensuring right relations with the gods.[15]

The situation was not markedly different in the Greek east. In Athens, the citizenry, meeting in formal assembly *(ekklesia,* a term early Christians appropriated for church), comprised the supreme arbiter of religion and served as the focus between the people and the divine. Only the citizenry thus constituted could seek divine sanction for any religious change—even deity was prevented from undertaking any initiative except at the invitation of the *ekklesia.*

After Greece was gathered under the Roman umbrella (146 B.C.E.), eventually the emperor and Roman law moved to center stage, but the dynamics of civic religion did not materially change; the citizenry, as formally constituted (emperor/senate/assembly), were the supreme arbiters between the people and the gods.

The important point, however, is the linkage among human welfare, the state, and the gods, a linkage that underscores the civic character of Greco-Roman religions.

V. *Divine Encounters*

However public and political, the religions of the empire were nonetheless private and personal.[16] They were civic but also domestic— even primarily so. Like that of the state, the individual's welfare also depended on right relations with the gods.

As with the state, so with the individuals that made it up: nature was experienced as life, spirit, and divinity. In a deeply personal way they sensed a presence that permeated their world, and they sought to feel it.

A Personal Spiritual World

The world at their hand was a world of spirits: for the Greeks, demons *(daimona);* for the Romans, divine agents *(numina)*—for both, these spirit-powers were found chiefly in the life of the family and the work of the field. People had the expectation that these spirits specially watched over life's hazardous moments: birth and child-rearing, marriage, recurrent illnesses, sea voyages, and the uncertainties of craft or trade.

But the *daimona/numina* were neither abstract nor impersonal. For Socrates the demon was that inner force that would prompt him to stop, to say no, to refuse the chance to escape, and to die—his invisible self. Among the Romans the *numina* (also, *lares familiares*) comprised one's true spirit: the "Genius" of a man, the "Juno" of a woman.[17] For Greeks and Romans alike, peoples' spirits were so one with them that they constituted their true identity. Demon, Genius, Juno pointed to one's character.

These intimate, guardian spirits, however, were not always benign. There was the evil genius and the bad demon. The spirits could be pleased or displeased by good or bad conduct in any and every aspect of life. Although the spirits brought in their train much anxiety, as we shall see shortly, the salient fact is that the ancients had a deeply personal sense of divine presence, especially at home. In both the Greek and the Roman household, the hearth was central. Among the Greeks it was the site of the family's *daimon;* among the Romans, the site of the family's *numina*. The Roman household strikingly emphasizes this divine domesticity: the Latin word for hearth is *focus,* meaning the abode of the hearth-goddess, Vesta, and the family spirits *(lares/numina)*. Thus, even in contemporary usage it is quite accurate to speak of the hearth as the focus of the family's domestic encounters with the divine.

Epiphanies

The ancients simply expected to see and to talk with gods and goddesses. Power, after all, bubbled up everywhere. But the occasion was usually the extraordinary: unexpected and breathtaking beauty, the flash of brilliant light, a violent storm, stillness, especially the tranquillity of the night. The well-known epigram of the astronomer Ptolemy (100–175 C.E.) captures the intimacy of the moment:

> Mortal though I be, yea ephemeral, if but a moment I gaze up to the
> night's starry domain of heaven. Then no longer on earth I stand; I
> touch the Creator, And my lively spirit drinketh immortality.[18]

The sense and expectation of the divine were almost always
linked to the pressure points of risk and danger. On a journey, especially at sea, the gods were always near; at a critical moment in battle,
Athena might stand astride the walls of Athens or Constantine might
see a pillar of light and the sign by which he was to conquer[19] or the
natives of Malta, seeing Paul shake off the scorpion without the slightest harm from its venom, might say that he is a god (Acts 28:6).

The overriding crisis was recurrent illness, which vaulted
Asclepius, the god of healing met earlier, and his sanctuaries, the most
famous of which was at Epidaurus (Greece), into ancient prominence.[20]
In contrast to the more clinical medicine of celebrated physicians like
Galen (129–199 C.E.), the medicine of Asclepius was designed to heal
the malaise of the spirit and, as a consequence, its physical symptoms.

A. INCUBATION

Prominent was the rite of incubation. After preliminary purification and sacrifices, the sanctuary's priests would attempt to divine the
presence of Asclepius and announce his invitation to the suppliant
patient. If bidden, patients would spend the night in the inner sanctuary,
where the god would come to them in a dream, perhaps as a serpent or a
dog, and either touch the afflicted part of the body or prescribe therapy.
An important inscription from Epidaurus describes what could happen:

> Ambrosia of Athens, blind of one eye. She came as a suppliant to
> the god. As she walked about in the Temple she laughed at some
> of the cures as incredible and impossible. . . . In her sleep she had
> a vision. It seemed to her that the god stood by her and said that he
> would cure her, but that in payment he would ask her to dedicate
> to the Temple a silver pig as a memorial of her ignorance. After
> saying this, he cut the diseased eyeball and poured in some drug.
> When day came she walked out sound.[21]

These intimations of divine presence and action were "epiphanies," reinforcing the adage that seeing is believing. Even the statues of
the gods, numerous in every city, were epiphanies: they embodied the
divine presence, marked out the sacred, and stood as deeply religious
symbols. Thus, Paul, seeing the ranks of divinities that stood as statues

in the Acropolis, could exclaim to the Athenians about their sense of divine presence, "I see how extremely religious you are in every way" (Acts 17:22).

B. ORACLES

But hearing was also believing. The clap of thunder almost always resonated divine presence and action. So also the voice of a child, like the one Augustine of Hippo (354–430 C.E.) heard in the garden of his retreat outside Milan, "Pick up and read."[22]

The most striking phenomenon was the oracle.[23] In almost every difficult or dangerous circumstance, personal or national—the troubled person, the individual at risk, the city or state on the brink of a grave decision—the ancients sought the mind and will of the gods through oracles. People needed to know: to know who they were, what was in store for them, what was real and what was not, and, finally, what to do.

There is a remarkable collection of oracular texts from the second and third centuries of our era that reflects this need to know. Egyptian and based on a common source of revelation—Hermes the Thrice-Great *(Trismegistus)* messenger and herald of the gods—the collection is called the *Hermetic Corpus*. The first tractate, "Poimandres," opens this way:

> One day, when I had begun to think about existence, and my thoughts had soared . . . it seemed to me that an immense creature vast beyond all measure approached, called me by my name and said to me: "What do you want to hear and to see and, by thought, to grasp and understand?" I said, "But you, who are you?"—"I," he said, "am Poimandres, I am the mind of the Sovereign Absolute. I know what you want and I am with you always." And I said, "I want to hear about the things that exist, to understand their nature, to know God." . . . With these words everything before me changed in aspect and were revealed in a moment. I saw a vision without limit, everything became light, serene, joyous, and I marvelled when I saw it.[24]

Similarly, some men in the small city of Oenoanda in Asia Minor (Turkey) cut the words from a god into a stone they lodged appropriately high up in the outer circuit of walls where the first rays of dawn would catch them:

Self-born, untaught, motherless, unshakable,
Giving place to no name, many-named, dwelling in fire,
Such is God; we are a portion of God, his angels.
This, then, to the questioners about God's nature
The god replied, called him all-seeing Ether: to him, then look
And pray at dawn, looking out to the East.[25]

The original site of the inscription was the oracular shrine of Apollo at Claros (southwestern Turkey), but here they are, high up on the walls of a major seat of Apollo's wisdom of Oenoanda, where they have been since the second or third century of our era.

Even more ancient and celebrated was the oracle at Delphi (central Greece), whose site was considered the very navel of the universe, and the riddle of whose prophecies remains shrouded in mystery.[26] City-states would come there to find out about economics or public health or their chances in war; individuals, about whether to marry, business matters, childlessness; an emperor might come, as did Hadrian (117–138 C.E.), to find out Homer's birthplace. Slaves were manumitted at Delphi.

A ritual surrounded the oracle. After purification and sacrifice, inquirers, in prescribed order, approached the oracle. A male prophet would put the inquiry to the Pythia (an aged priestess of Apollo rapt in a frenzy of divine possession) and then interpret her response, usually in verse.[27]

Increasingly questions of individual morality occupied the oracle, which authored the axiom that purity was indeed a matter of ritual but even more a matter of spirit. The most famous oracular utterance— thought to have captured Greek moral wisdom—is carved on Apollo's Delphic temple: "Know yourself; nothing to excess."

Whether by dream, augury, invocation, or oracle, divination was the ancients' attempt to hear the will of the gods and follow it. If one expected to see the gods, one expected also to hear them, for they impinged on the lives of everyone, even in the grave.

VI. Death and Beyond[28]

House of Death

Strung out for miles on the Old Appian Way that runs from Rome to Brindisi are ancient tombs, dominated by the tomb of Caecilia

Matella, and those famous burial grounds called catacombs. Monuments to death and life afterward, they can be found outside the ancient
walls of any Greco-Roman city, for the people, whether Greek or
Roman, had pretty much one mind on the subject of death, burial, and
beyond.

To be properly buried was overridingly important, lest one's spirit
wander a homeless (and dangerous) exile. Even the poorest of the poor,
whose fate would otherwise be a pauper's common grave (often an
open trench) formed funerary societies to ensure proper burial.[29]

Large monuments might be equipped with a dining room, some
even with a kitchen, which dramatizes one aspect of ancient expectations about death and beyond: the tomb was the house of the dead
where they would live as best they could within its walls. For people of
means great care was taken with both design and the amenities. The
reason was quite simple: "Since this is our fixed home, we better look
carefully after it." But whether tomb or trench, the confines of the grave
were oppressive; epitaph after epitaph bears the abbreviated petition,
"STTL," "May the earth be light for you" *(sit terra tibi levis)*.[30]

And there were rituals that reinforced the grave as the horizon
where present and afterlife met. A funeral feast at the grave immediately
followed the burial, and another, on the ninth day. The dead, after all,
needed food to maintain life in the grave, which sometimes was even fit-
ted with a spigot for pouring drink into it. The meals suggest what
inscriptions otherwise poignantly underscore, namely, belief about living on in the grave even to the point of a yearning for companionship.

Immortal Shades

That the dead live on in the tomb was perhaps the most primitive
and enduring conviction about death and afterlife in antiquity. Not
everyone, however, saw life in the grave after death so narrowly
enshrined. As we have already seen, kings, heroes, and emperors were
immortalized. Others lived a shadowy existence, like Odysseus'
mother, Anticleia, and Aeneas' father, Anchises. Homer records
Odysseus' journey to the ends of the earth to meet and talk with
Anticleia, who told him:

> [T]his is the appointed way with mortals when one dies. For just
> as soon as life has left the white bones, and the sinews no longer
> hold together bones and flesh, when the erupting force of blazing

fire undoes the body [the reference is to cremation], then the spirit wanders; like a dream it flits and hovers now here now there.[31]

So also Aeneas. The prophetess Sibyl leads Aeneas through the world below to the Elysian fields and to Anchises, his father, whom three times he tries to embrace, but "thrice the form, vainly clasped, fled from his hands, even as light winds, and most like a winged dream."[32]

Both poets reflect a widespread anxiety about life after death, and, if anything were to survive, surely it was not the body: for Homer it was the spirit *(psyche)* and for Virgil, the form *(imago)*. For both, what survived was elusive, like a dream or a breeze—a shade. Further, both depict what public painting confirms, that after death one might expect punishment or reward. When the Sibyl and Aeneas come to the great divide, for instance, off to the right runs the road to Elysium and reward; to the left, the road that "wreaks the punishment of the wicked, and sends them on to pitiless Tartarus."[33]

The philosophers, as will be clear in the next chapter, reflect on this anxious conviction. They clarify it, and reason to the immortality of the soul, especially Pythagoras (b. 531 B.C.E.) and Plato (429–347 B.C.E.) and their philosophical descendants. Despite these discussions, the anxiety proved ineradicable even for antiquity's most celebrated philosophers.

VII. Personal Religion

This ancient anxiety was fed by the deep-buried currents of ancient religion: a persistent sense of divine presence, an insistent need to feel it, and a pervasive fear that one's reach exceeds one's grasp. One distinguished scholar in the field calls these currents "personal piety," another, "votive religion."[34]

In either case, the currents surface in the mass of votive objects archaeologists have unearthed, ranging from lead "curse" plates through carefully wrought artifacts to moving inscriptions, some of which we have already considered.

The votive objects represent ways of coping with life's anxieties both here and now and hereafter. The core strategy, as we have seen in the discussion on worship, was a contract: *do ut des,* "I give that you may give [in return]." Petitioners sought salvation from present distress; they promised that, if gained, they would offer the deity a special gift, usually some renunciation: a prescribed loss for a petitioned gain.

The contract presupposed trust, the kind born of good faith; the promise was solemn—a vow *(votum)*. Thus, "votive religion," a form of religion that offends sensibilities ancient and modern. In the face of offense, perhaps the following advice from a distinguished contemporary scholar of ancient Greek religion is well heeded:

> There is the agonizing experience of distress, the search for some escape or help. . . . the experience of success. . . . In fact, votive religion did provide help by raising hopes, by socializing anxieties and sufferings: the individual is encouraged to try once more, and he encounters the interest and reinforcement offered by priests and fellow worshipers.[35]

Fate

Votive religion filled the painful gap between the personal and formal in Greco-Roman religion. One of the pressure points was the growing sense that humanity was at the beck and call of powerful forces omnipresent in the universe. People's successes and failures seemed only to be the result of fate.

In Homer's time (sixth century B.C.E.) fate meant a code of conduct in human affairs within which humans were free agents. The gods and goddesses were engaged with people's destinies, but on a general level. By our period, however, necessity *(ananke)* had entered the human drama to the detriment of free agency. Fate and necessity composed a script that governed the world at large and each individual life in detail. Fate became *heimarmene*—a mechanical chain of causes embodied in Chance—for the Greeks, *Tyche,* and for the Romans, *Fortuna.* And they in turn embodied the mysterious power that determines the course of nature, history, and human life.

Thus, the Roman poet Lucretius (99–55 B.C.E.) could give his long philosophic poem on the atomic generation of the universe the title, "The Way Things Are" *(De natura rerum)* and invoke Fortuna-Venus as the guiding power of the universe that "controls the way things are, since without [her] nothing has ever come into the radiant borders of light, nor is anything ever glad or lovable."[36]

The ultimate problem was how to cope with one's fate—without a way, nothing is ever glad or lovable. A fairly representative, if bitter, Roman epitaph runs: "I've escaped, I've got clear. Goodbye, Hope and Fortune. You've nothing on me. Play your tricks on others."[37]

The very word *fate (fatum)* suggests how one might cope, for it means something spoken about one's lot—a prophetic declaration, an oracle, a divine determination.

Cosmic Sympathy

Divination was the way for state and people alike. Especially important was astrology, which had become all the rage under the emperor Tiberius (14–37 C.E.) and thereafter. Astrology's starting point was that human life is intrinsically and harmoniously rooted in the universe, an axiom held to be true beyond any ancient doubt.

The term for the bonding was *cosmic sympathy (sympatheia)*— that ambient force that pervaded the universe and bound everything in it together. It was especially embodied in the sun, the moon, the planets Mercury, Venus, Mars, Jupiter, and Saturn, and the twelve constellations of the Zodiac. Newspaper horoscopes still bear the stamp of that ancient art, as does our language. We still speak of someone as jovial (after Jove, another name for Jupiter) or saturnine (after Saturn) or martial (after Mars) or even lunatic (after *luna,* moon).

The ancient "Hymn to the Stars" attributed to Orpheus captures the problem of existence under this oppressive but inconstant rule of fate:

> Heavenly stars, dear children of dark night,
>   on circles you march and whirl about,
> O brilliant and fiery begetters of all.
> Fate, everyone's fate you reveal,
>   and you determine the divine part for mortals
>   as, wandering in midair, you gaze upon the seven
>   luminous orbits.[38]

Magic[39]

Hand in hand with fate went magic, a vastly popular way of coping with fate. Since the inhabitants of the empire felt that they were puppets on a string, they needed to find a way of influencing the puppeteer. The key was cosmic sympathy; granted that the essence of divinity was power and that divine power pervaded all that exists, then channeling it became mandatory.

A. SHAMANS AND SHAMS

Enter the magicians *(magi/magoi),* the channels of cosmic sympathy—its agents. They appear most colorfully in a recently discovered collection of Greek magical papyri from Greco-Roman Egypt.[40] The magicians of the papyri are religious ministers. The venerable among them were associated with temples of Egyptian and Greek deities, usually members of the temple priesthood. They demonstrate mastery of the older languages and religious traditions and possess a galaxy of gifts, among which are visions, trances, speaking in tongues, prophecy, insight into psychic states, and miracles.

Their culture was what one scholar has called "shamanistic," and about shamans he writes:

> A shaman may be described as a psychically unstable person who has received a call to the religious life. As a result of his call he undergoes a period of rigorous training, which commonly involves solitude and fasting, and may involve a psychological change of sex. From this religious "retreat" he emerges with the power, real or assumed, of passing at will into a state of mental dissociation. In that condition, like the Pythia [the priestess at Delphi] or like a modern medium, he is not thought to be possessed by an alien spirit; but his own soul is thought to leave its body and travel to distant parts, most often to the spirit world.[41]

Others, far less venerable and shamanistic, were itinerant craftsmen who would adopt any and every religious tradition that seemed useful. With little or no understanding, these journeymen used words more for sound than sense, inserted their own material, and recognized no cultural differences between the deities of the Greeks, Egyptians, Romans, or Jews.

In a world alive with forces and charged with cosmic sympathy, the magician, with his handbooks of magic containing the wisdom of the past, gave people the feeling that he could make things work in a world where they did not work as they used to—he could tap, regulate, and channel the "invisible energies."[42] In short, the magician was the agent of worried, troubled, and troublesome souls.

B. KINDS OF MAGIC

Some were shamans, some were shams, but the ancients could distinguish between the two. They knew of a lower magic *(goetia)*—

generally harmful ("black magic").[43] They also knew of a higher magic, theurgy (*theurgia*: "white magic"), which sought to actualize the divine presence.[44] And there was a magic in between *(mageia),* which could be either. The world of theurgy was the place of the shaman; the world of *goetia,* the place of the sham.

In the next chapter, we will see theurgy at work among a community of philosophers, and *goetia* in the literary account of a young man with a dangerous penchant for the curious. Philosophers saw theurgy as a beneficent discipline designed to effect a divine encounter; the litterateur discovered disaster in *mageia* and *goetia.*

One of the many surviving theurgic texts details an extensive discipline, with stanzas interspaced with formulae, some of which use the abbreviation "Iao" for YHWH, God of Israel. The discipline concludes with this assuring rubric:

> Having done this, return as lord of a godlike nature which is accomplished through this divine encounter.[45]

The text underscores the ancient desire for divinization through the encounter with divinity, a transformation much sought in antiquity among Pagans, Jews, and Christians.

VIII. Conclusion

Religion for the Greeks and Romans demonstrates two forms, civic and votive. A clear set of convictions pervaded both: (1) power is the essence of divinity; (2) the universe is charged with the power, grandeur, and menace of divinity; (3) cosmic sympathy binds together the divine and human worlds; (4) individual and social well-being is rooted in establishing and maintaining the right relationship with the gods and goddesses; and (5) religion, especially civic and votive ritual, channels divine power for better or worse.

Although civic religion long played a leading role, votive religion, with its emphasis on the individual and personal, moved to center stage during the first three centuries of our era. The fragility of personal and imperial life began to dominate the script, and votive religion gradually upstaged the empire's civic religion.

A supporting cast of Fortuna-Tyche, astrologers, and magicians entered from the wings. The new religious drama drew frequent applause from educated and uneducated alike because it responded, often with remarkable effect, to life's frequent hostile demands, to people's vulnerability, and to the quest for security in the here and hereafter.

Behind the scenery, the theatrical masks, and the script of imperial Paganism, however, one can sense and sometimes actually glimpse a thoroughgoing piety that sought the holy, which it addressed in countless names for the profusion of Pagan gods and goddesses. Sometimes devotees forsook food, sex, and vice to know for sure whether Mandulis was indeed the sun-god. Sometimes they imitated a hero-sage like Apollonius of Tyana in the hope of ascending to heaven. Sometimes they entered the "golden house" of Asclepius to petition the healer for a cure of body and spirit.

Some there were who touched the creator in a momentary gaze at "night's starry domain of heaven." Some there were whom the god touched in a dream, curing a blind eye. Some there were whom the Thrice-Great Hermes taught "about the things that exist, to understand their nature, to know god." Some there were—little people in a small city of Asia Minor—convinced that they were "a portion of God, his angels." And some there were who knew the feel of divinization through theurgy.

We have considered major characteristics of the Greco-Roman Pagan religions to establish the background for conversion in ancient Paganism. But already, perhaps without realizing it, we have seen instances, albeit sporadic, of conversion in ancient Paganism. Perhaps most Pagans did not cross the boundaries into other religions; some, however, converted to a deeper piety in their own.

NOTES

1. Tertullian, *Apology* 12: 1, 13:1–6 (PL 1:338, 344–46; trans. Emily J. Daly, *Tertullian: Apology,* FC 10 [1950] 43, altered).

2. *Abodah Zarah* 1:2b (*The Babylonian Talmud: Seder Nezikin in Four Volumes,* ed. I. Epstein [London: Soncino Press, 1936] 4:3–4).

3. For text and translation, see Arthur Darby Nock, "A Vision of Mandulis Aion," *HTR* 27 (1934) 53–102, text and translation on 61–64. See also his "Later Egyptian Piety," in *Essays on Religion in the Ancient World* (Cambridge: Harvard University Press, 1972) 2:572. Mandulis was a solar deity, here associated with Ra; Isis (for whom, see Chapter 3) eventually took precedence over him.

4. John Ferguson, *The Religions of the Roman Empire* (Ithaca: Cornell University Press [Aspects of Greek and Roman Life, ed. H. H. Scullard], 1970) 65. I am indebted to Professor Ferguson for this and much else in this chapter.

5. Philostratus, *The Life of Apollonius of Tyana* 8:30 (F. C. Conybeare, ed., *The Life of Apollonius of Tyana,* Loeb [1921–1927] 2:402–3).

6. See Ferguson, *The Religions of the Roman Empire,* 88–98; S. Prince, *Rituals of Power: The Roman Imperial Cult in Asia Minor* (New York: Cambridge University Press, 1984) 23–73; and Lily Ross Taylor, *The Divinity of the Roman Emperor* (1931; reprint, Chico: Scholars Press, 1981).

7. Taylor, *The Divinity of the Roman Emperor.* In Rome the tradition started with Caesar, who saw divinity as an essential feature of the monarchy—he was chiefly influenced by Hellenistic regal traditions (58). Caesar's apotheosis was recognized in 43 B.C.E., if we are to credit the memoirs of Octavian, his adopted son and eventual successor (90–91), who, as Augustus, would be deified.

8. For a discussion of the god and his cult sites, see Károly Kerényi, *Asklepios: Archetypal Image of the Physician's Existence,* trans. Ralph Manheim (New York: Pantheon Books [Bollingen 65.3], 1959). For a collection of texts in English, see Emma J. and Ludwig Edelstein, eds., *Asclepius: A Collection and Interpretation of the Testimonies,* 2 vols. (Baltimore: The Johns Hopkins University Press, 1945); the second volume is a detailed study of Asclepius as hero and deity, temple medicine, cult, etc.

9. Cited without reference to source in Ferguson, *Religions of the Roman Empire,* 110.

10. E. Edelstein and L. Edelstein, *Asclepius,* vol. 2, texts 272, 273:126; see also vol. 1, 44–45:81–83.

11. Apuleius, *Metamorphoses* 11:5 (J. Arthur Hanson, ed. and trans., *Apuleius: Metamorphoses,* Loeb [1989] 2:298–99).

12. Arthur Darby Nock, *Conversion: The Old and the New in Religion from Alexander the Great to Augustine of Hippo* (Oxford: Clarendon Press, 1933) 7.

13. For what follows, see Mary Beard, "Priesthood in the Roman Republic," in Mary Beard and John North, eds., *Pagan Priests: Religion and Power in the Ancient World* (Ithaca: Cornell University Press, 1990) 19–48.

14. See John North, "Diviners and Divination at Rome," in Beard and North, *Pagan Priests,* 51–71.

15. See Taylor, *Divinity of the Roman Emperor,* 181–204.

16. For what follows, see Ferguson, *Religions of the Roman Empire,* 99–131; and André-Jean Festugière, *Personal Religion Among the Greeks* (Berkeley: University of California Press, 1954), especially 19–36.

17. Ferguson, *Religions of the Roman Empire,* 67–73.

18. Ptolemaeus (fl. 180 C.E.), cited in Festugière, *Personal Religion Among the Greeks,* 118. The translation is that of T. F. Higham and C. M. Bowra, *The Oxford Book of Greek Verse in Translation* (Oxford: Clarendon Press, 1938) 643 (n. 621).

19. Eusebius, *The Life of Constantine* 1:28; for Athena, see Zosimus, *New History* 5:6.

20. See Kerényi, *Asklepios,* 18–46; the other sites are Kos and Rome.

21. Testimony 423:4, in E. Edelstein and L. Edelstein, *Asclepius,* 1:230, cited in Luther H. Martin, *Hellenistic Religions: An Introduction* (New York: Oxford University Press, 1987) 51.

22. Augustine, *Confessions* 8:29 (James J. O'Donnell, ed., *Augustine: Confessions* [Oxford: Clarendon Press, 1992] 1:101); the scene and its implications are studied in detail in Chapter 9.

23. See Ferguson, *Religions of the Roman Empire,* 151–56.

24. Walter Scott, ed., *Corpus Hermeticum: Ancient Greek and Latin Writings Which Contain Religious or Philosophic Teachings Ascribed to Hermes Trismegistus* (1924; reprint, London: Dawsons of Pall Mall, 1968) 1:114–15. See also Luther Martin, *Hellenistic Religions,* 146–50; and Ferguson, *Religions of the Roman Empire,* 108–9.

25. Cited in Robin Lane Fox, *Pagans and Christians* (San Francisco: Harper & Row, 1988) 169; for source discussion, see 711–12, especially the introduction and n. 16.

26. See David E. Aune, "Oracles," *ER* 11:81–86.

27. For an extended discussion of the Asclepius religion, see E. Edelstein and L. Edelstein, *Asclepius,* vol. 2: the volume is devoted to interpretation based on the testimonies.

28. See Ferguson, *Religions of the Roman Empire,* 132–49; Franz Cumont, *After Life in Roman Paganism* (1922; reprint, Dover Publications, 1959); and A. Hilary Armstrong, *Expectations of Immortality in Late Antiquity* (Marquette: Marquette University Press, 1987).

29. For discussion of burial, funeral rites, and mourning in Rome, see Keith Hopkins, *Death and Renewal* (Cambridge: Cambridge University Press, 1983).

30. Cited in Ferguson, *Religions of the Roman Empire,* 34. For full discussion, see the entire chapter, 132–49; Fox, *Pagans and Christians,* 95–98; and Ramsay MacMullen, *Paganism in the Roman Empire* (New Haven: Yale University Press, 1981) 53–56.

31. Homer, *The Odyssey* 10:215–23 (V. Berard, *L'Odyssée* [Paris: Les Belles Lettres, 1968] 2:92); the word for spirit here is *psyche.*

32. Virgil, *Aeneid* 6:699–702 (R. D. Williams, *The Aeneid of Virgil, Books 1–6* [New York: St. Martin's Press, 1972] 147); the term is *imago.*

33. Virgil, *Aeneid* 6:540–44 (Williams, 147).

34. Thus, Festugière, *Personal Religion Among the Greeks,* 2:85–104; "votive religion" is Walter Burkert's, *Ancient Mystery Cults* (Cambridge: Harvard University Press, 1987) 12–29.

35. Burkert, *Ancient Mystery Cults,* 13–14.

36. Lucretius, *De rerum natura* 1:21–25 (W. H. D. Rouse, trans. and ed., *Lucretius: De rerum natura,* Loeb [1931] 4). The goddess is Venus. Lucretius was doubtless dead when the poem appeared in 55 B.C.E.; it is his only extant work. An Epicurean, he was grounded in the physical theory of Epicurus (d. 270 B.C.E.): man is mortal; the cosmos is an accident; there is no providential god; the criterion of the good life is pleasure.

37. Cited in Ferguson, *Religions of the Roman Empire,* 85, where he also considers additional reasons for the fatalism: Stoic ideas of destiny, the onset of astrology, association with Iris (goddess of the rainbow and massager of the gods).

38. *The Orphic Hymns* 7:3–8, cited in Martin, *Hellenistic Religions,* 101. The text and translation is in A. N. Athanassakis, ed., *The Orphic Hymns: Text, Translations, and Notes* (Missoula: Scholars Press, 1977) 12–13.

39. For discussion, see Georg Luck, *Arcana Mundi: Magic and the Occult in the Greek and Roman Worlds* (Baltimore: Johns Hopkins University Press, 1985). He presents collections of annotated texts on each of the arcane subjects with interpretive discussion. Luck defines magic as "a technique grounded in a belief in powers located in the human soul and in the universe outside ourselves, a technique that aims at imposing the human will on nature or on human beings by using supersensual powers. Ultimately, it may be a belief in the unlimited powers of the human soul" (3).

40. For the texts and interpretive introduction, see Hans Dieter Betz, ed., *The Greek Magical Papyri in Translation, Including the Demotic Spells,* 2nd. ed. (Chicago: University of Chicago Press, 1986).

41. E. R. Dodds, *The Greeks and the Irrational* (Berkeley: University of California Press, 1951) 141. See also Luck, *Arcana Mundi,* 11–15.

42. Betz, *Greek Magical Papyri,* xlvii.

43. See Apuleius, *Metamorphoses* 2:5 (Hanson, Loeb 1:68); here he is describing Pamphile, the witch, and her potions.

44. For discussion, see Luck, *Arcana Mundi,* 20–25.

45. See Betz, *Greek Magical Papyri,* 40–43 (*Papyri Graecae Magicae* IV. 154–285) for the entire rite.

Chapter 3

CONVERSION IN PAGANISM

Introduction

We have considered some primary characteristics of Greco-Roman Pagan religions and, in the process, seen glimpses of a piety that might easily indicate conversion. The subject of this chapter goes beyond glimpses to two extended examples of ritual and conversion in ancient personal religion. The first is a classic account of conversion in the mystery religions of Greece and Rome; the second, a detailed example of conversion in the philosophical schools of antiquity.

I. The Mystery Religions[1]

The most arresting expression of personal or votive religion in antiquity can be seen in the mystery religions. They first appeared in prehistory during the festive rites celebrated at Eleusis, the most important religious center in the Greek world. But for their development and spread we must turn to the Hellenistic period (336–63 B.C.E.), inaugurated by Alexander and his conquests (336–323 B.C.E.).

The soil was already well tilled for a new religious planting in the late Hellenistic period.[2] Civic religion with its formalities had come to stand aloof from the needs and aspirations felt by individuals, who began to look to other forms of religion for answers. In addition, colonization, both Greek and Roman, meant that the religions of the colonizers came face-to-face with the religions of the colonies—whether in Egypt, North Africa, the Middle East, or even India. The net result of the encounter was mutual assimilation. Sometimes assimilation expressed itself in syncretism, and sometimes, in a new religion. Egyptian

Isis is a familiar example. In our era she became the Greek Aphrodite, Lady Justice (Dike) of the poets and philosophers, Demeter of Eleusis, and finally the universal deity of the Mediterranean world.

Challenged by the new divinities and religions in a changing cultural world, people came to sense an emptiness in their public piety, a void that could be filled only by a piety more attentive to them as individuals, to their precarious position in the world, and to their deeply felt needs. They grew fascinated by the world beyond, with the underworld, death, and the universe itself, deifying in detail time (Kronos), destiny (Moira), nature (Physis), and the All (Aion).

The mysteries stepped in to fill the painful gap between the public and the private, between the formal in religion and the personal. The mysteries held out the promise of a better life here and hereafter, and the rites of initiation that were developed were designed to fulfill the promise.

Performed in honor of a given deity, the rites (1) required of their subjects' careful (and costly) preparation, (2) demanded personal decision, (3) consisted of dramatic ceremonies centered on the individual and her or his aspiration for a better way, (4) sought to induce in the adherent a direct and transforming experience of the sacred through intimacy with deity, and (5) encouraged lifelong religious formation and service.

The Rites[3]

The mysteries were symbolized by a covered wooden basket (cista mystica), which signified that the contents were shrouded in secrecy. Only those initiated could know what was within because the mystery involved revealing the inexpressible sacredness of the deity— the god or goddess unveiled!

The rule first formulated for Eleusis held sway: the holy rites [Demeter's] are "not to be transgressed, nor pried into, nor divulged. For a great awe of the gods stops the voice."[4] Secrecy covered all the main rituals and is responsible for the term *mysteries,* the root of which is *muo*—in Greek, "I close" (one's eyes or mouth). As a result, detailed knowledge of the rites and their meaning is difficult to acquire.

A. TERMINOLOGY

The terminology, at least, has been recovered. The rites initiated devotees into a specific cult—the Isiacists (initiates of Isis, *Isiakoi telesthenai)* or Dionysians *(Dionysiakoi telesthenai),* and so forth. Since their new condition was a matter of personal choice, ethnicity, birth, or status did not matter. A Roman as well as a Greek could be a Dionysian; an artisan as well as a senator could be an Isiacist; a Copt soldier as well as a wealthy merchant could be a Mithraist.

Central to the process of becoming an initiate was ritual: the rites *(teletai/orgia)* were celebrated *(telein)* by an initiation priest *(telestes/ hierophantes)* in an initiation hall *(telesterion),* which was the setting for a festal occasion. Processions, dances, and music framed the actual celebrations that took place there—sometimes in a temple, as among the Isiacists, sometimes in a cave, as among the initiates of Mithra, often in a crypt.

The rites consisted of a closely connected sequence of dramatic actions *(dromena)* that usually involved the showing of certain symbols *(deiknumena)* coupled with interpretations *(exegeses)* through sacred narrative *(legomena/hieroi logoi),* usually ancient myths, yielding a revelation of deity *(epopteia)* as the culmination of the rites and the highest stage an initiate could reach.

B. STAGES

But initiation into the mysteries was not just an isolated happening. The rites demanded attentive preparation, part of which was purificatory *(katharsis)* and part formative. Entry into the group of devotees *(systasis)* was graded. The ancient Eleusinian mysteries, for instance, consisted of two parts.[5] The "Lesser Mysteries," which assembled the candidates for instruction and a test of their worthiness, were celebrated in the spring and involved ritual purification and public sacrifice. The goal of these lesser mystery rites was to prepare the candidates by purification and form the candidates for initiation into the "Greater Mysteries," a ten-day festival held in the fall and consummated in the sacred precincts of Demeter's sanctuary at Eleusis.

The mysteries of Mithras, which came to the fore in the second century of our era, exhibited seven stages.[6] The first three were preparatory; the next three brought ever-deeper intimacy and union with the divine Mithra. The culmination was the seventh: called "Father," it signaled identification with Kronos/Helios, the father of Mithras, god of the universe and time. The seven stages, according to the second-century Pagan philosopher Celsus (c. 170 C.E.), represent the ascent of the initiate's soul through the planets to heaven via the "golden gate" of the sun.[7]

II. The Golden Ass

Although the discipline of the secret draws a curtain between us and the drama enacted, an account survives that raises the curtain: the racy Latin novel *Metamorphoses* (better known as *The Golden Ass*).[8]

A. THE WORK

Composed about 170 C.E. by Apuleius, a well-born North African rhetorician (b. 125), toward the end of his life, *Metamorphoses* recounts the exploits of Lucius, whose fascination with magic has remarkable consequences.

Thereby hangs a series of tales—comic, erotic, idealized, and tragic. In the first three books, Lucius comes to the Greek city of Hypata in search of magic, makes love to his host's serving girl in order to find it, comes face-to-face with magic, and is transformed into an ass. The next four books describe his experiences, linked to the fate of Charite, a girl whom bandits have taken hostage. The following three books (8–10) recount his wretched life at the hands of four successive owners.

The tales of the first ten books seem fantastic, at least until set in the context of Apuleius' second-century world, a world dominated, as we have seen, by the conviction that divine cosmic forces shaped one's lot and destiny: the individual was a puppet and fate was the puppeteer.

Enter magic with its promise and power to fix a world that did not work well for anyone but the favored few. So pervasive was the practice of magic that Apuleius himself faced a charge of using magic to make a rich widow his wife. He wrote his *Apology* in vigorous and successful defense of his innocence. Perhaps the experience chastened him. For all its humor and many bizarre accounts, *Metamorphoses* was a warning: "Know, esteemed reader, that you are reading a tragedy, and no mere comedy" (10:2). The tragedy—the tales and the way Apuleius tells them—seems to reflect his conviction that the world he knows turns people into beasts. Augustine, who spent the first year of his higher education at Madauros, thought Apuleius was recording his own experience.[9]

In the eleventh book we enter another world, the world of the mysteries, in which the divine will (providence) takes the initiative and imposes divine order.[10] The conflict between the earlier books and this last book is between the malignant will of the demon and the providential will of Isis.[11] The world of magic turns people into beasts; the world of the mysteries turns them into gods.

Lucius and the reader discover a world enhanced rather than debased, and experience divine rather than asinine transformation. The magic of the mysteries is theurgy; the magic of Greek Hypata is *goetia*.

B. AUTOBIOGRAPHY

Apuleius borrowed the Lucius tales from a now lost Greek work. Nonetheless, he composed *Metamorphoses* with a strong admixture of autobiography—especially in the twelfth book, entirely his own composition.[12] As an Isis initiate, he was thoroughly familiar with the rites. The religious experience reflected in the work bears the mark of authenticity, as does the conviction that binds the whole work together—Isis saves people from the vanities of this world, which make them little more than beasts, for a life of blissful service both here and hereafter.[13] Isis, not magic, saves.

III. The Mysteries of Isis

The First Stage

At the end of the tenth book, Lucius flees his fourth owner, a carnival showman, by galloping to Cenchreae, the port city east of Corinth. The eleventh opens with the eve of the Isis festival, celebrating the opening of navigation (March 5, the *Isidis Navigium*). Lucius is asleep on an abandoned part of the beach, but moonrise awakes him. Suffused by the "silent mysteries of dark night," Lucius has a vision of Isis in the rising moon and sees that human affairs are "wholly governed by her providence," and not by the practitioners of the "evil arts" (*artes maleficii: goetia*).[14]

A. THE DREAM

Lucius immediately performs a ritual immersion by plunging his head into the waves seven times; he then begs Isis to restore him to the Lucius he was—or to let him die. At that he falls back to sleep (or into a trance) and encounters Isis. She asserts that her divinity is one, though all the world worships her under different forms; then, she reveals her true name: Queen Isis (the *Metamorphoses* has all the overtones of an Isiac missionary tract).

Next, she assures him that his day of salvation is dawning: he will see a procession and a priest carrying a garland of roses attached to a sistrum (a distinctive Isiac musical instrument)—ironically, roses were the very flower that had gotten him into trouble in the first place (2:16). Without hesitation and relying on her good will, he should push through the crowd, join the procession, go right up to the priest and, as if he were going to kiss his hand, pluck the roses. Immediately he would slough off the hide of the beast. To assure him, Isis tells Lucius that just as she is present to him, she is simultaneously present to the priest also in a dream, instructing him what he must do next. We then learn that at the command of Isis the crowd will part for Lucius and that no one, thinking that he may be a sham magician, will misinterpret his sudden transformation.

The *do ut des* follows. In return for his regained humanity, she explains, he must pledge his life, even to his last breath, to her service—a benefit given for a benefit received. Under Isis' guardianship he will live in happiness and, she assures him, even when he must travel down to the dead, he will see her in the dark underworld, holding court, while he dwells in the Isles of the Blest at the ends of the earth (the Elysian Fields). In addition, she promises:

> I will favor you and you will constantly worship me. But if by assiduous obedience, worshipful service, and determined celibacy you win the favor of my godhead, you will know that I—and I alone—can even prolong your life beyond the limits determined by your fate.[15]

B. THE REALITY: TRANSFORMATION

Everything happens just as Isis foretold in the vision (11:9–12). The procession numbers women in white, men and women carrying lights, corps of pipers and flutists, a boys' choir in gleaming white chanting a hymn, and crowds of those to be initiated—men and women of every rank and age playing their sistrums. The mysteries are not restricted by age, sex, or status. In the position of honor at the back of the procession come six priests of Isis vested in white and bearing the symbolic insignia of the cult. They are followed by priests *(pastiphori)* who carry cult statues and mystery symbols, including the covered basket and a golden urn—symbols of the deeper holiness shrouded in silence. At the end walks the high priest, who carries Lucius' salvation:

> In his right hand he held, decorated exactly according to the pre-scription of the divine promise, a sistrum for the goddess, a crown for me; and it was fitting that it should be a crown of victory, by Hercules, since now, after enduring so many great toils and pass-ing through so many perils, by the providence of the great and mighty goddess I would overcome Fortune, who was so savagely battering me. . . . (11:12; Griffiths, 84–85)

Lucius eats the garland of roses, comes to his former self, amazes the crowd, receives a white garment from an initiate, and hears a homily from his priest about his wretched life and the responsibilities imposed by his rebirth (renata). Ill-starred curiosity and enslaving lust had turned him into an ass. Birth, status, and education had availed him nothing. Yet blind Fortuna, while she tortured him, led him through random wickedness to this holy event. Now she may rage at losing him, yet he can take heart:

> For hostile fate has no power over those whose lives have been claimed by the majesty of our goddess. . . . Now you have been received into the protection of a Fortuna who is not blind, but sees, and who illumines the other gods too with the radiance of her light. So, then, a happier face in keeping with the white cloak you have assumed. Follow the procession of the Savior Goddess with triumphant step. Let the unbelievers take note . . . behold here is Lucius! He has been freed from his former sufferings. . . . Accept of your own free will the yoke of service. For when you have begun to serve the goddess, then will you better realize the result of your freedom. (11:15; Griffiths, 86–89)

After a long and painful journey, Lucius has come to his true self. The crisis of his identity is over.

The Second Stage

The dream, the procession, and his ritual rebirth are but the first stage of initiation. Lucius' full initiation awaits him. He goes to Isis' temple—only the initiated could do so. There he makes his home, dedi-cates himself to Isis' service as a layman, and becomes "the inseparable companion of the priests and a constant worshipper of Isis" (11:19).

In their midst, his days are devoted to learning the obligations of the cult, testing the demands of chastity, and acquiring prudence and circumspection.

Another dream occurs (part of which is quickly fulfilled). Lucius' desire for further initiation grows to insistence. He entreats the high priest only to receive a double caution: further initiation is entirely in the hands of Isis, and he must discipline himself against either over-eagerness or obstinacy. "'For,' his mentor says, 'both the gates of death and the guardianship of life were in the goddess's hands, and the act of initiation was performed in the manner of voluntary death and salvation obtained by favor'" (11:21).

So he waits obediently, abstaining from meat as well as sex to prepare for initiation. Lucius has found his new religion, but it requires training and discipline, even asceticism.

A. FULL INITIATION

In another dream, Isis declares to him that the day has come, explains the cost he must bear, and identifies the priest who is to administer the rites.

After morning prayers and the sacrifice to open both temple and day, the priest brings out sacred books and reads to Lucius the preparations that have to be made (11:22).

During the day, the priest leads him to the baths for the customary washing, prays that Lucius receive divine forgiveness, sprinkles him for a final cleansing, and brings him back to the temple.[16]

Word has been passed, and crowds flow into the temple to honor Lucius. The uninitiated are dismissed. Then, at dusk Lucius, wrapped in a new linen robe, is led into the sacred room where Isis' statue stands in the temple (cella). Prevented by the rule of secrecy from describing in detail what took place there, he writes:

> Listen then, but believe, for my account is true. I approached the boundary of death and, treading on Proserpine's threshold [the realm of the dead], was carried through all the elements, after which I returned. At dead of night I saw the sun flashing with bright effulgence. I approached close to the gods above and the gods below and worshiped them face to face.[17]

In the morning he puts on special robes to mark his consecration to holiness, enters the temple, and stands on a platform before the statue of Isis. Over his "holy attire" he wears an expensive, embroidered linen cloak called the "Olympian Stole," in his right hand he carries a flaming torch, and on his head he wears a palm-leaf crown, the gold leaves of which jut out like the rays of the sun. Resplendent like the sun, he is attired like the statue of Isis, before which he stands.

Then the curtains open for the crowds to view him. Later in the day he hosts a banquet and, on the third day, a sacred meal—both to mark that his "initiation was duly consummated."[18]

With rash inquisitiveness and a thirst for novelty, a young man dabbled in magic rituals and became an ass. Isis sought and transformed him into the divine young man through richly articulated rites of initiation that occupied all his days from March 5 to December 12. His birth as an ass took seconds; his rebirth as an initiate nine (!) months.

B. SYMBOLIC DRAMA AND THE MEANING OF THE RITES

The key passage to understanding the religious convictions that course through the rites is Lucius' account about approaching the boundaries of death. Although the passage does not specify the rites, the terms he uses suggest their significance.

1. Death and the Elements

Whatever the actual rites were, they symbolized death. In other mysteries the candidate for initiation was considered a person about to die *(homo moriturus)*, a fact that Lucius confirms just before his own full initiation: "For the gates of hell and the guarantee of life alike were in the power of the goddess, and the very rite of dedication itself was performed in the manner of a voluntary death and of a life obtained by grace."[19]

The rites took place in a crypt within the temple. Evidence from other cults suggests that Lucius was placed in a coffin and that incense induced a state of trance, in the course of which he encountered "the elements." Depicted on the walls of the crypt, perhaps as planets, the elements were astral deities who represented the kind of vast cosmic regions to which Paul alludes when he speaks about the "elemental spirits" (Gal 4:9). A hypnotic spell doubtless encouraged Lucius' participation.

Lucius was literally on a trip that had actually started with his baptism for the remission of sins earlier in the day. But from beginning to end, the trip dramatized his death to the old Lucius, the ass, whom he came to regard as wrong, sinful, and abhorrent.

2. The Effulgent Sun

Yet in the "dead" of night, Lucius saw brilliant lights. His words suggest that there was a ritual reawakening from his coffin trance, a ritual that involved alternating brilliant light (torches?) and deep-dyed darkness.[20] The mythical context within which he understood his trip is the journey of the sun (Re-Osiris-Pharaoh) through the underworld at night—a world unable to extinguish the sun.

The religious significance is Lucius' safe journey through ritual death to the threshold of resurrection and rebirth. Like the sun, he is not extinguished.

C. TRANSFORMATION

Lucius—still in the crypt-tomb—then encountered the gods and worshiped them face-to-face. The principal deity of the underworld was Osiris, whom Isis, his wife, had brought back to life; the principal deity of the heavens was Re, the sun. Re and Osiris are the "gods above and below" of whom he speaks. But behind both is Isis, to whom Lucius later prays:

> The gods above honor you, and you are worshipped by those
> below; you revolve the sphere of heaven, and illumine the sun,
> you guide the earth, and trample hell under your feet.[21]

The goal of full initiation was a divine encounter that transformed. For Lucius the transformation, first experienced when he ate the roses, was fully dramatized and accomplished in the morning. Arrayed in his linen tunic and embroidered cloak, wearing a crown of gleaming, gold palm leaves, and carrying a torch, he was "adorned like the sun and set up in the manner of a divine statue. . . ."[22] Before the people who crowded in, he, once an ass, stood as a god.

The identity of Lucius with Isis is unmistakable and reminiscent of the words of Paul: "As many of you [Christians] as were baptized into Christ have clothed yourselves with Christ" (Gal 3:27).

D. CONVERSION

The characteristics of conversion in *Metamorphoses* are also unmistakable. Lucius' world is a world in crisis, one in which the mass of people are convinced that their lots are fixed by forces above and beyond their control. Such a man is Lucius, a man in crisis of identity:

how can he get control over his fate? His first attempt, he discovers, is a magical disaster. He is debased by a debased world.

But a long quest filled with tragedy leads him to a second attempt. Driven "by the wildest storms of Fortune, and her heaviest gales," he learns that he has come to the "haven of Rest and the altar of Mercy," to the savior goddess, Isis (11:15; Griffiths, 86–87).

Isis and her community of initiates is his new religious reality, and, with the discovery, his conversion from the old to the new Lucius begins.

The rites and the instructions are the key: they provide the continual interaction necessary for his gradual transformation, which takes the better part of a year. Even then he discovers that conversion is ongoing; in a vision of Isis he is told to seek initiation into the kindred rites of Osiris, mate of Isis and god of the underworld.

Although Lucius may or may not be a stand-in for Apuleius, he is clearly a stand-in for the many initiates in the ancient mysteries whose experience of conversion would be otherwise unknown. In Lucius we have the biography of a Pagan convert.

IV. Philosophy and Religion

The second example of conversion in antiquity's votive religions is philosophy—something of a paradox in the modern world, since philosophy and religion are often seen as adversaries. Yet the Roman Stoic philosopher Seneca (1–65 C.E.), a celebrated spokesman for ancient philosophy, held that the two were one:

> [The task of philosophy] is to discover the truth about things divine and human. Religion never departs from her side, nor does religious feeling, nor duty, nor all the rest of the virtues joined together in a closely knit association. Philosophy has taught us to worship what is divine and to cherish what is human, and that dominion lies with the gods and that fellowship is the way for humans. [23]

The Schools[24]

Seneca was simply giving witness to the fact that philosophy's concern is the cure of souls *(anagoge)* and that its proper setting is community. The result was the development of the philosophical schools that had taken deep root in the cultural and intellectual landscape: Stoics, Cynics, Neopythagoreans, Peripatetics, and Epicureans, among the most prominent.

The axial figure in their rise was Socrates (469–399 B.C.E.), who saw his primary task as inquiring into the right conduct of life. As one classical scholar puts it:

> Socrates marks the turning point. His sense of mission [that] led him finally to martyrdom, his preoccupation with personality and with the quest for a basis for right conduct, his power of attracting and influencing disciples, all these things, through the impress which they made on his disciples, set a standard for *lovers of wisdom* and the *love of wisdom,* philosophers and philosophy: it is now that the words acquire popularity and definite meaning. Adhesion to Socrates somehow meant giving your soul to him.[25]

Plato (429–347 B.C.E.), Socrates' disciple, gave this adhesion enduring form by founding the Academy around 385 B.C.E. Organized as a corporate body with a continuous life of its own and provided with successive heads, the Academy survived until dissolved by the emperor Justinian (527–565 C.E.) in 529 C.E. In its latter days, the Academy launched the Platonic revival known as Neoplatonism, the philosophy shaped by Plotinus (200–270 C.E.) and so instrumental in the conversion of Augustine of Hippo.[26]

The Academy inspired other schools as well. Aristotle (384–322 B.C.E.), tutor of Alexander the Great, remained a member of the Academy until Plato's death, when he struck out on his own, founding the Peripatetics—a name derived from the covered court *(peripatos)* of his school in a grove sacred to Apollo just outside Athens. It, too, survived to undergo a revival in the first two centuries of the empire, disappearing from view when the Neoplatonists assumed the work of commenting on Aristotle.

Not long after Aristotle's death, a Cypriot named Zeno studied at the Academy (Polemon was its head then), eventually to strike out on his own as well. He taught in the *stoa poikile,* a public hall in Athens, from which the name of the school he founded (300 B.C.E.) derives, the Stoics.[27]

The school went through several phases in its development, the most important of which was the middle period, when the founder's namesake, Zeno of Tarsus, became head (201 B.C.E.). He revised the

Stoic system from top to bottom in the light of Platonic and Aristotelian ideas, emphasized ethics, and focused them to meet the needs of active statesmen and soldiers. As a result of this second Zeno, Tarsus became a center of Stoic learning and philosophy, a fact that would leave its deep impress on another of its famous citizens, the Christian Paul.

Middle Stoicism influenced the Roman period deeply, producing masters like Seneca, Musonius Rufus (30–102 C.E.), and the latter's pupil, Epictetus (55–135 C.E.), all of whom influenced many leading Romans, not the least of whom was the emperor Marcus Aurelius (121–180 C.E.).

Philosophical disputes of the second century of our era between the Academics, Peripatetics, and Stoics brought ethical questions to center stage. The Stoic school faded into the wings during the third century, although it had a lasting effect on Neoplatonism and on a number of early Christian thinkers.

The Pythagorean Way

Although there are still other philosophical schools worthy of our attention (among them, the Cynics and the Epicureans), for our purposes the most striking is the Neopythagorean school, which revived for the Greco-Roman world the ancient school of Pythagoras. Although he is the subject far more of legend than fact, a sketch is possible.

A. PYTHAGORAS[28]

Pythagoras was born on Samos, an island in the Aegean Sea. After journeys to Egypt and Babylon, he eventually emigrated (was exiled?) to Croton in southern Italy (531 B.C.E.). Because of its Greek colonies and because of Pythagoras' work there, that part of Italy was known as *Magna Graecia*—the site of a vigorous philosophical and religious revival.

There Pythagoras organized a loose society that functioned as a political and religious group (518–513 B.C.E.), which spread until, with its strength broken, it merged with other groups and schools by the end of the next century (400 B.C.E.).

Pythagoras' followers experienced him as something of a shaman. Their experience gave rise to legends about him, legends rooted in their experience of him and his teachings and shaped by the promise and possibilities of a life lived under Pythagorean rule.

His system turned on two tenets: that one's hidden self (*psyche/*

soul) is one's true self, which stands in opposition to one's physical self, and that one's true self can be liberated from the physical through successive reincarnations. Undergirding the principles is the conviction that the freed self is capable of immortality and, therefore, of divinity.

The key to the soul's ascent to the divine is asceticism. Integral to Pythagorean asceticism was the therapeutic value of a life of inquiry: Philosophic investigation gave a means of developing right relations with the world and the ordering principles that govern it. Like ritual practice, which also characterized the community, philosophy was a way of purification and, therefore, a way of salvation, as we shall see in detail.

B. NEOPYTHAGOREANISM[29]

Pythagorean tradition remained alive, inspiring a number of attempts to revive it. An important revival, usually called Neopythagoreanism, appeared in Rome and Egypt in the first century B.C.E. and persisted until fused with Neoplatonism in the third century of our era.

Although discovery of mathematics and number theory are attributed to Pythagoras and his immediate followers, Pythagorean beliefs about the soul left an even more distinctive stamp on the world of Greco-Roman thought. Pythagorean teachings are actually a network of related axioms: (1) the true self ought not to be equated with the experienced or empirical self; (2) true freedom is to be gained apart from earthly existence; (3) salvation involves disentanglement from this world's demands, conditions, and history; (4) the afterlife is a better life by far than present life; and (5) the true self, with its intimations of immortality, is in principle divine.[30]

But of more direct importance for understanding philosophy, religion, and conversion is Pythagoras' impact on the later history of Greek and Roman philosophy, especially the biographies by Diogenes Laertius (latter half, third century), Porphyry (232–305 C.E.), Porphyry's younger contemporary Iamblichus (250–325 C.E.), and the anonymous life preserved by Photius (820–891 C.E.).[31] Of these, Iamblichus' biography is the most important for us, because he recounts the life of Pythagoras primarily by depicting, as the title—*On the Pythagorean Way of Life*—suggests, life in the philosopher's school.[32]

A genuinely remarkable man, Pythagoras quickly became the focus of legend, a fact that ought to caution any reader who picks up the biographies. In addition, the biographies tend to be apologies for

philosophy as a way of life, akin to the *Metamorphoses* as an apology
for the mysteries of Isis—protreptics that run to apologies. And they
were successful: Porphyry and Iamblichus have been credited with
the revival of Pythagoras' philosophy, especially Iamblichus, who attempted to pythagoreanize late Platonic philosophy (Neoplatonism).[33]

Although Iamblichus' picture of the philosophical life is conditioned by his own school experience and his keen desire to pythagoreanize Neoplatonism, his work articulates the school ideal that
flourished in the late empire—however imperfectly realized. For the
study of conversion, its value lies in his depiction of how candidates are
admitted and formed.

Probation (Iamblichus, On the Pythagorean Way 17:71–79)

Pythagoras carefully observed candidates to determine the quality
of spirit or soul within. He inquired carefully about their families and
studied their dispositions toward laughter, silence, and chatter and how
they spent their leisure. He inquired into what caused them joy or pain,
how they dealt with others, what kind of physique they had, and how
they moved. And he looked carefully into the nature and quality of their
desires. We read that he saw all these visible signs as pointing to "invisible character traits in their souls" (17:71–72; Dillon and Hershbell,
Iamblichus, 97).

Those admitted to the school were put under supervision for three
years to see whether they had the stability, love, friendship, and inner
equipment required for learning. If they passed this scrutiny, they were
subjected to a five-year period of silence to acquire self-mastery, especially control of the tongue.

During the period of silence their possessions were held in common, and they attended the master's discourses by hearing them outside
the curtain or veil behind which he taught. Thus, they were given the
name "hearers" *(akousmatikoi)*. When a hearer left or was dismissed,
he was given double the value of what he had brought to the community, but from that moment forward he was considered to have died. His
fellow hearers even built tombs for the departed.

Disciples (18:80–89)

Those who passed the scrutiny of eight years were initiated as
disciples with ritual celebrations (nowhere described) and "many great
cleansings and purifications of the soul" (17:74; Dillon and Hershbell,

Iamblichus, 98–99). They could then go behind the veil and hear the master's discourses face-to-face. Now, at last, they could study philosophy.

But all were not alike in ability or progress. Some were "Pythagoreans," disciples of high ability, considered models for all others. Their possessions were held in common, and they lived a communal life.

The less able were the "Pythagorists," who continued to manage their own affairs and, in place of a communal life, assembled frequently to pursue common leisure activities.

There were similar divisions among the "Pythagoreans." Since there were two kinds of philosophy, the metaphysical and the ethical, so there were two ranks of Pythagoreans. The second rank comprised the probationers or hearers *(akousmatikoi)*. Their discourses were designed to teach ethics or practical wisdom, which was divided into three kinds, "For some discourses indicate what a thing is, others what is the best in any category; and others, what is necessary to do or not to do."[34]

The true followers formed the first rank, the *mathematikoi*. Through scientific study and argument they learned the reasons behind the injunctions learned as hearers. The axiom that distinguished them was that true philosophers ask why things and people are the way they are.

A Typical Day

Presumably, once a Pythagorean, always a Pythagorean; it was a total way of life marked by silence and contemplation. Iamblichus describes a typical day (21:96–100) of the recently initiated Pythagorean (and, presumably, Pythagorist).

The morning was devoted to solitary walks in sacred places (groves and temples) to set their "souls in order and compose their intellects" (21:96). After the morning walk, they associated with one another, again in sacred places, devoting themselves to "instructions, lessons, and . . . the improvement of their characters" (21:96). Next followed physical exercise—track, wrestling, long jumps, and shadowboxing—for which they prepared with oil-rubs. Lunch of bread and honey concluded the morning.

The time after lunch was devoted to matters pertaining to the management of their communal life, especially business that engaged externs, and visiting with guests. Late in the afternoon, they again took walks, this time in twos and threes, reviewing the lessons of the day and "training themselves in noble pursuits" (21:97).

After the walk, they bathed; dinner in common (ten or more together) followed, timed to finish before sunset. They drank wine with the meal, had vegetables and meat, and rarely fish. After dinner, public reading and drinks would follow—the oldest did the selecting and the coaching; the youngest, the reading. The day concluded with ritual libation:

> And when they were about to leave, the cup-bearer poured out a libation for them, and when the libations were made, the oldest proclaimed these things: not to have or destroy a cultivated and fruitful plant, and in like manner, not to harm or destroy a living being harmless by nature to the human race. In addition to these proclamations, they were ordered to have a reverent and good attitude to the divine, daemonic, and heroic orders of being, and to think in like manner about parents and benefactors; to assist the law, and to war with lawlessness. After this exhortation, each departed to his house. (21:98–99)

At the end of the day, wearing linen, the students "purged" their minds with hymns and musical odes as they fell asleep, for music itself was therapeutic: it improved "human character and ways of life" (25:114).

"Such then," Iamblichus concludes, "were the things transmitted each day to the association of the men for their nurture, and for the elevation of their way of life" (21:100).

Widespread Popularity

Philosophical schools commanded wide attention because they offered a compelling and credible way of life coupled with a systematic explanation of the gods, human beings, and the world. Their goal was the contemplation of the All that stood behind the multiplicity of this world—a contemplation that led to union with the All.

The philosophical schools produced some remarkable people.[35] Plato, spoken of as the son of Apollo, received reverence as a deity immediately after he died. Pythagoras became the subject of endless legend. Epicurus was a deity to his devotee Lucretius (cited earlier, the author of *The Way Things Are*). Apollonius ascended to heaven. Epictetus became a Pagan saint.

V. Philosophy and the Mysteries

To enter a philosophical school required conversion. The language of conversion studded the language of philosophy. For Plato, its purpose was to turn the soul around *(epistrophe);* for Cicero, to turn people from carelessness to piety *(conversio);* for Seneca, to discover the truth about things divine and human *(verum invenire);* for the author of the *Poimandres*, to summon to repentance those who follow the path of error and ignorance *(metanoia)*.[36]

Protreptic

As a result, philosophers wrote missionary propaganda, which acquired a technical name, protreptic, a tradition that started with Aristotle, whose early work, *Protreptikos,* extols the supreme value of contemplation as a way of life. Protreptics were exhortations that appealed to people to cast off their old ways and adopt philosophy as the true way of life. Other disciplines, like rhetoric, readily took up the tradition—Apuleius' *Metamorphoses,* which extols the supreme value of life according to the Isiac way, is an example.

But the goal of protreptics was conversion, a fact to which Augustine would attest; when he came across Cicero's protreptic for philosophy, *Hortensius,* it forever changed the direction of his life.[37]

Conversion to Philosophy

The candidates who came to Pythagoras' school were on a quest for divine truth and union with divinity. Although their previous education inspired the quest (Iamblichus, 16:68–70), they came to see it as self-indulgent and debased. Indeed, much of their subsequent formation consisted of purification: ascetic, cognitive, and musical in a ritual setting—repentance coupled with a complex therapy designed to wean them away from a life immersed in the senses.

Only after careful screening were they admitted, and then only as probationers. The first stage was three years of supervision principally designed to test their aptitude for the philosophical life.

Dominated by silence broken only by instruction behind the veil, the second stage of five years followed. Although the intent was formation of the intellect, it is best described as the "cure of the soul" *(anagoge)*.

Since the philosophical school was a voluntary association, they were free to leave, and we may surmise that many did. But the school was also free to dismiss, and, given its demanding standards, we may also surmise that many left not of their own volition.

Admission was awarded to those who persevered. Iamblichus, perhaps taking a page from the mysteries, speaks of rites of initiation but discloses no details. Depending on ability and progress, the novices joined the ranks of either the hearers or the mathematicians. Whether the boundaries between the two were permeable we are not told. In any case, their subsequent formation—how long it took is not stated—was filled with days that combined contemplation, instruction, athletics, and communal ritual. At some point in the process they fully expected and were fully expected to attain the revelation of, and union with, the All.

Philosophy and the Mysteries

As Iamblichus describes it, the Pythagorean way has the ambience of a mystery religion. Pythagoras is a descending and ascending divinity, an uncorrupted soul sent down to communicate wisdom to souls that have fallen away from insight. Like a mystagogue, he leads the soul through the successive stages of Pythagorean philosophy to insight, *epopteia,* coupled with divine union.[38] Perhaps Pythagoras was himself an initiate.[39]

Whether in the mysteries or in the Pythagorean way, an initiate makes a personal decision to seek admission (Lucius, after some years embroiled in magic, and the Pythagorean, after the demanding disciplines of grammar and rhetoric). Both were subjected to a highly selective screening process and experienced a long period of intellectual, social, and religious formation laced with extended rituals (Lucius, for months, and the Pythagorean, for years). Full initiation enacted the entire process, evoked and stabilized commitment, and envisioned a permanent way of life. For both Lucius and the Pythagorean, conversion meant the cure of the soul *(anagoge),* a new vision of divinity, and the intimacy of divine union.

Although conversion to the mysteries was not conversion to philosophy, their similarity of goal and mode of reaching it are best understood in the context of the personal world of votive religion, a world within which Judaism and Christianity also flourished. They all breathed the same air.

NOTES

1. For what follows see Walter Burkert, *Ancient Mystery Cults* (Cambridge: Harvard University Press, 1987); Luther H. Martin, *Hellenistic Religions: An Introduction* (New York: Oxford University Press, 1987) 58–89; and Marvin W. Meyer, ed., *The Ancient Mysteries: A Sourcebook* (San Francisco: Harper & Row, 1987). Additional studies are cited at relevant points.

2. Burkert, *Ancient Mystery Cults,* 12–29, reviews the reasons.

3. See Burkert, *Ancient Mystery Cults,* 7–11, for what follows.

4. *Hymn to Demeter* 478–79 (Helene P. Foley, ed., *The Homeric Hymn to Demeter: Translation, Commentary, and Interpretive Essays* [Princeton: Princeton University Press, 1993] 26–27); for the theology of Eleusinian mysteries, see 84–97.

5. For detailed discussion of the degrees of initiation and the stages, see George E. Mylonas, *Eleusis and the Eleusinian Mysteries* (Princeton: Princeton University Press, 1961) 237–85.

6. M. J. Vermaseren, *Mithras, The Secret God* (New York: Barnes and Noble, 1963) 138–53 (the seven grades), 129–39 (initiation); David Ulansey, *The Origins of the Mithraic Mysteries: Cosmology and Salvation in the Ancient World* (New York: Oxford University Press, 1989) 3–13 (status of question about interpretation).

7. Cited in Meyer, *The Ancient Mysteries: A Sourcebook,* 209. For Celsus, see Henry Chadwick, ed. and trans., *Origen: Contra Celsum* 6:22 (Cambridge: Cambridge University Press, 1965) 334. Because Origen (d. 254) responds to Celsus extensively in his work, scholars have been able to reconstitute about 70 percent of Celsus' work *On the True Doctrine;* for a study and translation, see R. Joseph Hoffmann, *Celsus on the True Doctrine* (New York: Oxford University Press, 1987).

8. For the text and translation, see J. Arthur Hanson, ed. and trans., *Apuleius: Metamorphoses,* 2 vols., Loeb (1989); for text, translation, and commentary on the eleventh book, which deals with initiation, see J. Gwyn Griffiths, *Apuleius of Madauros: The Isis-Book (Metamorphoses, Book XI)* (Leiden: E. J. Brill, 1975); for a recent interpretive study, see Carl C. Schlam, *The Metamorphoses of Apuleius: On Making an Ass of Oneself* (Chapel Hill: University of North Carolina Press, 1992). See also Martin, *Hellenistic Religions,* 16–34; and Arthur Darby Nock, *Conversion: The Old and the New in Religion from Alexander the Great to Augustine of Hippo* (Oxford: Clarendon Press, 1933) 138–55, who retells the story, but is ambivalent about whether it represents conversion to the mysteries of Isis (especially 155). For Nock the problem is that the cult of Isis did not require the total allegiance of its

adherents: his view of prophetic—and therefore true—religion is that it is all or nothing.

9. Augustine, *De civitate dei* 18:18, cited in Griffiths, *The Isis-Book,* 6.

10. For a masterful commentary, see Griffiths, *The Isis-Book.*

11. Schlam, *The Metamorphoses of Apuleius,* 50.

12. For discussion, see Griffiths, *The Isis-Book,* 1–7. What follows Lucius' transformation back into a human being has few points of contact with "Lucius or Ass," and, as Griffiths comments: "The whole atmosphere is one of spiritual expectation and tension, and it is hard to avoid the impression that a personal experience is being portrayed" (3).

13. H. J. Rose, *Handbook of Latin Literature* (London, 1936) 151, cited in Griffiths, *The Isis-Book,* 10.

14. *Metam.* 11:1 (Griffiths, *The Isis-Book,* 70–71). I follow the Griffiths text and translation for Book XI. For magic as *maleficium,* see Griffiths, 49.

15. *Metam.* 11:6 (Griffiths, *The Isis-Book,* 76–77; commentary 158–67).

16. *Metam.* 11:23 (Griffiths, *The Isis-Book,* 98). For discussion, see Griffiths, *The Isis-Book* 286–90: he interprets the bathing *(lavacro)* and the ablution *(purissime circumrorans abluit)* as a purification from sin, calls it baptism, considers that it was linked with triumph over death, and comments that there was a similar rite in the Mithraic mysteries. Tertullian, who was writing only a generation after Apuleius, speaks of both mysteries as initiating subjects by baptism (*De baptismo* 5 [Ernest Evans, ed., *Tertullian's Homily on Baptism* (London: SPCK, 1964) 12–13]).

17. *Metam.* 11:23 (Griffiths, *The Isis-Book,* 98–99; commentary, 294–308).

18. *Metam.* 11:24 (Griffiths, *The Isis-Book,* 100–101 and 318–19). The banquet celebrated his rebirth; the sacred meal, the completion of initiation. Such sacred meals are well known in the other mysteries as well.

19. *Metam.* 11:21 (Griffiths, *The Isis-Book,* 94–95; commentary, 296–301).

20. For comparative evidence, see Griffiths, *The Isis-Book,* 303–6.

21. *Metam.* 25 (Griffiths, *The Isis-Book,* 100–101, altered; commentary, 306–8).

22. *Metam.* 11:24 (Griffiths, *The Isis-Book,* 100–101; commentary, 308–18).

23. Seneca, Letter 90:3 (C. Costa, *Seneca: Seventeen Letters* [Warminster, Wilts., U.K.: Ars & Phillips, 1988] 86–87).

24. See, Nock, *Conversion,* 164–86; Robert L. Wilken, "Collegia, Philosophical Schools, and Theology," in Stephen Benko and John J. O'Rourke, eds., *The Catacombs and the Colosseum: The Roman Empire as the Setting of Primitive Christianity* (Valley Forge: Judson Press, 1971) 271–78.

25. Nock, *Conversion,* 165–66.

26. Augustine, *Confessions* 7:20 (James J. O'Donnell, ed., *Augustine: Confessions* [Oxford: Clarendon Press, 1992] 1:86); see Chapter 9.

27. For a valuable and accessible study, see J. M. Rist, *Stoic Philosophy* (Cambridge: Cambridge University Press, 1969).

28. For a collection of ancient biographies of Pythagoras, see David R. Fideler, ed., *A Pythagorean Sourcebook and Library: An Anthology of Ancient Writings Which Relate to Pythagoras and Pythagorean Philosophy* (Grand Rapids: Phanes Press, 1987). For a recent biography, see Peter Gorman, *Pythagoras: A Life* (London: Routledge & Kegan Paul, 1979), who assesses the ancient biographies, 1–13.

29. For the revival, its wellsprings, and its leaders, Porphyry and Iamblichus, see Dominic J. O'Meara, *Pythagoras Revived: Philosophy and Mathematics in Late Antiquity* (Oxford: Clarendon Press, 1989).

30. For discussion, see R. Bennett, "Pythagoras," *ER* 12 (1987) 113–15, and his valuable selective bibliography. See Walter Burkert, *Lore and Science in Ancient Pythagoreanism,* trans. E. Minar (Cambridge: Harvard University Press, 1972) for a study of the Pythagoras that stands behind the legends. See O'Meara, *Pythagoras Revived,* for Pythagoras and his system revived.

31. For translations of all four, see Fideler, *Sourcebook,* 57–156.

32. For text, translation, and commentary, see John Dillon and Jackson Hershbell, eds., *Iamblichus: On the Pythagorean Way of Life, Text, Translation, and Notes* (Atlanta: Scholars Press, 1991).

33. Thus, O'Meara, *Pythagoras Revived,* 210–15. Iamblichus' pythagoreanizing of Neoplatonism is explored in detail in the second part of the study.

34. *De vita Pythagorica* 18:82 (Dillon and Hershbell, *Iamblichus,* 106–7); see also Fideler, *Sourcebook,* 76–77.

35. Thus, Nock, *Conversion,* 175–76.

36. Cited in Nock, *Conversion,* 179–80: Plato, *Republic* 518D; Cicero, *De natura deorum* 1:77; Seneca, *Epistle* 90:3 (Costa, *Seneca: 17 Letters,* 86); and *Poimandres* 1:26–28 (the translation Nock gives does not indicate an elision; repent *[metanoésate]* is in 28). For the text, see Walter Scott, ed., *Corpus Hermeticum: Ancient Greek and Latin Writings Which Contain Religious or Philosophic Teachings Ascribed to Hermes Trismegistus* (1924; reprint, London: Dawsons of Pall Mall, 1968) 1:129–33.

37. Augustine, *Confessions* 3:4.7 (O'Donnell, 1:25). See Chapter 9.

38. See O'Meara, *Pythagoras Revived,* 214–15.

39. Iamblichus, *De vit. Pythag.* 3:19 (Dillon and Hershbell, *Iamblichus,* 44): *pásas theôn teletás.*

Chapter 4

CONVERSION IN ANCIENT JUDAISM:
THE SECOND-TEMPLE PERIOD

Introduction

Out of the innumerable religions and religious movements of the Greco-Roman world, only two—one the mother, the other the daughter—outlasted the Roman Empire to survive into the present: Judaism and Christianity. This chapter considers conversion in early Judaism.

The religious history of ancient Judaism turns on a series of pivotal events from about 1750 to 587 B.C.E.: Abraham and the patriarchs, Moses and the Exodus, the conquest of Palestine, the founding of the Davidic kingdom and the building of the temple at Jerusalem under Solomon, the split of the kingdom into Israel and Judaea, the fall of Israel in 722 B.C.E., and the fall of Jerusalem and destruction of the first temple in 587 B.C.E. All told, for about twelve hundred years nationality was the only way one could acquire identity as an Israelite: one had to be born an Israelite; birth *(natio)* was the way.

People of foreign birth lived and worked in Israel; so did their children and children's children. Such people had formal status as "resident aliens" (in Hebrew *gerim,* singular, *ger;* in Greek, *proselytoi, proselytos*); like the widow, orphan, and Levite, they were landless and powerless. If they were somehow absorbed into Israel, it was not by conversion; there is no evidence of conversion in preexilic Israel.[1] Once a *ger,* always a *ger.*

Exile

To answer the questions about becoming a Jew, however, we must consider a second series of pivotal events, from 587 B.C.E. to 70 C.E.

The first event begins with the fall of Jerusalem to Nebuchadnezzar, king of Babylon (2 Kgs 24:10–17). In 587 the king, provoked by the inhabitants, returned with his troops to destroy the temple, devastate the city, and carry off to Babylon the king (Zedekiah) and high priest (Seriah) and most of the city's remaining population (2 Kgs 25:1–21). Thus began the exile and the possibility of conversion as a way of becoming an Israelite.

I. Second-Temple Judaism

In 539 B.C.E., King Cyrus and the Persians conquered Babylon. A royal edict permitted Israelites to return to Palestine. Many returned to Judaea and Jerusalem—residency in Judaea would eventually give the returned Israelites the name "Jews" (Greek, *Judaioi,* inhabitants of Judaea) and their religion the name "Judaism" (*Judaismos,* the religion of the Judaeans).

The return begins the "postexilic" period, marked at its outset with the rebuilding and dedication of a new temple circa 520–515 B.C.E. (Ezr 3:1—7:16), which stood until destroyed by the Romans in 70 C.E. Thus, it is referred to as the second-temple period.

Conversion and the Returnees

The return took place in waves. In the middle of the next century, Ezra led a group of exiles back to Judaea (458 B.C.E.), only to discover that many of the earlier contingents had married Pagan residents, a fact that, as he saw it, jeopardized Israelite identity (Ezr 9:1–15). In Ezra's view intermarriage made them and their children *gerim.*

A question arose almost immediately: if they repented and sent away their foreign wives, could they reenter the covenanted people? The answer was that all who had married Gentile women must send "them away with their children" (Ezr 10:44). Ezra's proscription was ratified by Nehemiah, the Israelite governor (Neh 13:23–31). For both Ezra and Nehemiah the issue was of the utmost gravity: intermarriage threatened the identity and survival of the people of Israel. As before the exile, conversion was out of the question for the wives and the children.

The Maccabees and After

The Persians and their hegemony fell before the conquests of Alexander the Great (336–323 B.C.E.), who sought to evangelize his vast empire for Greek culture and civilization. Thus began (323 B.C.E.) the Hellenistic period for the Jews, which lasted until the Romans entered the scene in 63 B.C.E.

Under the Hellenistic kings that succeeded Alexander, the first of a series of Jewish revolts against foreign rule wracked Palestine. In 198 B.C.E., Syria displaced Egypt as the power in Palestine and, with some encouragement from the wealthy and well-placed in Israel, began a policy of Hellenization there. In the decade of the 160s the Hellenizing crisis culminated in a Jewish revolt under the Maccabees (167–166 B.C.E.) and the violation of the temple by the Syrian king, Antiochus Epiphanes. His form of Hellenism was extreme.

The Maccabean revolt was successful; in 164 B.C.E. the insurgents regained the temple, which they rededicated. Syrian oppression halted, and Israel acquired a measure of sovereignty under the Maccabean leaders (the dynasty was called Hasmonean), but not the old, preexilic sovereignty. Nor was the independence they gained what they knew under the Persians. But the sovereignty and independence they did have lasted until the Romans came a hundred years later, only to stay until ousted seven centuries later by Islam—prompting more than one wag to define Jewish history as "one damned thing after another."

Nonetheless, the years between the Maccabean revolt and the Roman invasion witnessed the clarification of identity, belief, and institutions that gave face and form to the Judaism of antiquity with which we are concerned.

Religious Identity

Ezra's solution—sending Gentile wives and children away—did not stick. The focus shifted from intermarriage to a more direct question: could Gentiles become Jews? The answer, though long in coming, points to a crucial shift that made conversion a possibility.

After the exile, the conception of Israel as a nation necessarily began to alter. Though the ancient idea of tribes, according to which early Israel had been organized, hung on, composition of the returnees came to be by clan, with classification by ritual status. Rather than a "Benjaminite," for instance, a person was a priest, Levite, or Israelite. Postexilic Israel gradually identified itself on cultic grounds rather than ethnic: ethnicity began to be defined by birth and religion. As a result, avenues into Judaism other than birth opened up.

II. Conversion in Second-Temple Judaism

At some point between the return in 537 B.C.E. and the Maccabean revolt, Jews developed a way of initiating non-Jews into the people of Israel. Precisely when is extremely difficult to determine, though an important document indicates that the date cannot be later than the second century B.C.E.

A Well-Established Tradition: Judith

The document is the Book of Judith. Authored in the late second century B.C.E., it takes conversion for granted.[2] Set in Nebuchadnezzar's Babylonian kingdom, the book is about the Assyrian Holofernes' legendary invasion of Israel, or more accurately, how Judith, with the help of Achior, Holofernes' Ammonite army commander, saved Israel. Not only was Israel saved but also Achior became a Jew in the process: "He came to full belief in God, and was circumcised, and admitted as a member of the community of Israel, as his descendants still are" (Jdt 14:10).

The author sets down three components for conversion: belief in God, circumcision, and admission into the Jewish community (more would be added in time). Although it is not at all clear whether they were necessary conditions or the expected norm,[3] the three components meant an entirely new religious reality for the convert: (1) a new doctrine of God, (2) a new code of worship and conduct, and (3) a new community.

A. BELIEF

Although Judaism is not a creedal religion, conversion involved a change of some fundamental convictions, especially about God. Specifically, converts had to reject any other divinity and adopt Israel's God as the only God. Modern scholars call such a belief "radical monotheism" because it rejected, root and branch, the very idea of more than one God.

In the period before the exile, monotheism does not apply—at least not across the board. Preexilic Israelites generally believed that their God was mightier than the gods of other nations, but not necessarily materially different from them—henotheism, as we have seen, is the technical term for such a conviction.

The prophets wrought the change. They insisted that the God of Israel was Lord of the entire universe, before whom there were no other gods. By the sixth century B.C.E., the prophetic view had won out: Israel's God was embraced as omnipotent, omniscient, creator of the universe, beyond the reach of the human mind—in short, the one, true God. If ancient Judaism had a creed, it was formulated in a prayer, the *Shema* (from its opening word) recited morning and evening (still): "Hear, O Israel: The Lord our God, the Lord is one. . . . "[4]

B. PRACTICE

Jewish monotheism did more than anything else in antiquity to distinguish Jew from Gentile and Judaism from the other religions of the Greco-Roman world. But ancient Judaism's monotheism was "practical" monotheism, which leads directly to the second component in conversion—conduct—a component made explicit by the end of the second century of our era, when the rabbis insisted that two related items pertaining to belief be required of Jews and potential converts: (1) the recognition of the binding authority of the Torah and (2) the acceptance of its 613 precepts.[5]

Neither item was an innovation, for biblical religion was a matter of practices; conduct mirrored conviction and required enactment in ritual. The Torah, "the Teaching [of Moses]" (for Greek-speaking Jews, the Law, *nomos*), was considered the revealed will of the Lord: its precepts were accepted as his indispensable code of conduct. As a result, obedience to God's will and its counterpart, observance of his code, were the litmus tests of belief.

Although it implied belief, practice (i.e., observance of the precepts) determined who was a Jew and defined the boundaries of the Jewish community. This is especially the case after the Maccabean revolt (164 B.C.E.). Scholars (scribes, doctors of the Law or lawyers, and, finally, rabbis) might endlessly argue about interpretation of the Torah and its application to conduct, but the Torah's centrality and binding character were beyond dispute: when one accepted the "yoke" of the Torah, one accepted the obligation to observe all its precepts. Observance was no mean enterprise, since the precepts ranged widely across matters about the proper worship of God (sacrifice, prayer, and the study of scripture), ritual observances (the Sabbath, and the like), and ethics (both virtues and morals).

C. CIRCUMCISION[6]

By the beginning of our era, the Sabbath, the dietary laws, and circumcision were the most distinctive Jewish practices. Yet Gentiles considered circumcision as *the* mark of the Jew. Although circumcision is clearly biblical (Gn 17:1–14, 34:1–29; Ex 4:24–26, 12:43–49; and Jos 5:2–9), it does not command anything like the attention the other laws do.

Nonetheless, biblical interpreters increasingly took circumcision to signify both the covenant between God and Israel and membership in the covenanted people. Inevitably, circumcision came also to signify submission to the demands of the Torah—once one was a Jew, one was obligated to keep all the prescriptions of the Torah.

From the Maccabean period on, circumcision achieved prominence as the distinctive mark of Jewishness. By the end of the first century B.C.E., the rite was the usual practice in the land of Israel for males, whether Jewish offspring or converts.[7]

Whether the same can be said for the Jews who lived outside Palestine (the diaspora) is a matter of continuing dispute.[8] Jewish literature addressed to Gentiles makes no direct appeal for Gentile circumcision. Even literature intended primarily for a Jewish audience registers ambiguity about circumcision as a requirement.

Philo and Paul

Philo of Alexandria (d. c. 50 C.E.), whose writings reflect the variety in Judaism at the turn of the era, notes that some of Alexandria's Jews dispense with circumcision for both offspring and proselytes. He agrees with them that the inner or spiritual meaning of circumcision is "the excision of pleasure and all passions, and the putting away of sacrilegious opinion that the soul can engender itself. . . . "[9] He has in mind ethical circumcision as opposed to physical. With most of the city's Jews, however, he insists on the literal observance of circumcision, arguing that just as the body enfleshes the soul, physical circumcision enfleshes its spiritual meaning.[10]

The problem about the ethically circumcised, however, persisted. At what precise point in the process of conversion did the inquirer cross the boundary and become a Jew? Some think Philo means that the ethically circumcised were truly Jews; others dispute that interpretation.[11] Philo's argument is, however, clear: circumcision is one of the commandments converts must follow as Jews.

Paul's bitter dispute (50 C.E.) with Christian opponents in Galatia (modern Turkey) about the necessity of circumcision must be seen against this background of ambiguity. It suggests that diaspora Jews other than Alexandrians dispensed with circumcision.[12] Paul's opponents taxed the apostle with two charges: that he did not require circumcision for Gentile converts and that he, nonetheless, continued to preach circumcision (Gal 5:2–11). His settled opinion required ethical circumcision: "The true Jew is he who is such inwardly, and the true circumcision is of the heart. . . . " (Rom 2:25–29). Unlike Philo but like Alexandria's spiritualists, he abrogated physical circumcision for Gentiles.

Izates of Adiabene

At about the same time but considerably further east (modern Iran), the same ambiguity can be found. According to the Jewish historian Flavius Josephus (35–100 C.E.),[13] Izates, the future king of Adiabene, was won over to Judaism. His contact was a Jewish merchant, Ananias, whose strategy was first to win over Izates' wives and through them, their husband. In the meantime, the queen mother, Helena, was converted by another Jew, Eleazar.

When Izates' father, the king, died and Izates returned home to assume the crown, he learned with pleasure about his mother. Then, thinking that he was not a devout convert without the one final step, he determined to be circumcised. His mother cautioned him: should he do so, he risked uproar among his subjects, sensitive as they were to "foreign" ways.

Caught between regal prudence and religious commitment, the king sought advice. Eleazar, who, Josephus reports, was extremely strict in applying the law, insisted that he be circumcised; Ananias, his mentor, countered, arguing: "The king could worship God even without being circumcised, if indeed he had fully decided to be a devoted adherent of Judaism."[14]

Although Eleazar won out and Izates was circumcised, the dispute underscores the point that circumcision under certain circumstances appears to have been dispensable.[15] It also underscores the point that circumcision had become the sign of the Jew, regularly expected of one who sought to be a convert. Circumcision was part of the process, the expected norm.

D. MEMBERSHIP IN THE COMMUNITY

The dispute about circumcision and conversion paints a picture of sharp contrast to earlier days: a community-based religion open to and accepting Gentiles. But how were they persuaded to enter? And what was their status on entering?

Jewish Mission[16]

The author of the Gospel of Matthew insists that lawyers and Pharisees travel "over sea and land to make one convert" [*prosêlyton*, Mt 23:15]; there is the Izates account just discussed. Both suggest a mission-minded Judaism.

Quite apart from the question of Matthew, Izates, and mission, however, Judaism had long been attractive to many in the Greco-Roman world. Jewish monotheism appealed to intellectuals searching for the One behind the many. For the Greco-Roman in the street, the attractions were more tactile: how Jews took care of their own, the synagogue's rich religious and social life, and what seemed high moral standards. As a result, many Gentiles attended the synagogue regularly, celebrated the Sabbath and other Jewish festivals, observed the dietary laws, and became benefactors of the local Jewish community.

Cornelius, a professional officer (centurion) in the Roman legion (Acts 10:1–3), was just such a benefactor. The Neopythagorean philosopher Numenius of Apamea (late second century C.E.) had such admiration for the Torah that he commented, "For what is Plato but Moses speaking in Attic [Greek]?"[17] Judaism's attraction penetrated whole families even in Rome itself. The satirist Juvenal (60–130 C.E.) lamented that when Roman fathers observed the Sabbath and abstained from pork, inevitably their sons ended up abandoning Roman law to follow Jewish law and to be circumcised.[18]

The attractions of Judaism won many Pagan sympathizers, often called "God-fearers."[19] Some just admired one or another aspect of Judaism; some simply acknowledged the power of the Jewish God; and some were overtly friendly to Jews to the point of benefaction. Others adopted Jewish practices, still others venerated the God of the Jews to the point of denying or ignoring Pagan gods, still others achieved an informal but intimate status within the Jewish community. These sympathizers constituted the pool from which converts came.

Outside Matthew's statement about the Pharisees and scribes scouring land and sea for converts, however, there is no corroborating evidence that points beyond some (a few? many?) mission-minded Jews to a mission-minded Judaism in antiquity. Although there had long been apologists for Judaism like Philo of Alexandria, their effort was directed to exposition and defense in service of Jewish identity and survival rather than conversion. If there was mission, the attractions of Jewish religious belief, practices, and institutions constituted it.

The Synagogue

The place where Gentile could meet Jew face-to-face and be accepted into the Jewish community—the third component in conversion—is that distinctive creation of the second-temple period, the *synagogue* (Greek, "assembly").[20] There the potential convert could hear the Jewish voice in both Hebrew and the vernacular; there the sacred book (*biblos,* in Greek) was chanted, interpreted, and studied; there the God of the Jews was available and could hear the petitioner.

Already in existence by the third century B.C.E., two hundred years later the synagogue was a major institution in Judaism: house of prayer, study center, meetinghouse, hiring hall, philanthropic center, and hospice for Jewish travelers, all rolled into one. From what Philo says, there may have been close to fifty in Alexandria; archaeologists have found traces of twelve in Rome; and in rural Egypt, there was perhaps one per town or village where Jews lived.[21]

Some synagogues were converted shops, others, houses, and still others, built for the purpose. Some were unadorned, others richly adorned, like the third-century C.E. synagogue in Dura-Europos—an important Roman military and trade center on the Euphrates River—that has yielded a striking collection of biblical mosaics.[22] Still others were vast, sited in the public business center of the city, like the synagogue in Sardis (modern Turkey).[23] It was longer than a football field, fronted on the business center of the city *(agora/forum),* and sided on the silk road to Persia and China.

Ambivalence Toward Proselytes

In spite of Judaism's appeal, an ambivalence about conversion and converts persisted in ancient Judaism. To be sure, the converts became members of the synagogue and Jewish polity, participated in the religious meals, were entitled to bring their legal cases before Jewish courts, shouldered their share of communal taxes, sat in the sections allotted for Jews in the theater, and were buried with other Jews.[24] To the outsider, the convert became a Jew.

But to the insider, or at least to some insiders, converts did not achieve full equality with the native-born: membership in the community, yes; full equality, no.[25]

The usual term for converts underscores the problem: *proselyte* meant in Greek what the Hebrew *ger* meant: resident alien, foreigner, stranger.[26] Although it could designate a sympathizer rather than a convert, by the first century C.E., proselyte was well on its was to becoming a technical term for a convert. It suggested a special status—not an outsider, but not an insider. In fact, the Jewish sectaries that produced the Dead Sea Scrolls divided Israelites into four groups: priests, Levites, Israelites, and proselytes; they also forbade proselytes entering the temple.[27]

The ambivalence was rooted in the fact that while the grounds for Jewish identity were cultic and religious, birth as a Jew continued to be the surest grounds for Jewish identity. Proselytes were not native-born.

Contradictory attitudes toward both proselytism and proselytes persisted in the rabbinic period.[28] On the one hand, the rabbis felt that righteous Gentiles could enter into the "world to come" without converting to Judaism. Gentiles, the argument went, need only observe the pre-Sinaitic "commands given to the sons of Noah" (Noahide Laws) that forbid idolatry, blasphemy, bloodshed, illicit sex, and robbery, to which was added the obligation to establish and submit to a legal system.[29] To observe them was to be on the road to salvation.

On the other hand, key figures in Israel's history are depicted as missionaries—Abraham, Jacob, Joseph, and Moses. In addition, Israel as a people was to be a light for the Gentiles, to sanctify God's name, and to proclaim his existence and glory to all.

The early rabbis did not formulate any explicit doctrine of proselytism—the onus was on the righteous Gentile to seek conversion. Nonetheless, the rabbis of the third, fourth, and fifth centuries took a more engaged approach—winning and welcoming proselytes in response to Christian missionary theory and practice.[30]

III. Ancient Jewish Sects and Conversion

The evidence from the second-temple period discloses that conversion was possible, that there was a normative process, and what it was: belief in Yahweh as the one and only God, observance of the Torah, and membership in the community. But was that the only kind?

Second-Temple Sectarianism

The increasingly sectarian character of second-temple Judaism discloses another kind of conversion, one that emphasized repentance and entailed return, reconciliation, and rededication to the terms of the covenant.[31] Such converts were Israelites who sought to become Israelites in more than name and birth.

As Jewish identity shifted its focus from nationality to religion in the Hellenistic period, Jews found themselves faced with many reform movements, especially in the period after the Maccabean revolt (164 B.C.E.–63 B.C.E.).[32] Like Joseph's celebrated coat (Gn 37:3), the Judaism of the period was many-colored.[33] Jewish sects thrived, generating a literature that flourished alongside the Bible, yet without achieving canonical status in the Hebrew canon—the works are called "Apocrypha" and "Pseudepigrapha."[34]

From Philo of Alexandria, the New Testament, and the Jewish historian and apologist Josephus (c. 73 C.E.), we learn the names of the sects—Pharisees, Sadducees, Essenes, and Zealots are particularly prominent—and second-temple sectarianism is particularly important for a full and rounded understanding of conversion in ancient Judaism. Today the term *sect* has a negative valence (dissident or erroneous belief); then the term was neutral, designating "mode of life," and hence "school" or "school of thought" (Greek: *hairesis;* Latin: *secta*).[35]

The sects in second-temple Judaism tended to separate from the larger Jewish community, thinking of themselves as reformers and as the authentic Israel. Not surprisingly, they demanded a thoroughgoing conversion from those who would join them.

Essenes

Although the evidence does not permit a single profile of Jewish sectarian life and the requirements for conversion, one sect has ridden to prominence in the past few decades, providing a documentary sense of sectarian Judaism. The sect in question is the Essenes, about whom a good deal is known from ancient authors.[36]

A. ANCIENT AUTHORS

From the Latin writer Pliny the Elder, we learn that the Essenes had withdrawn to the solitude of the desert just to the west of the Dead Sea, where they lived celibate lives in voluntary poverty, attracted a "throng of newcomers" to their community, and founded two other communities to the south (Engedi and Masada).[37]

A good deal more has been learned from Philo: agriculturists, the Essenes had no slaves, devoted themselves to the study and punctilious observance of the Law, and possessed no private property. Their food, clothes, and other needs were supplied by the community; furthermore, they stood out as "athletes of virtue" and withstood fierce persecution.[38]

About 75 C.E., the historian Josephus provided the world with the most comprehensive account of the Essenes. He considered their ideals, daily life, virtues, organization, social stratification, and beliefs, and he recorded a variety of intriguing details. We learn, for instance, that they possessed the gift of prophecy, observed a rule of silence, bathed daily in preparation for their (cultic) noon meal, had Essene colonies in numerous towns, and had an order of married couples for the propagation of the race (presumably, those in the town colonies).

About entry into the sect, we read in Josephus, the postulant waits outside the community for a year, living in continence, wearing a loin-cloth, and hacking out his own living in the desert while following a prescribed rule of life. Once he has proved himself, he "draws closer to the way of life and participates in the purificatory baths" and enters the community, "but he is not yet admitted to intimacy." His character is then tested for another two years, and if he perseveres, he is received into the community permanently:

> [At entry he] swears constant loyalty to all, but above all to those in power; for authority never falls to a man without the will of God. He swears never to show insolence in the exercise of his duty should he ever happen to be in command himself, nor to outshine his subordinates in his dress or by increased adornment. He swears always to love truth and to pursue liars; to keep his hands pure from theft and his soul pure from wicked gain. Also he swears to conceal nothing from the members of the sect, and to reveal nothing to outsiders even though violence unto death be used against him. In addition, he swears to transmit none of the doctrines except as he himself received them, abstaining from all [alteration], and to preserve the books of their sect likewise, as also the names of the Angels. Such are the oaths by which they secure the fidelity of those who enter the sect.[39]

B. QUMRAN[40]

The site of what many think was the main community of the Essenes was located only in 1947. More accurately, some of their "books," the celebrated Dead Sea Scrolls, were found in caves on the high ground at the northwest tip of the Dead Sea.

Two Scrolls[41]

Two of the Scrolls address in some detail requirements for entry into the community. The first, difficult to date, is the *Damascus Document* (abbreviated *CD,* also know as the *Zadokite Work[s]* and the *Damascus Covenant).*[42] The document achieved its present form some-where in Palestine before the foundation of the community at Qumran. Perhaps it originated in one of the "colonies" Josephus mentions.[43] The work is organized in two sections. The first section (devoted to ad-monitions) may well have been a missionary instruction or catechesis directed to outsiders.[44] The second section consists of selected interpre-tations of the Law *(halakha),* as well as precepts for the community.

The second scroll pertinent to conversion, composed between 100 and 75 B.C.E., is the *Rule of the Community* (also known as the *Manual of Discipline,* and abbreviated 1QS).[45] The scroll envisages a monastic community (very much as Pliny, Philo, and Josephus depict it) that seeks to pattern its life after the desert wanderings of Israel during Moses' time and to be the nucleus of a new and true Israel—the Israel destined to enter the Promised Land at the end of time.

Most modern scholars are persuaded that the sectaries of the scrolls were the Essenes of Pliny, Philo, and Josephus.[46] Seen in con-text, they were part of the movement of religious and national reforma-tion in Judaism that began to emerge early in the third century B.C.E., expressing itself in variety of sectarian movements and in the Maccabean revolt.

Community Structure

The Dead Sea community (and its branches) was highly struc-tured, with each member assigned his rank. At the highest level were the priests (the "sons of Zadok"), with a Guardian *(paqid/mebaqqer)* or Master *(maskil)* as the leader. Of the sect's institutions, the most influ-ential was the Council of the Community ("the Many," sometimes called the "Congregation") composed of the "mature members," within which was a Supreme Council of twelve men and three priests (the total may have been twelve, nine plus three). The "mature" or full-scale members (very likely, the entire council) practiced celibacy. Through celibacy, together with their constant ritual washings (Josephus' baths), they sought to embody the purity that the Bible required of priests before sacrifice.

The Council and Conversion[47]

The daily round of life in the priestly community at Qumran combined work, prayer, and study, centered around religious meals, especially the cultic noon meal. In addition, the *Damascus Document* indicates that the community enrolled children and that women shared its life—both facts confirmed by the archaeological work at Qumran.

One of the important functions of the Council of the Community was to admit new members. Already members of Israel, they were not converts from one religion to another (as a Pagan becoming a Jew or Christian). They were converts in that they sought to move from a life of lax or erroneous observance of the Law to one of fully committed observance—to move from the old and unfaithful Israel to the new and true Israel. Thus, the scrolls speak of a "new covenant" that fulfills the great covenants of the past, calling it the "Covenant of [divine] Mercy" *(berith hesed)* and the "Covenant of Repentance" *(berith teshuba).*[48] Indeed, both documents confirm Josephus' account that conversion entailed an extended probation and ritual process of entry into the "Covenant," and, fleshing out Josephus' account, disclose four stages in initiation.

First Pentecost: Preliminary Probation

The postulant's first move is to appear before the Guardian, who conducts an intense inquiry; if his "wisdom and deeds" prove satisfactory, on Pentecost he takes a preliminary vow in a ritual setting that involves a promise to turn to the truth (the community teachings) and to depart from evil—a vow that "brings [the candidate] into the Covenant." The newly admitted candidate then spends a year of probation devoted to instruction in the teachings, rules, and traditions of the community (1QS 6:15a/CD 15.11). His contact is solely with the Guardian.

Second Pentecost: Provisional Membership

After this probation, on the second Pentecost he comes before the council in its plenary session. Another inquiry ensues, and the Council of the Community members cast lots for or against admission.

If successful, the candidate takes an oath (above, Josephus) to live strictly by the Law as interpreted by the priest experts. He then takes a ritual bath of purification (immersion), coupled with a public confession of sin.

As if to remind all in attendance of the fragility of the human will, the rite included an instruction on the wellsprings of human action, namely, the spirit of truth and the spirit of falsehood, which bear on the meaning and perception of conversion to the sect. Conversion meant the expiation of "iniquity," sanctification through the washing, submission to God's precepts to the point of walking "perfectly" in them, and consciousness of the two spirits in which he walks until God comes: the spirits of truth and falsehood.

> Those born of falsehood spring from a source of darkness. All the children of righteousness are ruled by the Prince of Light and walk in the ways of light, but all the children of falsehood are ruled by the Angel of Darkness and walk in the ways of darkness (1QS 3:9–21; Vermes, 75–76).

At the end of the second year the now newly professed candidate has been "brought near"—he is a member, though not fully.

Third Pentecost: Preliminary Full Membership

Two more years of probation await, devoted to further catechetical instruction and scrutiny about the spirit according to which he walks and how he would fit into the community and its life.

At the end of the first of the two years, he hands over his property, which has been preserved for him—he is still able to leave, taking his property with him. His status remains ambiguous. A preliminary stage of full membership, it is signified by the fact that although he lives in community, he sits at table in a place lower than those of full members and can be excluded from the "Pure Meals," that is, the bread and new wine that reflect the Messianic purity of the temple. If he is not excluded, he may eat the bread but not the new wine.[49]

Fourth Pentecost: Full Membership

On the fourth Pentecost (the following year) the community again scrutinizes his life and character and votes on admission, which confers full membership and with it participation in the pure Meal and in government of the community. The names of the newly admitted are inscribed among the members in the order of rank; their property is merged with the community's, and the newly admitted no longer have the right to leave.

Conversion at Qumran is far more demanding than conversion to Judaism. Converts at Qumran move gradually from postulancy to mature membership over a course of four years; initiation is divided into two cycles. During the first two years (first and second Pentecost) they are outsiders, creatures of flesh subject to ritual and moral impurity. Their status is signified by the (repeatable) ritual washing and confession enjoined for the second rite of entry. The second two years (third and fourth Pentecost) are devoted to deepening their spirituality: preliminary full membership signified by participation in the bread but not the wine, and then by full membership in the community signified by the perquisites: seating by order, speaking one's mind in assembly, and sharing in the "Drink of the Many" (the pure wine).

This last stage, full incorporation into the community, was the decisive moment: the initiates now partake of the Spirit of Holiness resident in the community (which Christians might call "baptism of the Spirit").

Community Renewal

It is easy to overlook a major dimension of the rite of entry, namely, that it was a rite for the entire community. Both the *Community Rule* and the *Damascus Document* see a twofold purpose built into the rite: to initiate converts *and* to renew the community. Initiation was a ritual of renewal that says eloquently that no conversion is a once-for-all event.

The documents know of lapses, some serious enough to merit permanent excommunication. The in-course conversion of postulants to the community was, in fact, the annual occasion for the reconversion of the full members. It was at once a rite of entry and renewal, and, as anthropologists have long noted about rites of initiation, the rite of entry had much to do with the endurance of the community in the face of the most severe hardships and consequent defections.[50]

In 68 C.E. Qumran disappeared, not through decline but through destruction—destruction wrought by Roman legions headed for Jerusalem and bent on its annihilation. In the subsequent dispersion some of its members, with their traditions and practices, entered other sects, including Christian communities, a number of which lay to the east of the Jordan River and Dead Sea.

Baptizing Movements

Ritual immersion was at the heart of Qumran's rite of entry, the necessary condition for advancing to full membership.[51] The Essenes were but one among many sects for whom ritual washing was central: Hemerobaptists, Masbotheans, Sebueans, Sibyllinians, Elchasaites, Ebionites (the last two were Jewish-Christian). All protested against ebbing Jewish piety and oppression by the ruling aristocrats in Jerusalem.

John the Baptist[52]

The best-known sect claims John the Baptist as its founder. He came from a family of rural priests that were alienated (like the members of Qumran) from the aristocratic priesthood of Jerusalem's temple. He might even have been a Qumran initiate.

In Josephus' *Antiquities* (18:5.2:116–19) and the gospels, John appears as an ascetic solitary in the tradition of Israel's alienated prophets (like Elijah and Jeremiah). His preaching is aimed at the powerful—very likely the Jerusalem aristocracy, including the temple priests.[53] His goal was repentance and his message was *metanoia*:

> Now is the time to repent. God is about to execute his wrath on unrepentant perpetrators of injustice. His wrath will destroy those who refuse to repent. Those who do will receive a baptism of forgiveness now. Then they will do deeds of justice, and only then can they anticipate a second baptism of final and perfect purification. But now is the time to repent.[54]

Many in his audience respond by repenting, receiving his ritual immersion—the gospels call it by a distinctive name, "baptism" *(baptisma)*—and changing their lives, often dramatically. Some return home to live according to the ethical standards he preaches. Others remain with him, adopt his ascetic, ritual piety of prayer and fasting, and themselves preach the master's vision of the imminent end and baptize—the most familiar of them being Jesus of Nazareth.[55]

As it turned out, John and his followers cast a long shadow in early Christian history, a shadow that is the subject of Chapter 6. But they soon established a pattern that shaped earliest Christianity:

preaching, repentance, a new way of living, and the anticipation of a final purification, with baptism as the focus—in a word, *metanoia*. In its earliest formulation, we read:

> In those days John came, preaching in the wilderness [a baptism of repentance *(baptisma metanoias)*]; as is written by the prophet Isaiah, "A voice of one crying in the wilderness, 'Prepare the way of the Lord, make his paths straight'" [Is 40:3]. And he went into all the region about the Jordan. And he said to the multitudes coming for his baptism, "You brood of vipers! Who warned you to flee from the wrath to come? Bear fruit therefore that befits repentance *[karpous tes metanoias],* and do not begin to say to yourselves, 'We have Abraham for our father'; for I tell you that God is able from these stones to raise up children to Abraham. Even now the axe is laid to the root of the trees; every tree therefore that does not bear good fruit is cut down and thrown into the fire. . . . "[56]

IV. Conclusion

We have considered the two kinds of conversion that developed in the reform movements in the Hellenistic period of second-temple Judaism: conversion to Judaism and conversion to "true" Judaism. Read in the light of contemporary criteria for conversion, both kinds exhibit the characteristics of genuine conversion.

In both kinds, ritual was the decisive moment: for conversion to Israel, circumcision; for conversion to Qumran, the Pentecostal rite of immersion, followed in a year with admission to the community, participation in the "pure Meal," and possession of the community's spirit of holiness; for conversion to the Johannites, baptism.

Interaction with the community that embodied the new religious reality was continual and sometimes dramatic. The Gentile sympathizers who converted generally had a long synagogue association with Judaism; the Johannites, a brief but intensive association with John the Baptist and his disciples; the Essenes at Qumran, an increasingly intimate association that extended over four years.

The active search for a new identity, meaning, and purpose in life is dramatically evident among the postulants at Qumran and among the Johannites and can easily be inferred from the Gentile sympathizers who move through the synagogue into the Jewish world. And the search implies a crisis of identity that inspired it, a search confirmed by the history of the Hellenistic period, marked as it was with revolt of the Maccabees and the reforming sects. It was a history that points to a social world in crisis.

The evidence shows that both kinds of conversion required a clear-cut choice between an old way of life and new way, a choice that demanded commitment. Choice and commitment permeate the process from beginning to end, with repentance as the cutting edge. The evidence, however, yields one caveat: conversion is a gradual and continuing process. Although there is a decisive moment when one is a Jew or, as at Qumran and among the Johannites, a true Israelite, the road to it is long and hazardous. Conversion is not sudden. And the road beyond conversion is equally long and hazardous. Not every Johannite persevered in doing justice. Some Essenes followed a spirit other than the spirit of holiness. Some proselytes apostatized.

Yet the ritual life of synagogue and temple, of immersion and meal at Qumran, of prayer, fasting, preaching, and baptizing among the Johannites—not to mention observance of the Torah for all—functioned effectively to maintain and renew conversion.

NOTES

1. For this brief background I am indebted to the recent study and annotated bibliography of Shaye J. D. Cohen, *From the Maccabees to the Mishnah* (Philadelphia: Westminster Press, 1987).

2. In the Hebrew Bible Judith is apocryphal (and also for Protestants); in the Greek Bible (Septuagint/LXX) it is canonical. For discussion of the passage and its interpretation, see Carey A. Moore, *Judith: A New Translation with Introduction and Commentary,* AB 40 (1964) 86–90, 235–36. One of the reasons that Judith was omitted from the Hebrew canon may have been because of the rite of conversion: the rabbis would later insist that a convert must also be baptized—Achior was not baptized.

3. Thus, Martin Goodman, *Mission and Conversion: Proselytizing in the Religious History of the Roman Empire* (Oxford: Clarendon Press, 1994) 62.

4. For its themes, see Reuven Kimelman, "The *Shema* and Its Blessings: The Realization of God's Kingship," in *The Synagogue in Late Antiquity,* ed. Lee I. Levine (Philadelphia: The American Schools of Oriental Research, 1987) 73–95.

5. For discussion, see "Commandments, the 613," *Jewish Encyclopedia* 5:760–83. A rabbinic tradition is recorded that the 613 were revealed to Moses

at Sinai, 365 being for prohibitions equal to the number of solar days, and 248 being mandates corresponding in number to the limbs of the human body. The article contains a list of 365 compiled by the great medieval commentator on the Talmud, Maimonides.

6. On circumcision and its rise in postexilic Judaism, the literature is extensive. For recent treatment, see Alan Segal, *Paul the Convert: The Apostolate and Apostasy of Saul the Pharisee* (New Haven: Yale University Press, 1990) 72–114; Shaye J. D. Cohen, "Crossing the Boundary and Becoming a Jew," *HTR* 82 (1989) 13–33, and his "Conversion to Judaism in Historical Perspective: From Biblical Israel to Postbiblical Judaism," *Conservative Judaism* (1983); and John J. Collins, "Circumcision and Salvation in the First Century," in Jacob Neusner and Ernest S. Frerichs, eds., *"To See Ourselves as Others See Us": Christians, Jews and Others in Late Antiquity* (Chico: Scholars Press, 1985) 163–86, especially 170–86.

7. Circumcision achieved such prominence that for Jews and Gentiles alike it was *the* Jewish ritual. Thus, Cohen, "Crossing the Boundary and Becoming a Jew," 27. He goes on to state: " . . . as far as is known no [non-Christian] Jewish community in antiquity accepted male proselytes who were not circumcised" (ibid.). The issue is a matter of debate. Cohen here precludes the possibility, urged by Segal (*Paul the Convert,* xiii–xvi passim), that Paul and early Christianity can be taken as sound historical witness for first-century Judaism.

8. For discussion, see John J. Collins, "A Symbol of Otherness," in Neusner and Frerichs, *"To See Ourselves as Others See Us,"* 164–70. Goodman concludes that the evidence for uncircumcised proselytes is minimal and should be discounted (*Mission and Conversion,* 81).

9. Philo, *On the Migration of Abraham* 92 (F. H. Colson and G. H. Whitaker, trans. and eds., *Philo,* Loeb 4 [1932] 184–85). See also Philo, *On Special Laws* I:9 (Colson, Loeb 7 [1971] 104–5); Philo, *Questions on Genesis* III:52 (Ralph Marcus, ed., *Philo: Supplement* I, Loeb [1953] 253); and Philo, *Questions and Answers on Exodus* II:2 (Ralph Marcus, ed., *Philo: Supplement* II, Loeb [1953] 36–37). The mystical interpretation of circumcision is a constant in Philo.

10. Philo, *On the Migration of Abraham* 93 (Colson and Whitaker, Loeb 5:184–85).

11. For the disputants, see Neil J. McEleney, "Conversion, Circumcision and the Law," *NTS* 20 (1974) 319–41; and John Nolland, "Uncircumcised Proselytes?" *Journal for the Study of Judaism* 12 (1981) 173–94. The former had answered the question yes; the latter, no. For recent comment, see Goodman, *Mission and Conversion,* 81, where, citing McEleney and Nolland, he concludes that the evidence is minimal.

12. See Peder Borgen, *Philo, John, and Paul: New Perspectives on*

Judaism and Early Christianity (Atlanta: Scholars Press [Brown Judaic Studies 131], 1987) 237–49, for what follows. For commentary and literature, see Hans Dieter Betz, *Galatians: A Commentary on Paul's Letter to the Galatians* (Philadelphia: Fortress [Hermeneia], 1979) 5–9, 253–69. In his examination of the evidence, however, Goodman writes: "But in fact the evidence for uncircumcised proselytes is anyway minimal and should be discounted" (*Mission and Conversion,* 81; see 81–83). The presumption, however, is that Paul is not a witness of Jewish practice in the first century C.E.

13. For the account, see his *Jewish Antiquities* 20:32–47 (Louis H. Feldman, ed., *Josephus: Jewish Antiquities VIII–XX,* Loeb 9 [1965] 406–14).

14. Josephus, *Antiquities* 20:41 (Feldman, Loeb 9:408–10). See also note "a," where Feldman comments on the dispute between the two, relating it to rabbinic casuistry and the talmudic position.

15. At the end of his study, Nolland (n. 14) concludes his analysis of the Izates account (against McEleney) that the furthest the evidence can possibly take us is to the suggestion that there might have been those prepared to offer dispensation to particular highly placed individuals on the grounds of threat to life and property posed by their receiving circumcision. Indeed, even to go this far is "conjectural" (194). Nonetheless, there is the case of the hemophiliac Jews mentioned by Goodman "for whom the operation would endanger life and could therefore be forgone" (*Mission and Conversion,* 67).

16. For the state of the question and the literature, see Goodman, *Mission and Conversion,* especially 60–90; Gary C. Porton, *The Stranger Within Your Gates: Converts and Conversion in Rabbinic Literature* (Chicago: University of Chicago Press, 1994); and Scot McKnight, *A Light Among the Gentiles: Jewish Missionary Activity in the Second Temple Period* (Minneapolis: Fortress Press, 1991).

17. Thus, Clement of Alexandria, *Stromata* 1:150, 4, cited in Menahem Stern, *Greek and Latin Authors on Jews and Judaism,* 2 vols. (Jerusalem: Israel Academy of Sciences and Humanities, 1976, 1980) 209, n. 363a. Numenius implied the similarity of their teachings, not that Plato got his doctrine from Moses, which is the way Eusebius understood him—cited in Stern, 210–11, n. 363e.

18. *Saturae* 14:96–106; Stern, *Greek and Latin Authors,* 2, no. 301, 102–3.

19. The literature and disputes about the "God-fearers" are extensive. Some scholars think that there was no such entity as a defined class of God-fearers; thus, A. T. Kraabel, "The Disappearance of the God-fearers," *Numen* 28 (1981) 113–26, to which I responded in "The God-fearers Reconsidered," *CBQ* 47 (1985) 75–84. Others take a diametrically opposed position; see, for instance, Louis J. Feldman, "The Omnipresence of the God-Fearers," *Biblical Archeology Review* 12.5 (1986) 58–59. The results of the discussion indicate

that the term *God-fearers* refers to Gentiles sympathetic to Judaism that exhibit the range of interests outlined above. For the present state of the question that takes into account the diverse evidence that ranges from the barely interested to full adherents, see Cohen, *From the Maccabees to the Mishnah,* 55–58. The most recent examination of the evidence, however, is Goodman, *Mission and Conversion.*

20. For the most recent treatment and up-to-date bibliography, see Lee I. Levine, ed., *The Synagogue in Late Antiquity* (Philadelphia: The American Schools of Oriental Research, 1987). For a helpful pictorial study of the synagogues mentioned in what follows, see Herschel Shanks, *Judaism in Stone: The Archaeology of Ancient Synagogues* (New York: Harper & Row; Hagerstown, Md.: Biblical Archaeology Society, 1979).

21. See Avigdor (Victor) Tcherikover, *Hellenistic Civilization and the Jews,* trans. S. Applebaum (Philadelphia: The Jewish Publication Society of America, 1966) 299–304 passim; and Harry J. Leon, *The Jews of Ancient Rome* (Philadelphia: The Jewish Publication Society of America, 1960) 135–66.

22. For which, see Shanks, *Judaism in Stone,* 78–96.

23. For an accurate and visual account of recent discoveries, see Shanks, *Judaism in Stone;* he discusses Sardis and Ostia in 162–75 (see archaeological reports in the notes).

24. For discussion, see Cohen, "Crossing the Boundary and Becoming a Jew," 13–33, especially 28–29; and Tcherikover, *Hellenistic Civilization and the Jews,* 296–332.

25. See Cohen, "Crossing the Boundary and Becoming a Jew," 13–33, especially 24–27; and Martin Goodman, "Proselytizing in Rabbinic Judaism," *JJS* 40 (1989) 176–85.

26. For derivation, see David Novak, *The Image of the Non-Jew in Judaism: An Historical and Constructive Study of the Noahide Laws* (New York: E. Mellen, 1983) 14–20.

27. *Damascus Covenant* 14:3–6, cited in Cohen, "Crossing the Boundary," 30, n. 59.

28. Thus, Goodman, "Proselytizing."

29. See Novak, *The Image of the Non-Jew,* xiii–35, 257–73, 407–13. He regards the Noahide laws as the necessary condition for the revelation at Sinai, providing an essential link between the orders of creation and revelation. Observance of Noahide laws expressed a desire for communion even before its "Ultimate Object revealed himself to them" (409).

30. Thus, Goodman, *Mission and Conversion,* especially 60–90, where he explores all the evidence and arguments for an active Jewish mission and concludes that although there is some evidence of a Jewish mission to win Gentile *sympathizers* in the first century, the intensity of the mission varied

according to place and time period, and it was not a response to a mission theology (86–87). Similarly McKnight, *A Light Among the Gentiles,* 116–17.

31. See Chapter 1, "III. Conversion: A Biblical View."

32. For historical background, see Richard A. Horsley and John S. Hanson, *Bandits, Prophets, and Messiahs: Popular Movements at the Time of Jesus* (San Francisco: HarperCollins, 1988) 20–43; and Seán Freyne, *Galilee From Alexander the Great to Hadrian, 323 B.C.E.–135 C.E.: A Study of Second Temple Judaism* (Wilmington: Michael Glazier; Notre Dame: University of Notre Dame Press, 1980) 27–71.

33. Gn 37:18–24. The Hebrew word for "ornamented tunic" can also mean "a coat of many colors."

34. For the rise of scripture in the second-temple period, see James L. Kugel, "Two Introductions to Midrash," in David Kraemer, ed., *The Mind of the Talmud: An Intellectual History of the Bavli* (New York: Oxford University Press, 1990) 77–103; and James L. Kugel and Rowan A. Greer, *Early Biblical Interpretation* (Philadelphia: Westminster Press [Library of Early Christianity, ed. Wayne A. Meeks], 1986) 13–39.

35. The bibliography is extensive. Two studies, however, are extremely helpful in acquiring a sound sense of the multiform Judaism of the period: (1) Michael E. Stone, *Scriptures, Sects and Visions: A Profile of Judaism from Ezra to the Jewish Revolts* (Philadelphia: Fortress Press, 1980); (2) W. E. Nickelsburg and Michael E. Stone, eds., *Faith and Piety in Early Judaism: Texts and Documents* (Philadelphia: Fortress Press, 1983).

36. For the texts, see André Dupont-Sommer, *The Essene Writings from Qumran,* trans. Geza Vermes (Cleveland: World [Meridian], 1962) 21–38.

37. Pliny, *Natural History* 5, 17:4 (cited in Dupont-Sommer, *Essene Writings* 37).

38. Philo, *Quod omnis probus liber sit;* for the citations in *Quod omn. prob.* and their translation, see Dupont-Sommer, *Essene Writings,* 21–26.

39. Josephus, *The Jewish War* 2, 8, 7:137–42 cited in Dupont-Sommer, *The Essene Writings,* 30–31.

40. For a recent account of the discovery, see Jerome Murphy-O'Connor, "Qumran, Khirbet," *ABD* 5:590–94.

41. The literature on Qumran and the scrolls is vast and the controversies numerous, the most recent being about the monopoly of the scrolls by the International Oversight Team, for which, see Michael Baigent and Richard Leigh, *The Dead Sea Scrolls Deception* (New York: Summit Books, 1991). For a recent bibliography, see Joseph A. Fitzmyer, *The Dead Sea Scrolls: Major Publications and Tools for Study,* rev. ed. (Atlanta: Scholars Press, 1990). For valuable studies, see John J. Collins, "Dead Sea Scrolls," *ABD* 2:85–101, and his "Essenes," *ABD* 2:619–26; Geza Vermes, *The Dead Sea Scrolls: Qumran in Perspective* (Cleveland: Collins World, 1978); and

Matthew Black, *The Scrolls and Christian Origins: Studies in the Jewish Background of the New Testament* (New York: Charles Scribner's Sons, 1961). For an accessible and comprehensive English translation, see Geza Vermes, *The Dead Sea Scrolls in English,* 3rd ed. (New York: Viking/ Penguin, 1987).

42. For the state of the question, see Philip R. Davies, "Damascus Rule (CD)," *ABD* 2:7–10.

43. Thus, Philip R. Davies, *The Damascus Covenant: An Interpretation of the "Damascus Document"* (Sheffield: Journal for the Study of the Old Testament Supplement series 25, 1983) 202.

44. Thus, Davies (catechesis), but see also Jerome Murphy-O'Connor, "An Essene Missionary Document? CD II, 14–VI, 1," *Revue Biblique* 77 (1970) 201–29.

45. For a recent account of the scroll and scholarship on it, see Jerome Murphy-O'Connor, "Community, Rule of the (1QS)," *ABD* 1:110–12.

46. For the consensus, see James H. Charlesworth, ed., *Jesus and the Dead Sea Scrolls* (New York: Doubleday [Anchor Bible Reference Library, David Noel Freedman, ed.], 1992) xxxii–xxxv.

47. See B. E. Thiering, "Qumran Initiation and New Testament Baptism," *NTS* 27 (1981) 615–31, especially 615–23.

48. 1QS 1:8; CD 9:15. For discussion of the entry rite, see Black, *The Scrolls and Christian Origins,* 91–115. For commentary on the text of 1QS, see A. R. C. Leaney, *The Rule of Qumran and Its Meaning: Introduction, Translation, and Commentary* (London: SCM Press, 1966) 111–43. For a commentary on CD, see Davies, *The Damascus Covenant.*

49. Thus, Thiering, "Qumran Initiation," *NTS* 27:617–18.

50. Victor Turner, *The Ritual Process: Structure and Antistructure* (Chicago: Aldine, 1969) 181.

51. *Damascus Document* 11; *War Rule* 14; *Community Rule* 3:5. The rite, coupled with "humble submission of his soul to all the precepts of God," effected the candidate's and the member's purification. For wide-ranging discussion, see Joseph Thomas, *Le mouvement baptiste en Palestine et Syrie (150 av. J.-C.–300 ap. J.-C.* (Gembloux, J. Duculot [Dissertation, Louvain], 1965) 10–22. Thomas holds that the cultic concentration especially on purification functioned to substitute for temple liturgy, especially the sacrifices that brought atonement.

52. See Chapter 6 ("John and Jesus") and the following: Walter Wink, *John the Baptist in the Gospel Tradition* (Cambridge: Cambridge University Press, 1968); Paul W. Hollenbach, "John the Baptist," *ABD* 3:887–99; and John P. Meier, *A Marginal Jew: Rethinking the Historical Jesus,* (Garden City, N.Y.: Doubleday [Anchor Bible Reference Library], 1994) 2:19–99.

53. For the historical background of the dissidents and a typology of

popular movements, see Horsley and Hanson, *Bandits, Prophets, and Messiahs,* 1–47.

54. I am indebted to Hollenbach, "John the Baptist," *ABD* 3:896, for the elements of this construct.

55. The disciple who carried on a mission parallel with John's was Jesus (Jn 3:6, 4:1); thus, there is reason to suppose that other Johannites did.

56. This represents Athanasius Polag's reconstruction of Q, for which, see Ivan Havener, *The Sayings of Jesus: With a Reconstruction of Q [by Athanasius Polag]* (Wilmington: Michael Glazier, 1987) 123. The brackets that include "baptism of repentance" contain Polag's reconstruction of the Q-saying. For a wide-ranging set of parallels and the Greek text, see John S. Kloppenberg, *Q Parallels: Synopsis, Critical Notes, and Concordance* (Sonoma, Calif.: Polebridge Press, 1988) 4–17.

Chapter 5

CONVERSION IN THE RABBINIC PERIOD

I. Background

The last chapter concentrated on the second-temple period. We encountered a normative process of conversion for Gentiles and two sectarian processes for Jews who sought to be true Israelites. The concern of this chapter is the rabbinic period. We shall encounter the rabbis' clarification and codification of the way Gentiles became Jews in Palestine and the elaboration of a distinctive rite of initiation for women in the Egyptian diaspora.

The period, which comprises the formative period of rabbinic Judaism, begins and ends with two pivotal and wrenching events: the destruction of the temple (70 C.E.) and the Islamic conquest of the Near and Middle East (640 C.E.).[1] It was marked early on by two more Jewish revolts against Rome: the revolt in Egypt, Libya, and Cyprus (115–117 C.E.) and the Bar Kokhba revolt in Palestine (132–135 C.E.).

The Judaism that survived to flourish was forever changed. By 132 C.E., Egyptian Judaism was in a shambles; Jewish Palestine was decimated. The old leadership and the second temple were long gone; Jerusalem had been destroyed, rebuilt as a Pagan city, renamed Aelia Capitolina, and dedicated to Jupiter. Under pain of death, Jews were forbidden to enter the city, and vital Jewish practices, like circumcision and the recitation of the traditional prayer honoring God as the one and only God *(Shema),* had been proscribed. Added to the depredations of war, much Jewish land in Palestine had become Roman booty, and its residents, a large, landless, and desperate peasant class. Palestinian

Judaism faced extinction, and diaspora Judaism, without the land called holy, risked evaporation.

Enter the rabbis, who rebuilt Judaism on the shattered foundations of the old. To understand their rise, we must briefly revisit the rise of the sects covered in the last chapter.

Sectarianism

The sectarianism we have encountered in Qumran and the Johannites had it roots in the political, social, economic, and cultural turmoil of the second-temple period as far back as Ezra and Nehemiah (c. 450 B.C.E.).[2] The Maccabean revolt simply raised the curtain on a religious drama already playing, one about temple, Torah, and scripture, and exemplified by the sectaries at Qumran.

A. TEMPLE

The new temple and its rituals were no match for the grandeur and authenticity of Solomon's temple, yet it acquired a centrality and importance the first never had.[3] Like Israel of old, the Israel of the return from exile saw the new temple as the place where God was intimately and actively present, the residence of infinite holiness.

But it was a source of trouble almost from the beginning. Not everyone approved of its building; those who remembered the first temple wept at the dedication of the second (Ezr 3:12). It was authorized by a Gentile king (Cyrus), who had nothing of the wisdom and magnificence of Solomon. The high priesthood had been usurped and illegally transferred, which led to lax observance, especially of the temple purity laws. Thus, ambivalence persisted from Ezra and Nehemiah onward.

The second century B.C.E. revealed the problem. The priestly rulers and well-placed aristocrats engaged in a reform guided by Syrian Hellenism. Antiochus IV Epiphanes increasingly interfered in Israelite affairs, treating Judaism as just another local cult. He even forbade certain central Jewish religious practices and began to enforce Pagan rites (168 B.C.E.), and as part of a failed attempt to invade Egypt, he invested Jerusalem and defiled the temple. Revolt led by the Maccabees was the response (166 B.C.E.).

When the dust settled, the Maccabees rededicated the temple (164 B.C.E.), invested themselves with the high priesthood, even though not of high priestly lineage, and took over the reins of power for the next hundred years.[4] Known as the Hasmoneans (142–63 B.C.E.), the new high priestly leaders sought power and position, grew corrupt, and oppressed the people. A warring aristocracy became a military monarchy. King Herod (37–4 B.C.E.) piled on the last straw: he, a half-Jew, completed the temple (even though magnificently).

The Qumran sectaries had already fled from Jerusalem and the temple. They saw their community in its desert fastness as the replacement for the temple, at least until God built it anew at the "End of Days," and they regarded their leaders as heirs of the true priesthood, stemming from Solomon's high priest, Zadok. They were also persuaded that the temple's spirit of holiness had fled with them. In relocating the temple they sought to retain God's intimate and active presence among at least a holy remnant of Israel.

B. TORAH

Like the temple, the Torah was also a target of the sects, not as the record of salvation history, but as the record of God's will expressed in law. In addition to the laws of purity, the laws about marriage, Sabbath, and festival liturgy came under sustained scrutiny; divisive disputes about interpretation of their meaning arose.

The centrality of laws in the disputes disclose a major component of ancient Judaism: the laws of the Torah represent God's will and stand as the terms of his covenant with Israel. Many were convinced that widespread lax observance jeopardized the covenant and endangered Israel.

The Hellenism that provoked the Maccabees was a dramatic example. Faced with a temple and a priesthood defiled by lax observance (as well as illegitimacy), Qumran had become a sect of the strict observance. As the pure remnant of Israel, the sectaries saw themselves as the bearers and protectors of the covenant and its terms.

C. SCRIPTURE[5]

At some point between the fifth and the third century B.C.E., the living voice of the prophet was heard no more in the land. The word of God fixed in writing stepped to the fore, enshrined in the books of the Hebrew Bible. Although the contents of the Bible were fluid, all Jews believed in the Torah (Genesis, Exodus, Leviticus, Numbers, and Deuteronomy) as scripture, and by the end of the first century C.E., the prophetic books *(Nebi'im)* and the writings *(Kethubim)* had been added to the canon of scripture.

Sects might argue about what should be in the canon, but their principal disputes were about interpretation, especially how the written word of God applied in the press of daily life. For some, strict construction was the only way: If a teaching or practice were not explicitly in the Mosaic books, it was unwarranted and therefore false. Others adopted different and distinctive methods of interpretation.

Qumran exemplifies one method. The sectaries interpreted revelation in the light of their community, especially its history and opponents, and its mission to prepare for the throes of struggle at the end of time. The method is called "pesher" (peser), derived from the frequent and distinctive use of the term (psr). A word used in the sense of interpretation, realization, or "presaged reality," pesher introduced an interpretation of a biblical text.[6]

Qumran's Book of Habakkuk is an example. It contains historical allusions that point to different periods of Israelite history and their impact on the community. In the pesher on Habakkuk, the author cites: "For there is yet a vision concerning the appointed time. It testifies to the end, and it will not deceive (Hb 2:3)." The author then writes, "Its interpretation is that [psrw'sr] the last end will be prolonged."[7] The interpretation concerns events that delay the "End of Days," for which the community is preparing.

Pharisees[8]

Qumran stood at one extreme—a small separatist group convinced that it embodied the ideals of Israel and that it alone understood the mind and will of God.[9] At the other extreme stood the Pharisees, who also flourished from the middle of the second century B.C.E. to the destruction of the temple in 70 C.E.

Although Josephus considers them a sect, he means by the term a school of thought with a cohesive set of teachings and a distinctive way of life. In contrast to the Qumran separatists, the Pharisees were socially and politically active.

The sources of information about the Pharisees (New Testament, Josephus, and Rabbinic literature) are difficult to assess, but contemporary scholarship has sketched a brief profile.[10]

Pharisees were members (haberim) of an educated, voluntary association (habura) that sought to influence the Jerusalem leaders, change society, and reform Judaism. Their communal life was based on a strict adherence to the covenant and its terms. The laws that concerned them most were those regarding ritual purity, tithes, food laws, and Sabbath and festival observances—laws that, as they interpreted them, set out an agenda of holiness for both the land and the people.

The Pharisaic vision included a distinctive program for Jewish life: the holiness required of the temple and its priests was required of all Israelites. The purity laws demanded a new mode of Jewish life, for which all were accountable. As experts in the Torah and accurate interpreters of its laws *(halakha),* they were popular with the people of the towns and villages—effective guides for the perplexed, who sought to be holy in everyday life. And in their interpretive work they showed themselves reassuringly dedicated to the ancestral traditions that supplemented the Torah.

When the Romans destroyed the temple (70 C.E.), the Pharisees' vision of holiness opened a road to survival: the actively intimate God was in the people's midst. Destruction of the temple did not put God to flight. Pharisaic life showed the way to the Holy One. The role of daily prayer in their communal life, their concentrated study of the Torah and the application of its fruits to the everyday life of the people, and the central place accorded both the synagogue and the Jewish home established a model for the new mode of a Jewish life, a life no longer bound to temple, land, or nation whose capital was Jerusalem.

II. Mishnah and Talmud

As a way of holiness independent of place, the Judaism of the Pharisees could travel. This did not happen instantly, of course. A historical continuity between the Pharisees and those who claimed to be their heirs—the rabbis—remained. The major figures of first-century Judaism were the Pharisees Gamaliel I, Simon, his son, and Gamaliel II, Simon's son, who, after the destruction of the temple, assumed leadership over the fledgling rabbinic movement.

The Rabbis: Mishnah and Talmud

Although it took many decades, precisely when the Judaism of the rabbis became normative Judaism need not delay us. Far more important is the fact that the rabbis early established themselves in academies devoted to the authoritative interpretation of the Torah as the guide to daily life. By the beginning of the third century C.E. they largely dominated Palestinian Judaism and their influence had spread to Jewish communities outside the land of Israel.

A. MISHNAH

In the course of their rise, the early rabbis, called *tannaim* ("repeaters" of the teaching of Moses), achieved the canonization of the Hebrew Bible and compiled the *Mishnah* ("that which is learned by repetition"). A topical collection of rabbinic interpretations and applications of law *(halakha)* in the Torah, the Mishnah functioned as a law code for Jews under the patriarch of Jewish Palestine, Judah the Prince, at the beginning of the third century (c. 200 C.E.). Beneath its patterns of legal formulation, however, the Mishnah comprises a work of religious imagination—extended essays that deal with topics like the nature of sacred time and space, holiness, marriage and the family, and how to live day to day in an unbelieving world.[11]

Underlying the legal discussions in the "Tractate on Appointed Times," for instance, is the rabbis' intent to create in the homes and villages of ordinary Israelites a matrix of holiness, one comparable to the holiness required of the temple and its cult—now long gone.[12] So fundamental is the work to Judaism that the later rabbis (c. 300 C.E.) reckoned the Mishnah with the Torah as inspired: it was oral Torah.

B. TOSEFTA, GEMARA, AND TALMUD

At about the same time as the Mishnah was being compiled, the tannaim also compiled the *Tosefta* ("addition" or "supplement"), a work organized like the Mishnah, amplifying it. Their successors— the rabbis of the third, fourth, and fifth centuries (*Amoraim,* "spokesmen")—continued deliberations about the Mishnah. Their work is known as the *Gemara* ("completion" or "tradition").

Mishnah, however, was the building block for the most influential work in the history of Judaism, the *Talmud* ("learning" or "study"), both in its Jerusalem (Yerushalmi) and in its Babylonian (Bavli) versions.[13] Although based on the earlier deliberations, especially the Mishnah, and incorporating later rabbinic deliberations, the Babylonian Talmud was composed in its present form in the sixth century. It became the foundation document of Judaism.[14] Over these early centuries, then, Judaism assumed its definitive form, and is often referred to as rabbinic or talmudic Judaism.

The Talmud on Conversion[15]

An important aspect of rabbinic Judaism in antiquity concerned who is a Jew, a question still under debate in modern Israel. Among the range of answers in Jewish antiquity, the normative answer was that the Jew is an Israelite who believes in Yahweh as the one and only God, who is circumcised, and who is a member of the covenanted community of Israel.

A. CONVERSION: CRITERIA

The criteria for specifying who is a Jew naturally affected the requirements for becoming a Jew. The rabbis assumed these traditional requirements for membership in Israel as the basis of discussion. Rabbinic debate, however, indicates two additional requirements: (1) a sacrifice of atonement, while the temple still stood, and after its fall, an atonement offering; (2) ritual immersion *(mikveh/tebilah)*.[16]

A twofold problem about the offering arose: (1) what constituted an offering after the temple's destruction, a fowl (bird, birds?) or money? (2) whether it was for sin or a purifying rite. No definitive resolution appeared.

Debate also continued about circumcision, especially whether both circumcision and immersion are required for a Gentile to become a Jew. Again no definitive solution appeared, but both proved to be major components of the rite of entry.

The rabbis' principal concern was to make the entire process of becoming a Jew more explicit. Although precisely when is the subject of scholarly debate, the substance of the rite was in place in rabbinic circles by the end of the second century C.E.

B. THE RITUAL PROCESS

The Talmud contains a text for the ritual in one of its tractates, *Yebamot* ("sisters-in-law"). A similar discussion is found in an extra document known as *Gerim* ("resident aliens"). The latter (the title suggests its contents) presents the laws governing converts and Gentiles who have renounced idolatry. *Yebamot* is a tractate that deals with conversion in the context of levirate marriage, of forbidden sex, and of prohibited marriages. The introductory phrase "Our Rabbis taught" indicates that this tradition was believed to be a tannaitic one, dating from the same period as the Mishnah. The text from *Yebamot* is as follows:

Our Rabbis taught: if at the present time a man desires to become a proselyte, he is to be addressed as follows: "What reason have you for desiring to become a proselyte; do you not know that Israel at the present time are persecuted and oppressed, despised, harassed, and overcome by afflictions?" If he replies, "I know and yet am unworthy [of the privilege of membership]," he is accepted forthwith, and is given instruction in some of the minor and some of the major commandments. He is informed of the sin [of the neglect of the commandments of] Gleanings, the forgotten Sheaf, the Corner of the Field and the Poor Man's Tithe.[17] He is also told of the punishment for the transgression of the commandments. Furthermore, he is addressed thus: "Be it known to you that before you came to this condition, if you had eaten [forbidden fat] you would not have been punishable with *kareth* [extirpation]; were you to profane the Sabbath you would not be punishable with stoning; but now were you to profane the Sabbath you would be punished with stoning." And as he is informed of the punishment for the transgression of the commandments, so is he informed of the reward guaranteed for their fulfillment. He is told, "Be it known to you that the world to come was made only for the righteous, and that Israel at the present time are unable to bear [47b begins here] either too much prosperity, or too much suffering." He is not, however, to be persuaded or dissuaded too much. If he accepted [all the restrictions and disabilities pointed out to him], he is circumcised forthwith. Should any shreds which render the circumcision invalid remain, he is to be circumcised a second time. As soon as he is healed arrangements are made for his immediate ablution [immersion], when two learned men must stand by his side and acquaint him with some of the minor commandments and with some of the major ones [so that he can submit to the "yoke of the commandments"]. When he comes up after his ablution, he is deemed to be an Israelite in all respects.

In the case of a woman proselyte, women make her sit in the water up to her neck, while two learned men stand outside and give her instruction in some of the minor commandments and some of the major ones.[18]

C. THE STRUCTURE OF THE RITE

The structure of the rite is clear: (1) the presentation and examination of the potential proselyte, (2) preliminary instruction, (3) circumcision of male candidates, and (4) a second (apparently, a review) instruction coupled with a ritual immersion *(tebilah/mikveh)*. The other version, *Gerim,* has the following brief postbathing instruction, a practice that may not have obtained in the early days:

> When he has immersed and risen [from the water], they speak to him kind words, words of comfort, "To whom have you attached yourself? Happy are you, [for you have attached yourself] to him who spoke and the world came to be, blessed is he. The world was created only for the sake of Israel, and only Israel are called children of God, and only Israel are dear before God. And all those [other] words that we said to you, we said them only to increase your reward.[19]

D. SCREENING

This first stage of the conversion rite engages a subject already considered: proselytes and proselytism in ancient Judaism.[20] We can presume that the recruits were from the ranks of the God-fearers also already considered, especially those who had abjured other gods and embraced the God of Israel.[21]

Unfortunately, the tractate *Yebamot* tells us little about what motivated those who presented themselves and even less about their status and vital statistics, save that they ranged in age from children to grandfathers, were slaves and free, and were male and female.[22] The tractate *Gerim* is more expansive: some sought to marry Jewish women; others came over simply out of fear of being an outsider in the land of Israel; still others, out of hope for material gain. But to emphasize the need for true conversion the tractate insists: "Anyone who is not converted from purely religious motives is not a proselyte."[23]

Two aspects of proselytes' situations come across with force. Jeopardy, the first, was part and parcel of the proselyte's social setting: "Israel," we read, "at the present time are persecuted and oppressed, despised, harassed and overcome by afflictions." Conversion to Judaism in late antiquity was a hazardous course to follow. As the consequence of the Jewish revolts in the late first and early second centuries, Roman hostility toward Judaism escalated. At one point, the emperors prohibited circumcision altogether (Hadrian, 117–138 C.E.), then prohibited the circumcision of non-Jews (Antoninus Pius, 138–161 C.E.), and even later are said to have prohibited conversion to Judaism altogether (Septimius Severus, 193–211 C.E.). And when Christianity achieved toleration under Constantine and establishment under Theodosius I (381 C.E.), the peril of conversion escalated further.

The second aspect, we learn, is that the proselytes were in a "sorry state" and why.[24] Some rabbis argued that the proselytes' sense of affliction was God's punishment, springing from the fact that they had not observed the Noahide commandments.[25] The rebuttal insisted that as proselytes they were "like a child newly born," implying that the proselyte bears no guilt for what has happened before conversion. As neophytes they are as yet ill instructed and not well established in the Jewish life and observances—a sorry state. Others thought that their sorry state was the result of fear: they had dallied in their decision to convert. Finally, as we have seen, there was an ambivalent attitude toward proselytes; in the discussion of the rite and its requirements, the Talmud records the rabbinic saying: "Proselytes are as hard for Israel [to endure] as a sore. . . ."[26]

What the rabbis have noticed is that conversion involves an identity crisis. Although Erikson (and others, as we have seen) concentrated on the elements of crisis in the individual, social scientists have gone on to show that groups, communities, indeed entire civilizations and cultures, undergo crises of identity.[27]

The crisis for many God-fearers was compounded of an old identity and way of life dying and a new identity and way of life aborning. Their "sorry state"—their anguish—nonetheless brought them to the Judaism of the rabbis, who could facilitate entry into what they saw as the covenanted people of Israel.

Why did they want to convert? As it turns out, a résumé of reasons was not the point, just a humble disposition in the face of the reality: "I know, yet I am unworthy."

E. INSTRUCTION

The humble of disposition, once accepted, were the subjects of the second stage, instruction. The syllabus: commandments "minor and major." The selection of the precise commandments (Gleanings, the forgotten Sheaf, the Corner of the Field, and the Poor Man's Tithe) is puzzling at first glance. They are based on agricultural practice that distinguished the Israelite from the Gentile and sought to develop group solidarity.[28]

Viewed from a wide-angle lens, the subjects exemplified indispensable Jewish topics: commandments, punishment, and reward. The general purpose was clear: preliminary instruction about Jewish law and how one was to live as a Jew. How long the period of instruction lasted is nowhere indicated; nor are we told whether the topics indicated exhausted the instructions. Clearly the candidates had some previous and fairly intimate association with Jews and the synagogue; they entered on the stage of instruction often with a good deal of knowledge about Judaism.

F. CIRCUMCISION[29]

The talmudic rite divulges little about circumcision, save that a repeat might be necessary, but there is an attendant ritual. When an Israelite baby was circumcised, customarily eight days after birth, his father, according to the Talmud, recited a blessing that specifically refers to the "covenant of Abraham." For the convert, the one who performed the rite offered the same blessing. Although without reference to Abraham, the blessing clearly states that circumcision signifies the convert's entry into the covenant and the covenanted people:

> Blessed are you, YHWH, our God, king of the universe, who has sanctified us with your commandments and has commanded us to circumcise converts and to cause the drops of the blood of the covenant to flow from them, because if it were not for the blood of the covenant heaven and earth would not endure, as it is said, "If not my covenant by day and by night, I would not have appointed ordinances of heaven and earth" [Jer 33:25].[30]

G. IMMERSION

The final component of the rite is immersion in a pool of clear water (mikveh) constructed according to talmudic requirements in the tractate Mikva'ot.[31] In general it contained enough natural spring water for an average standing adult (four feet?) to immerse and wash away any ritual impurity. It also contained enough space for the two instructors to stand on either side of the candidate to conduct their continued discussion of commandments "major and minor."

Although, as we have seen, there was some dispute about whether both circumcision and immersion were necessary for conversion, the text cited above requires both as the norm.[32] Another matter of dispute was whether the convert is a full Israelite upon emerging from the mikveh. Our text leaves no doubt that at least at that point he or she was "an Israelite in all respects."

Conversion and Initiation

Conversion in Jewish antiquity was no easy affair. The first step was an attraction that drew the candidate close to Judaism and then to the gradual realization that it was not only *a* new religious reality but *the* new religious reality: Israel's God was the only one, and the community of Israel was the place to embrace him. This produced the "sorry state" we have examined—a crisis both personal and social—and we have called such a person a God-fearer or sympathizer.

At some point in the crisis, the candidate seeks out the rabbis and asks for the rites we have just discussed. How long the ritual itself then took is hard to estimate: for a male, a week or so; perhaps less for a woman.

But was the rite of entry a rite of passage or initiation? Some think that it was simply an attempt to regulate what had been a personal and chaotic process.[33] Considered as an integral part of the process we have sketched, however, the ritual focused for the candidates their experience of crisis and change, dramatically enacting their journey across the boundaries of their old religion and way of life into a new religious reality. They were every bit as initiated into Judaism as Lucius was into the community of Isis initiates.[34]

III. Conversion in the Diaspora

From the time of the Babylonian exile, at least, Jews of antiquity lived in dispersion (Greek, *diaspora*)—outside the land of Israel. Although the oldest and most influential diaspora community was in Babylon (Iraq), where the Talmud was composed, large Jewish communities existed in all the major cities of the Mediterranean and the Middle East. Archaeological evidence, which continues to mount, underscores the fact that the Jews of the diaspora were active and important participants in the cultural and social life of their cities.[35] It underscores as well how deeply the culture and tradition of their several worlds influenced them.

Hellenistic Judaism

A case in point is Hellenistic Judaism. The adjective, as already noted, refers to the Greek language, culture, and way of life that pervaded people of the eastern Mediterranean. Hellenism was not ingested without spasm by the conquered peoples—recall the Maccabean revolt in 166 B.C.E. Nonetheless, it shaped the language, literature, and religion of Greek-speaking Jews. As a result, scholars are inclined to speak of Hellenistic Judaism as an antonym for Palestinian Judaism. The distinction is useful as long as one does not think of Judaism in Palestine as untouched by Hellenism or of Hellenistic culture as untouched by Judaism.

Joseph and Asenath[36]

We have already seen different ways in which Gentiles became Jews in Alexandria and elsewhere. One more way remains to be illustrated by the widely circulated story of the patriarch Joseph and his wife, Asenath. Although told in many tongues and subject to many editorial hands (including Christian), the original story was written in Greek, very likely during the second century C.E. by an Egyptian Jew thoroughly versed in the Greek version of the Bible (the Septuagint/LXX), rabbinic biblical interpretations *(midrash),* and Greek legend.

Based on the traditions about the patriarch Joseph that occupy the last chapters of the book of Genesis (39–50), *Joseph and Asenath* elaborates in romantic and religious detail the laconic biblical statement that the pharaoh gave Asenath, the daughter of Potiphera, priest of On (Pentephres of Heliopolis in the LXX), to Joseph and that they had two sons, Manasseh and Ephraim (Gn 41:45, 50).

A romance with a missionary purpose, the work has two parts; only the first, the conversion of Asenath, is our direct concern. The social situation of Jews and Gentiles in the diaspora is the crux of the plot; because of the rigid separation between Jews and Egyptians, marriage between them is out of the question.

The problem is idolatry, which makes even the food Asenath eats the cause of impurity. Thus, Joseph may not even approach her, much less respond to any advance. Even so, Pentephres, his family (save for Asenath), and even the pharaoh are God-fearers. They confess "the Lord, the God of Jacob" (Philonenko, 21:3) and accept Joseph as the "Strong One" or "Son of God" on whom the spirit and grace of the Lord rest (4:8–10; 8:1; 20:6). Indeed, Pentephres very much wants Joseph to marry his daughter. The trouble is that Asenath must become a Jew: conversion is the rub.

A. THE ENCOUNTER

Asenath, "eighteen, tall and comely," is besieged by royal suitors (1). She lives, however, quite apart, in a tower attached to the family's residence, with seven maids of her very own birth date and age. One chamber (room is too informal a term) in her tower is filled with "the gods of Egypt [whom] Asenath venerates, fears, and offers sacrifices [to]" (2).

Joseph enters the story early. Cleared of charges that he had seduced pharaoh's wife (Gn 39:7–23), he had become pharaoh's vizier and notified Asenath's father, Pentephres, of his official visit to Heliopolis (3).

Pentephres and his wife, away at one of their estates, hurry home and alert Asenath that they want her to marry Joseph. She responds with hauteur and anger: Joseph, after all, is an alien and had been a slave, and rumor has it that he had slept with the pharaoh's wife (4).

Joseph arrives, splendid in raiment and visage; Asenath sees him from her window on the courtyard. Smitten, she begins to think better of her earlier attitude: "Miserable and insensitive I am, for I have spoken evil words to my father. Now may he give me to Joseph as a servant and as a slave, and I will serve him forever" (5:8). Joseph also sees Asenath. Initially annoyed (he remembered how much trouble the flirtatious wife of the pharaoh had caused him), he, too, has a change of heart when he learns who she really is and says, "If she is your daughter, Pentephres, may she come down, then, because she is my sister and from this day forward, I will love her as my sister" (7:11). So, Pentephres' wife goes to bring Asenath downstairs, Joseph blesses the girl, and Pentephres, looking to Joseph, encourages her to kiss him. But Joseph protests, saying:

> It is not fitting that a pious man, who praises the living God with his mouth, and who eats the blessed bread of life, and who drinks the cup blessed with immortality, and who is anointed with the oil blessed with incorruptibility, kiss a foreign woman, one who has praised with her mouth dead and silent idols, and who has eaten at their table the bread that chokes [out life], and who drinks their libations from the cup of deceit, and who is anointed with the ointment of ruin.[37]

B. REPENTANCE

Asenath is stunned at Joseph's words. Undaunted, he proceeds to seek her conversion, praying that the Lord who gives life to the universe and who calls [people] from darkness to light, and from error to truth, and from death to life, [may] you yourself, Lord, give life to this [chaste] young woman and bless her. And renew her by your spirit and refashion her with your [hidden] hand . . . (8:10–11).

Heartened by his words, Asenath goes to her tower chamber. Torn by emotions of joy that Joseph had prayed thus for her transformation and of terror that she must turn in penitence *(metanoiei)* from her venerable gods, she throws herself down on her bed and awaits in this torment "the coming of evening" (9).

In the meantime, Joseph, with the promise to return in eight days, had departed. So also had her family—to the country. Alone (but for her maids), Asenath tosses and weeps. At last, she rises, sneaks outside, and brings up to her chamber a sack of ashes.

Then she exchanges her fashionable, even regal, robes for the black clothes she had worn when her eldest brother had died. She then throws her finery, including her tiara, out the window and proceeds to smash her idols, casting the gold and silver fragments out the window for the poor to find and take. Then, she casts away her luxurious dinner. Finally, she covers the floor with ashes, puts on a girdle of sackcloth, lets her hair down, covers her head with ashes, and lies on the ash-covered floor, beating her breast and weeping until morning. The account of her repentance concludes:

> In the morning Asenath rose and saw that the ashes under her, mixed with her tears, had become like clay. And anew Asenath fell face down on the ashes until sunset. And thus Asenath conducted herself for seven days without tasting any [food]. (10:18–20)

C. THE TURNING POINT

The eighth day dawns; the critical moment in her conversion has arrived. Asenath finds herself in no-man's-land: exhausted by her long ordeal, she feels disowned by parents and kin alike. Unable to go back or to go on, she is caught in the throes of a deep quandary. Attracted by what people had told her about the mercy and gentleness of the "God of the Hebrews" and painfully aware of her orphaned state, she senses her unworthiness to become a Jew ("I know and yet am unworthy!" we read above). As a result, she kneels and offers a long and now celebrated prayer in which she confesses her sinfulness, depicts her plight as one orphaned, desolate, and defenseless against the deaf and dead idols who are, nonetheless, in close pursuit, and professes her faith in the Lord of Israel and her commitment to Joseph (12–13).

D. THE ARCHANGEL'S REVELATION

At the end of Asenath's prayer, the archangel Michael visits her in a vision that recalls her first sight of resplendent Joseph. Michael says to her:

> Lay aside the tunic that you have put on, take off the sackcloth with which you girded yourself, shake the ashes from you hair, and wash your face with living water. Then, put on a new and stainless gown, and gird yourself with the brilliant cincture, the double one of your virginity. Then return to me and I will tell you the words destined for you. (14:12–14)

Asenath does as she was told, and returns to Michael, who tells her that God has seen her penitential ordeal, has written her name in the book of life, and will renew, refashion, and revivify her. Michael also assures her that she will eat the bread of life, drink from the cup of immortality, and receive anointing with the ointment of incorruptibility. He then consoles her: "Courage, Asenath, behold, the Lord has given you to Joseph in marriage and he will be your spouse" (15:5—the words of comfort we read above in *Gerim*).

In the process her name would be changed to "City of Refuge," for many nations (Gentiles) would find shelter under her wings through repentance (15:6).

E. MICHAEL AND THE MIRACULOUS HONEYCOMB

A table is spread for Michael in anticipation of his departure. Michael asks for a honeycomb to be brought, together with the bread and wine Asenath has promised. Although the honeycomb's presence in the castle is quite unknown to her, Asenath finds it in her storehouse, all white "like snow and overflowing with honey and its odor was like the scent of life" (16:4). When she comes to Michael, he puts his hand on her head and says:

> "Happy are you, Asenath, because the mysteries of God have been revealed to you, and happy are those who attach themselves to God in repentance, because they will eat from this honeycomb. For this honeycomb—the bees of the Paradise of delights made it, and the

angels of God dine on it, and whoever eats it shall never die" (16:8).

Michael gives Asenath a piece of the honeycomb. Its bees cover her from head to foot and eat from the piece in her mouth. At Michael's command, however, they fly to heaven, save those who wish to harm her—they fall dead. He restores them to life, however, and they inhabit the fruit trees surrounding the house. As Michael prepares to go, Asenath intercedes for her seven maids, calling them to come. Michael then blesses them in God's name, assures them of God's favor forever, and, as Asenath turns to put away the table, Michael disappears "as in a chariot of fire rising to heaven, towards the East" (17:6).

F. TRANSFORMATION AND MYSTICAL MARRIAGE

With the series of Michael visions, Asenath's conversion is complete. But there is more to the story. Asenath dresses in the brilliant clothes Michael has spoken of; her face, haggard from her long ordeal, is transformed as she prepares to wash with pure water (18).

Joseph then comes back as he has promised and as Michael has confirmed. Then, although Pentephres proposes to give them both in marriage, Joseph seeks her hand from the pharaoh, who marries them, saying to Asenath: "The Lord, the God of Joseph, will bless you, he who has chosen you for him to be his wife, because he is the firstborn son of God, and you shall be the daughter of the Most High and Joseph will be your spouse forever" (21).

G. THE TEST

The second part of the romance (22–29), which need not detain us, recounts the postconversion struggle. Joseph, Asenath, and their children, Manasseh and Ephraim, journey to the land of Israel to see Jacob. But the enmity of the pharaoh's son pursues them, even to the point of his conspiring to kill Joseph; indeed, he even attempts to kill his own father. But the son is killed, and Joseph and family return to a now peaceful Egypt and live faithful to each other and the covenant.

IV. Conclusion

Joseph and Asenath forms a surprising—almost eccentric—conclusion to our study of how one became a Jew in antiquity. Its approach and ambience reflect a world quite different from Palestine. Yet it is an appropriate conclusion because is sets in high relief a Judaism as many-hued as the coat the patriarch Jacob had made for his son Joseph (Gn 37:3, 39). It also focuses attention on Judaism in the Greek-speaking diaspora and reveals at close quarters the gap that stood between Gentiles and Jews abroad. Further, it allows the reader an intimate view of a persistent problem, intermarriage, and its solution, the conversion of a non-Jewish woman.

Finally, the story, albeit with romantic drama, discloses that conversion in Jewish antiquity involved a personal crisis embodied in a dramatic rite of passage from an old way of life to a new one, exhibiting the classic phases of such rites: separation, transition, and incorporation.[38]

For Asenath, the old way, represented by her familiar "gods," began to recede when Joseph refused to embrace and kiss her and when he and her family departed: she was left alone, orphaned, so to speak. The turning point or transition was the seemingly endless seven days of ritual mourning in mourning clothes, sackcloth, ashes, and lament. The encounter with Archangel Michael, the revelations of God's mysteries, and the return of Joseph mark the beginning of her transformation and new way of life. Pharaoh seals it by giving Asenath to Joseph in marriage.

Although it might be useful to analyze the other rites we have studied in this chapter as rites of passage, if one makes the necessary adjustments for their differences, they can be seen as rites whose function is to effect the passage of the candidate from an old way of valuing and living to a new way.[39] Although more could be said, space permits only a brief review of what we have so far seen.

Until postexilic Judaism modified its ethnic sense of identity to include religion, Gentiles becoming Jews was problematic. By the second century B.C.E. the problem is solved in favor of conversion as a way into the people of Israel. A solidly established rite of entry appears in Palestine: declaration of belief in the God of Israel as the one true God, circumcision, and acceptance in the Jewish community.

With the destruction of the temple and the rise of the rabbis, acceptance into the Jewish community involves a complex rite of examination, instruction, circumcision, and immersion which both focuses the process of conversion and enacts it. From the *mikveh,* the convert emerges an Israelite in every respect. For converts, drawn usually from the circle of God-fearers, conversion meant both a new world and a new identity, specifically, a new doctrine of God, a new code of religious observance and conduct, and a new people—and, to some extent, an uncomfortably ambiguous status within Judaism.

In the diaspora, however, if Philo, Paul, Josephus, and the author of *Joseph and Asenath* are to be credited, uniformity did not prevail, at least not until rabbinic Judaism became normative—comparatively late in our period.

NOTES

1. I am indebted to Shaye J. D. Cohen, *From the Maccabees to the Mishnah* (Philadelphia: Westminster Press, 1987) 122–74 for what follows. But see also Michael E. Stone, *Scriptures, Sects and Visions: A Profile of Judaism from Ezra to the Jewish Revolts* (Philadelphia: Fortress Press, 1980); and Uriel Rappaport, "Maccabean Revolt," *ABD* 4: 433–39.

2. Cohen identifies the following as the best attested "proto-sects": the congregation of the (returned) exiles in the Book of Ezra, the group represented by Nehemiah 10, and the group represented in Isaiah 65. But see also Stone, *Scriptures, Sects and Visions*.

3. For what follows, see Cohen, *From the Maccabees to the Mishnah*, 124–72, especially 124–44.

4. In 142 B.C.E., Simon, the Maccabee, succeeded Jonathan, his elder brother, who succeeded Judas. Simon, we read, became the great high priest, general, and leader of the Jews (1 Mc 13:42). For discussion of the reign, see Michael David McGehee, "Hasmonean Dynasty," *ABD* 3:67–77.

5. For what follows, see James L. Kugel, "Two Introductions to Midrash," in David Kraemer, ed., *The Mind of the Talmud: An Intellectual History of the Bavli* (New York: Oxford University Press, 1990) 77–103; and James L. Kugel and Rowan A. Greer, *Early Biblical Interpretation* (Philadelphia: Westminster Press [Library of Early Christianity, ed. Wayne A. Meeks], 1986) 13–39.

6. See Devorah Dimant, "Pesharim, Qumran," *ABD* 5:244–51, especially 244.

7. Cited in ibid., 248.

8. For what follows, see Cohen, *From the Maccabees to the Mishnah,* 143–50; Martin Goodman, *The Ruling Class of Judaea: The Origins of the Jewish Revolt Against Rome, A.D. 66–70* (Cambridge: Cambridge University Press, 1987) 51–108, especially 82–85; and Anthony J. Saldarini, "Pharisees," *ABD* 5:289–303.

9. I am indebted to Cohen (*From the Maccabees to the Mishnah,* 125) for this definition of sect, which reflects the contemporary analytic research of

Brian Wilson in the sociology of religion.

10. For the sources and their assessment, see Saldarini, "Pharisees," 294–301; and Goodman, *The Ruling Class of Judaea*, 182–85.

11. For discussion, see Alan Avery-Peck, "Judaism Without the Temple," in *Eusebius, Christianity, and Judaism*, ed. Harold W. Attridge and Gohei Hata (Detroit: Wayne State University Press, 1992) 409–31.

12. Thus, ibid., 419. Avery-Peck analyzes each of the Mishnaic tractates from the standpoint of their underlying religious meaning.

13. For a discussion of the Talmud and its two versions, and their editorial and textual history and contents, see Gary G. Porton, "Talmud," *ABD* 6:310–15. For an intellectual history, see David Kraemer, ed., *The Mind of the Talmud*, especially 9–25.

14. Thus, Porton, "Talmud." Kraemer *(The Mind of the Talmud,* 28) holds that Bavli reflects the work of Amoraim from the first through the sixth generation (third to sixth centuries) and that it was composed between the late fifth and early seventh centuries (115).

15. For what follows, see Gary G. Porton, *The Stranger Within Your Gates: Converts and Conversion in Rabbinic Literature* (Chicago: University of Chicago Press [Chicago Studies in the History of Judaism, ed. William Scott Green], 1994) 71–154; Shaye J. D. Cohen, "Crossing the Boundary and Becoming a Jew," *HTR* 82 (1989) 13–33; and his "The Rabbinic Conversion Ceremony," *JJS* 41 (1990) 172–203.

16. For discussion, see Porton, *Stranger Within Your Gates,* 132–48.

17. These concern agricultural gifts to the poor: Jews to other Jews. They gave money to the Gentile poor but not the fruits of God's holy land.

18. *Yebamot* 47a–b, in I. Epstein, ed., *The Babylonian Talmud, Seder Nashim, Yebamot I* (London: Soncino Press, 1936) 310–11. For an alternate translation and for what follows, see Cohen, "The Rabbinic Conversion Ceremony," especially 186–95.

19. *Gerim* 60a, 1:4 (translation in *The Minor Tractates of the Talmud,* vol. 2, ed. A. Cohen [London: Soncino Press, 1965] 603–4); Cohen, "The Rabbinic Conversion Ceremony," 180.

20. See Chapter 4 and Martin Goodman, "Proselytizing in Rabbinic Judaism," *JJS* 40 (1985) 176–85. That Gentiles could be righteous without conversion was generally accepted in rabbinic circles—all they had to do was to observe the Noahide laws. Nonetheless, some rabbis assumed the desirability of proselytizing. He concludes that "the notion that existing worshippers should put effort into attracting others to their cult was rarely, if ever, found outside Christianity before the third century" (183). But see Chapter 3, "The Mystery Religions."

21. See Chapter 4.

22. See the discussions in *Yebamot* 46b–49a (Epstein, Soncino, 306–20).

23. *Gerim* 60a, 1:7 (Cohen, Soncino, 604).

24. *Yebamot* 48b (Epstein, Soncino, 20).

25. See Chapter 4 and David Novak, *The Image of the Non-Jew in Judaism: An Historical and Constructive Study of the Noahide Laws* (New York: E. Mellen, 1983), 14–20.

26. *Yebamot* 47b (Epstein, Soncino, 312). In *Gerim* 61b (Cohen, Soncino, 611–12) the rules insist that the proselytes are "beloved by God." The example of Abraham is cited: he was ninety-nine (rather than in his early twenties!) before he circumcised himself. God, it appears, kept putting it off to keep open the door for proselytes.

27. See Chapter 1. For discussion of the social dimensions of the rise of new religions and of religious reform or revitalization movements, see John Gager, *Kingdom and Community: The Social World of Early Christianity* (Englewood Cliffs: Prentice-Hall, 1975) 21–65. Gager, relying on the work of social scientists like Peter Berger, Thomas Luckmann, Mary Douglas, Yonina Talmon, and Kenelm Burridge, focuses on Christianity and is particularly interested in why Christians joined. He concludes that their situation exhibits an uneven relationship between their expectation and the means of satisfying it. He calls this disinheritance. The God-fearers were likely subjects of disinheritance.

28. For a detailed analysis, see Gary G. Porton, *Goyim: Gentiles and Israelites in Mishnah-Tosefta* (Atlanta: Scholars Press [Brown Judaic Studies, ed. Jacob Neusner], 1988), especially 1–37, 285–307. He observes that Israelites were different from Gentiles, and these differences left their mark on all areas of activity. Indeed, that the Gentiles appear at all is to exemplify the ethnic borders of the Israelites. Thus, the Israelites treat the crops that grow in the Holy Land their own way, observe their own sacred times, have sexual relations only with Israelites, and the like.

29. See Porton, *Stranger Within Your Gates,* 139–41.

30. *Shabbot (Bavli)* 137b, cited in Porton, *Stranger Within Your Gates,* 140. According to Porton (327, n. 58), the reading, from which something seems to be missing, is a *Gemara* reading.

31. See "Mikveh," in *Encyclopedia Judaica* 11:1534–44.

32. For the dispute, see Porton, *Stranger Within Your Gates,* 141–48. Exactly when both were required is an open question (148).

33. Thus, Cohen, "The Rabbinic Conversion Ceremony," 203. He concludes that it lacks the rites of separation, transition, and incorporation (for which, see above, Chapter 1, Arnold van Gennep) and concludes that it is simply halakhic, an attempt to regulate and formalize what until then had been "an entirely personal and chaotic process" (203).

34. For discussion of rites of passage, see Chapter 1, Arnold van Gennep et al., and below, n. 38.

35. In addition to Herschel Shanks, *Judaism in Stone: The Archaeology*

of Ancient Synagogues (New York: Harper & Row; Hagerstown, Md.: Biblical Archaeology Society, 1979); see also Erwin R. Goodenough, *Jewish Symbols in the Greco-Roman Period,* 13 vols. (New York: Pantheon Books [Bollingen Series 37], 1953–1968).

36. For what follows, see Marc Philonenko, ed., *Joseph et Asenath: Introduction, texte critique, traduction et notes* (Leiden: E. J. Brill, 1968). Citations are those of the text. Especially valuable is his introduction (1–123). E. W. Brooks has translated the work into English: *Joseph and Asenath: The Confession and Prayer of Asenath, Daughter of Pentephres the Priest* (London: SPCK, 1918).

37. *Joseph and Asenath* 8:5–6 (Philonenko, 154–56). Some have thought this account the result of Christian interpolation, largely because of the cultic references, which evoke Christian initiation liturgy. In his introduction, however, Philonenko, the editor, discusses the "Christianization" of the text (98–102) and cites linguistic cross references to pseudepigraphal literature, such as the Wisdom of Solomon, Jubilees, the Sibylline Oracles, the Testament of Levi, IV Esdras, and the Testament of Solomon (154–57 and notes). In addition, as he points out, Goodenough has studied in depth the evidence for what he calls a "mystic Judaism," which, like the biblical mosaics of Dura-Europos, points to a Judaism quite different from the picture drawn by traditional studies.

38. The classic study is by Arnold van Gennep, *The Rites of Passage,* trans. Monica B. Vizedom and Gabrielle L. Caffe (Chicago: University of Chicago Press, 1960). The phases he established have become standard classifications and very useful tools of analysis: (1) separation, in which the subjects are segregated from family, associates, and their previous way of life; (2) transition or liminality, in which, individually and as a group, they are subjected to ordeals that efface their previous identity and during which they live on the margins, or *limina,* of their society or group; and (3) incorporation or reincorporation, through which they are reintegrated into their group or society with a new identity and new status (or, as in conversion, into a new community).

39. See Cohen, "The Rabbinic Conversion Ceremony," 203. The difference between the Talmud's rite and Joseph-Asenath is one of detail and human drama. In my analysis, the rabbinic and the diaspora rituals have the classic phases of an initiation ritual. The form of the former is halakhic; the latter, romantic.

Chapter 6

CONVERSION IN EARLIEST CHRISTIANITY

I. The First Century

Christian origins lie in the shadowland over which we have traveled in the last chapter: the Palestine of the Jewish sects that produced the Dead Sea Scrolls, the apocrypha, and baptizing movements. Two converts and a rite stand out from the shadows: John, Jesus, and baptism.

John[1]

In the fourth chapter we considered John and his community, noting that Jesus and his earliest disciples came out of the Johannite movement.[2] In the synoptic gospels, Jesus steps onto the Palestinian stage as a disciple of John, receives John's baptism of repentance for the forgiveness of sins, and becomes a co-worker, adopting John's mission and way of life.

Although little can be discovered about John's origins, some early Christians believed that he came from a family of rural priests alienated from the same priestly establishment in Jerusalem that had alienated the Qumran community and other apocalyptic groups (Lk 1:5–25). He may even have been associated with Qumran.[3]

In his early adult life, John left home, became a desert ascetic, and attacked the systematic injustices emanating from the capital by proclaiming an imminent day of wrathful judgment for those who did not submit to baptism and change their ways. Many came to him. Some converted, received his once-for-all baptism, and returned home to walk justly in their individual lives. Others converted and formed an

137

inner circle around John, practicing his ritual way of immersion, asceticism, prayer, and fasting in preparation for the final purifying judgment. They formed what came to be the Johannite community.[4] John was arrested and beheaded in the prime of his dissident life, but the Johannites continued after his death.

John and Jesus[5]

Jesus, whose origins were almost as obscure as John's, was one of John's converts and a member of the inner circle.[6] He left his family, parted from his former way of life in Nazareth as an artisan (carpenter?), and joined the Johannites. His baptism signals his conversion.

Although the accounts of Jesus' baptism say nothing about his decision and what led up to it, what he came to see through John's preaching is fairly clear: (1) the endtime was fast approaching, (2) Israel had gone astray and was in danger of God's fiery, imminent judgment, and (3) only those Israelites who underwent a thorough change of mind and heart would know salvation.[7] Further, if we credit the gospel traditions about John and Jesus, especially John's gospel (Jn 1:29–45; 3:22–30; 4:1–2),[8] Jesus worked for some months with John, proclaiming a baptism of repentance to prepare for the coming judgment and end of time. At some point, the two co-workers went in different directions, John to Samaria, and Jesus to Judaea and, eventually, to Galilee.

Although it is impossible to say how long they cooperated as baptizers, both were men whose lives were transformed by a prophetic vision of the imminent end of time and how to prepare Israel for it. Whether they saw their previous lives as wrong and sinful—one of the characteristics of conversion—can only be a matter of speculation. Perhaps John and Jesus saw their previous lives as evil because in pursuing them they had, in effect, collaborated with the oppressive system headquartered in Jerusalem; the prophetic call summoned them actively to oppose the injustice rampant in their society.[9]

Thus, out of the Palestinian shadows came two converts on an eschatological mission in the tradition of Israel's prophets, yet tinged with the apocalyptic view of Jewish authors in the Greco-Roman period.

Jesus the Convert[10]

Something, however, happened; the mission and message of Jesus changed dramatically. The vision that John and Jesus initially shared was of the imminent end of time and the searing judgment: "Even now the ax is lying at the root of the tree; every tree therefore that does not bear good fruit is cut down and thrown into the fire" (Mt 3:10; Mk 1:4–6; Lk 3:7–9).

But the Jesus of the gospels moderated John's message of God's wrath.[11] For Jesus, the judgment was not entirely future, nor was its arrival to be accompanied by felled trees thrown into the fire. Rather, the judgment was the benign reign of God, whose kingdom was already here. Healing made its presence evident, and baptism graphically symbolized the extinguishing of the fire—at least initially, though the rite would take on different meanings as it passed from John through Jesus to the early church.[12]

At some unrecoverable point in his work with John, then, Jesus experienced the kingdom present, reaching people in the here and now, especially through his work as an exorcist and healer. The gospel text that reflects the heart of the experience is recorded by Luke: "If it is by the finger of God that I cast out demons, then the reign of God has come upon you" (11:20).

A present and benign kingdom (though not without judgment) is central to the gospels;[13] the early chapters of Mark are representative. Not only is the kingdom near (1:15), but wherever the kingdom is, everything wrong is made right. And the individual is its goal. Through Jesus its agent, the kingdom touches and heals the man in the synagogue (1:23), Peter's mother-in-law (1:30), the leper (1:40), the paralytic (2:11), the man with the withered hand (3:1), the Gerasene demoniac with his legion of devils (5:5), the hemorrhaging woman (5:25), and the dead daughter of the leader of the synagogue (5:35).

Jesus' new vision is that through him the imminent end of the ages—the kingdom—is God visiting, healing, and redeeming his people as individuals, not just Israel as a people. The critical moment of the change—conversion[14]—seems to have been Jesus' experience of the finger of God healing through him. Healing, rather than punishment, was the sign of the reign of God. In such a view, Jesus is first a convert of John and his vision of the kingdom, and then a convert to a present and future kingdom, in which God is visiting and redeeming his people through healing.[15]

Baptism

In turning away from the Johannites, Jesus departed from their communal life and rituals. He consorts with sinners, he is a wine drinker, he does not fast, and if the silence in Matthew, Mark, and Luke is indicative, he turned away from baptism. Except for the "Great Commission" at the end of Matthew (28:19) and the mention of Jesus and his disciples baptizing found in John (Jn 3:22–30; 4:1–2), the rite virtually disappears from the gospels.

How, then, can baptism be the hinge on which Christian conversion turned?[16] Jesus instituted the eucharist at the Last Supper, but for baptism there is only the account of John's baptism of Jesus, to which early Christians regularly appealed as the pattern that shed meaning on Christian baptism.

Some link the persistence of baptism among Christians to proselyte baptism; others, to Qumran's entry rite; and still others link it to Jesus—the rite flowed from John through Jesus into early Christianity.[17] But the link was the end of the age, the *eschaton,* especially repentance, forgiveness of sins, and the imminence of the last day—related images that come into sharp focus in John's baptism. As a symbol of eschatological expectations, purification through water is rooted in the visions of Isaiah (1:16–17) and Ezekiel (36:25–28), and it is abundantly evident in works like the Dead Sea Scrolls and especially *First Enoch,* which features both a new flood as the final cleansing (54:7—55:2; 60:1–10; 65—68) and the resurrection of the dead (51; 61:1–5).

Further, John's selection of the Jordan evoked the image of the Exodus, when the Israelites crossed over both the Red Sea and the Jordan in their trek to the Promised Land (Ex 14:21; Jos 3:14–17). There was also Elijah, who ascended to heaven from the Jordan (2 Kgs 2:6–12).

Finally, John looked forward to the "more powerful one that is coming after me" (Mt 3:11; Lk 3:16), whom the evangelists unanimously identified as Jesus. With that identification made at the outset, their accounts move single-mindedly to the denouement of the gospels—the risen Jesus, who, as firstborn from the dead, embodies the kingdom fully arrived.

The earliest Christians retained John's baptism because its eschatological core effectively symbolized the kingdom and their entry into it by rebirth. John the Evangelist put the matter quite plainly: "Unless a man be born over again he cannot see the kingdom of God. . . . no one can enter the kingdom of God without being born from water and the Spirit" (Jn 3:3–5).

Precisely when the earliest Christians adopted John's baptism as the hinge on which conversion turns is impossible to say. As we have already noted, there is no compelling reason to think that it did not flow into the early church from John through Jesus. In any event, within two decades of Jesus' death Paul spoke of baptism as if it had been in place from the beginning, and the evangelists seemed to take the centrality of baptism for granted.[18]

Christian Baptism

A. IN THE NAME OF JESUS

Except for the eschatological link and the pivotal character of baptism in John's mission, the meaning of baptism was not in place; the documents of the New Testament propose many meanings. Paul and his heirs had the most to say about it, the synoptic gospels the least. Although the New Testament has no single doctrine of baptism, differences presuppose something—a ground—in which the differences are rooted.[19]

To distinguish it from other baptisms, especially John's, earliest Christian baptism was performed "in the name of the Lord Jesus," as one learns from both Paul's letters and Luke's Acts of the Apostles. Although some take it as a form for the administration of baptism—which it may be—to do so obscures the primary meaning of "in the name of."[20]

First and foremost, the phrase seeks to distinguish Christian baptism from others by asserting that the rite is centered on the person and work of Jesus as Lord—thus, "in the name of the Lord," "in the name of Jesus (Christ)." What sharpened the focus further was the foundational conviction of the earliest Christians, namely, (1) that Jesus had risen from the dead, (2) that his resurrection established an entirely new relationship between God and humankind, and (3) that baptism symbolized that relationship. Although Jesus himself had linked baptism and his death (Mk 10:38–39; Lk 12:50; Jn 18:11), Paul and his heirs soon developed a telling way of expressing the relationship between death, resurrection, and baptism:

Do you not know that all of us who have been baptized into Christ Jesus were baptized into his death? Therefore we have been buried with him by baptism into death, so that, just as Christ was raised from the dead by the glory of the Father, so we too might walk in newness of life. For if we have been united with him in a death like his, we will certainly be united with him in a resurrection like his. (Rom 6:3–5)[21]

B. BAPTISMAL PREPARATION: PREACHING AND TEACHING

Preaching and teaching in the Pauline churches continually emphasized the link between baptism, Christ's death and resurrection, and the kingdom. In the second and early third centuries, however, Pauline teaching about baptismal death and resurrection vanishes.[22] By the fourth century, baptism into Jesus' death and resurrection would rank with Jesus' baptism in the Jordan and the outpouring of the Spirit at Pentecost as a paradigm of Christian baptism—all three revealing the source from which conversion flowed.

From the outset, baptism was crucial to conversion but was only part of the process. Converts had to be prepared, often at length. The early preachers and teachers worked from an extensive syllabus that embraced all three paradigms—the Jordan, death and resurrection, and Pentecost—but emphasized the kingdom and how to enter it: (1) the arrival of the messianic age foretold by the prophets; (2) its inauguration in the life, death, and resurrection of Jesus; (3) Jesus' exaltation to his Father's right hand; (4) the presence of the Holy Spirit in the church as a sign of Christ's exaltation; (5) the imminent return of Jesus as the consummation of the messianic age; and (6) the call to repentance, the offer of forgiveness, and the summons to be baptized for initial conversion.[23] Those who responded were baptized.

The elements of the outline continued to shape preaching and teaching in the early communities: if conversion were to be both understood and sustained, continual instruction was indispensable for both potential converts and the baptized.

Some scholars distinguish between preaching about the dead, risen, and returning Jesus, which they call *kerygma,* and the subsequent teaching of its meaning and implications, which they call *didache.* According to this distinction, the goal of the *kerygma* is to elicit faith in candidates, whereas the goal of *didache* is to maintain and develop the religious life of converts. But the distinction is too sharp: it is based on a preconceived notion of what constitutes conversion, namely, that conversion is the response of faith to the *kerygma*. But the syllabus permeates both *kerygma* and *didache* in the New Testament and early Christianity. Both were intimately involved in the process of conversion. They comprised the first stage of a two-stage process: instruction and baptism.

C. BAPTISM IN THE SPIRIT

The issue about baptism in Jesus' name, then, discloses baptism as a work of Jesus who brought the kingdom. But there is a second issue that also discloses the ground of baptism—also a paradigm of baptism—baptism in the Holy Spirit, a subject broached especially by John the Baptist (the coming one who will baptize with the Holy Spirit and fire [Mt 3:11 and Lk 3:16; see Mk 1:8 and Jn 1:32–33]) and Luke's Acts.[24]

The focus of Johannite baptism was both repentance to escape God's imminent judgment and preparation for the "coming one"—for John the phrase may have meant an agent like Elijah or, perhaps, God himself. For the evangelists, the phrase meant Jesus, as already noted. Although Mark, John, and Acts do not speak of fire, the traditions behind Matthew and Luke do, disclosing a continuity with the Baptist's fiery judgment theme. All four evangelists, however, single out the Spirit, though each has his own emphasis.

Mark and Matthew

In Mark, the Spirit is the Spirit of Holiness, which at Qumran meant the atoning Spirit of God resident in the community—he heals both members and neophytes, making them holy.[25] Mark's Holy Spirit drives Jesus into the desert to encounter and defeat that other spirit, Satan, and, thereafter, to heal countless people as the exorcist par excellence.

Matthew agrees with Mark but expands the concept; the Spirit of Holiness is the source of righteousness (obedient fidelity) and prophecy. Jesus is the righteous man and the prophet as well as the healer: "Whoever receives a prophet because he is a prophet will receive a prophet's reward, and whoever receives a righteous man because he is righteous will receive a righteous man's reward" (10:41). Matthew's understanding of the Spirit's descent on or empowerment of Jesus as the righteous one underlies Matthew's account of the formula for baptism: "Go therefore and make disciples of all nations, baptizing them in the name of the Father and of the Son and of the Holy Spirit . . . " (28:20). People are made righteous—that is, set right—by the work of the Father, of the Son, and of the Holy Spirit, all three of whom are manifest in John's baptism of Jesus, the original pattern of Christian baptism. The members of Matthew's church were thereby empowered as exorcists, healers, prophets, and the righteous—all characteristics of Matthean Christianity.

Luke

Luke's account, however, differs from Matthew's and Mark's in an important detail: the Spirit descends on Jesus in the bodily form of a dove only *after* "he was praying" (Lk 3:22). Perhaps Luke was projecting back into the Jordan account the sequence of the baptismal rite in his own day: baptism, and only later, prayer and the imposition of hands (and possibly anointing) for the outpouring of the Spirit.

Whatever the ritual sequence, there is a disjunction between baptism in the water and baptism in the Spirit which continues strikingly in his second volume, Acts. The die is cast right at the outset of Acts—Jesus speaks to his disciples about the Baptist: "John baptized with water, but before many days you will be baptized with the Spirit" (1:15). The "many days" end on Pentecost, when, according to the account, the Spirit descended upon them like a violent wind (2:2).

The disjuncture persists through other accounts in Acts. Philip and the Samaritans (8:4–19) provide an example. The evangelist preaches, teaches, heals, and baptizes in Samaria with great success—he even converts the celebrated Simon, former magician. But only later are Peter and John sent to pray and lay hands on Philip's converts: they had only been baptized "in the name of the Lord Jesus" (8:16) and had not yet received the Spirit.

The separation between baptism and the gift of the Spirit in Luke's work has led many to think of baptism in the Spirit as a second baptism quite apart from water baptism; some even deny to baptism any efficacy in conveying the Spirit.[26] In fact, the disjuncture in Luke's accounts may reflect the two "baptisms" at Qumran: the initial lustrations that allowed the candidate provisional membership in the community and, later, the giving of the Spirit of Holiness that allowed full membership.[27]

But the disjuncture does not appear in the other gospels; there baptism and the gift of the Spirit are one event (Mt 3:16; Mk 1:10; Jn 3:3–9). Although the Spirit abounds in the life of Paul's communities, the implication of the Pauline letters, especially the Corinthian correspondence, Colossians, and Ephesians, is that the Spirit and his gifts are given in baptism. Nevertheless, Luke seems to attest to a differing ritual practice, symbolized by the outpouring of the Spirit at Pentecost—baptism in water for forgiveness and provisional membership, and baptism in the Spirit for holiness and full membership.

Succeeding generations of early Christians, as later chapters will show, tended to insist on a single baptism, allowing the Pentecost paradigm of baptism to slip into the background. Most Syrian Christians, for instance, held that the gift of the Spirit was adequately symbolized within the rites of prebaptismal anointing and baptismal immersion without any additional rites. Christians in North Africa, Italy, and Egypt developed postimmersion rites to symbolize the gift of the Spirit: when the newly baptized emerged from the baptismal waters, prayer, anointing, and the laying on of hands symbolized the baptismal gift of the Spirit.

Nonetheless, in later Syrian authors (fifth century) one finds a two-baptism framework, the second an unfolding or full flowering of the gift of the Spirit given in first baptism (normally in infancy) and restricted to those converted to an ascetic life.[28] And in the West (also fifth century) one finds the separation of postbaptismal anointing and imposition of hands into a separate rite, symbolizing the fullness of the gift of the Spirit and called confirmation in the High Middle Ages. Although early Christians agreed that baptism conveyed forgiveness, reconciliation, and the gift of the Spirit, they managed only with difficulty to keep firm the ground from which baptism sprang. The Jordan paradigm along with the Pentecost paradigm (at least within the empire) tended to slip into the background, while death and resurrection moved center stage.[29]

A Recapitulation: The First Century

Baptism was the hinge upon which conversion turned among both Johannite and Christian Jews. The reason was eschatological: baptism was linked with the kingdom and its coming. Among the disciples of John, baptism was a penitential preparation for a fiery judgment; among the disciples of Jesus, it was a redemptive healing for entry into the kingdom. Although John instituted baptism, the earliest

Christians appropriated the rite to symbolize and enact what happened in John's baptism of Jesus, in Jesus' death and resurrection, and in the descent of the Spirit at Pentecost. What happened to Jesus happened to the baptizand.

The Christians to whom Mark, Matthew, and John addressed themselves tended to emphasize the baptism of Jesus in the Jordan as the way in which Christians entered the kingdom. For his Gentile Christians, Paul emphasized entry into the kingdom through the baptismal imitation of Jesus' death and resurrection. For his audience, Luke chose to emphasize Pentecost as the revelatory event: baptism in water brought them forgiveness, while baptism in the Spirit brought them full initiation.

Nonetheless, all three baptismal paradigms were eschatological and required a systematic preparation of proclamation and teaching about Jesus, the kingdom, and discipleship, as well as the Johannite rituals of prayer, fasting, and moral reformation. Although the general outlines of the New Testament process of conversion are clear, the details are difficult to ascertain because the documents assume baptismal conversion and concern themselves primarily with the preaching and teaching needed to sustain it. Luke alone makes explicit what is implicit in Mark, Matthew, and John; he is writing his account so that Theophilus may know the truth concerning "the things about which you have been instructed" (Lk 1:4).

II. The Second Century

Other New Testament documents (Ephesians, 1 John, 1 Peter, and the Book of Revelation) avail themselves of the rituals or liturgy of baptism as the setting for preaching and teaching.[30] But for clarity about the details of the process and their development, we must go outside the canon to look at the early Christian literature springing up in the fertile soil of the Near East.

The *Didache*[31]

Recovered only in 1873, the one extant baptismal document that bridges the New Testament and early Christian literature is the *Didache (The Doctrine of the Lord [Brought] to the Nations by the Twelve Apostles*—in Greek, *didache* means doctrine/teaching).

Appropriating the mantle of apostolic authority, the work is a compilation made between 50 and 150 C.E. about teaching, liturgy, and church structure—sixteen chapters in all. It is the first of a distinctive type of literature called "Church Orders"—the forerunners of the medieval and modern missals, sacramentaries, the Book of Common Prayer, and hymnals. The importance of the *Didache* for a study of conversion is enormous; it records the rites of entry or initiation into the community, including a distinctive form of instruction.

The *Didache* originated in a community of Christian Jews (in the environs of Antioch) devoted to the Torah who felt that their relationship with Jesus in no way countered their identity as Jews.[32] Some see a special relationship between Matthew's community and the Didachist's; both communities observed the whole Torah as understood by Christian interpreters.

For us the important point is that the work bridges the New Testament and subapostolic period.[33] According to the most recent work (*The Didache in Context,* edited by Clayton N. Jefford; the material in *Didache* 1–5 (6 is a later addition) reflects types of Christian experience, practice, and community between the years 50 and 70 C.E., and the material in *Didache* 7–15 was composed prior to the final composition of Matthew's gospel (c. 80 C.E.).

What we learn from the oldest part of the document is vital for understanding conversion as a process. The first five chapters are devoted to a distinctive form of instruction given to candidates for entry into the community. The distinctive form is indicated at the outset:

> There are two ways, one of life, the other of death, and between the two ways there is a great difference. Now the way of life is this: you shall love first the God who created you, then your neighbor as your self, and do not yourself do to another what you would not want done to you. . . . And the way of death is this. Above all, it is evil and full of accursedness: acts of murder, adultery, passion. . . . (*Didache* 1:1–2; 5:1)[34]

New Testament ethical instruction made regular use of this "two ways" form—a type of Jewish wisdom-teaching—though in a more muted way. The dualism that it expresses is the dualism of ethical choice: turning from one way of life to another, the radical change that typifies conversion.[35] Jesus' parables reflect it, as do Paul's exhortations to put off the "old man" and put on the "new," and John's "sons of dark-ness" and "sons of light."

But it was the Didachist who spelled out with blinding clarity the "two-way" motif that interlaced early Christian moral teaching. In the back of his mind, of course, was the conviction that the one who chooses and lives the "way of life" is the one who truly observes the Torah—Matthew's observant or righteous one. Once the choice is made, the candidate is ready for the next step:

> As for baptism, baptize this way: Having said all this [the two ways], baptize in the name of the Father and of the Son and of the Holy Spirit [see Mt 28:20], in running water [recall the Jordan]. If you [singular] do not have running water, however, baptize in another kind of water; if you cannot in cold, then [do so] in warm [water]. But if you have neither, pour water on the head thrice in the name of the Father and Son and Holy Spirit. Before baptism, let the person baptizing the one being baptized—and others who are able—fast; tell the one being baptized to fast one or two [days] before. (7:1–4; trans. Cody, *The Didache in Context*)

The *Didache* shows several layers of revision, indicating, among other things, that the community had a long life. Of course, the quality of their religious life set forth in chapters 8–16 had much to do with their collective stamina: communal fasts (twice a week) and thrice daily prayer (the Lord's Prayer), the celebration of the eucharist (Sundays), the authority structure (apostles and prophets), rules for hospitality, and vigilance as they awaited the return of Jesus.

But the process of conversion occupies half the document: it emphasizes the importance of initial conversion and the effectiveness of the rites of initiation. Given that the substance of the two parts of the text do not appear to have been revised, the rites of initiation continued to require for more than a hundred years a distinctive two-way teach-ing. This teaching demanded (1) clear choice; (2) communal fasting; (3) water baptism in the name of the Father, of the Son, and of the Holy Spirit; and (4), without doubt, the eucharist—a two-stage process of conversion involving the cognitive and the ritual.[36]

The Pseudo-Clementine Recognitions[37]

Such was the process in one early Palestinian Jewish Christian community. In a Judaean community several decades later, it shows development both in the preparation phase of conversion and in its ritual phase.

The *Recognitions* is a complex work, the plot of which attempts to describe the conversion of Clement of Rome (c. 96 C.E.) and in the process describes the spread of Christianity, largely through the preaching of Peter. Clement, in his search for assurance about immortality, it appears, abandoned the philosophical schools (Chapter 3) and the Pagan diviners and theurgists (Chapter 2). In the preaching of the apostles, he encounters the history of God's saving acts in Christ and is convinced. Although the two ways of the *Didache* are not in evidence, the philosophical quest is and will continue to be.

But baptism does not immediately follow. The process is more elaborate than that in the earlier work, perhaps because of later revision. The candidates hand in their names to the bishop, who instructs them in the "mysteries of the kingdom of heaven" (*Recognitions* 3:67). In the interim, the candidates fast and otherwise "prove" themselves for three months. On the day of the "festival" (Passover?), they are anointed with consecrated oil, immersed in "living" waters in the name of the Trinity, and attend their first eucharist.

A Convert: Justin Martyr

The first autobiographical conversion account comes from a former neighbor of the Didachist and Pseudo-Clement, a man named Justin, born to a wealthy, Greek-speaking Gentile family in Flavia Neapolis (modern Nablus) in Samaria about 100 C.E.

The account is contained in one of his two major works, the *Dialogue with Trypho, a Jew*. The setting is the city of Ephesus sometime in the decade of the 130s, and the form is a dialogue. Justin's interlocutor is a well-born and well-educated Jew, Trypho, with whom he shares his conversion experience at the beginning of the dialogue (chs. 1–8).[38]

The opening question is about the nature of true philosophy, to which Justin gives a five-part answer: (1) true philosophy (as distinguished from the philosophical schools: Aristotelians, Platonists, Pythagoreans, Skeptics, and Stoics) is "knowledge of that which really exists, a clear perception of truth," with happiness the reward; (2) the schools have successively distorted rather than handed on the original and true philosophy; (3) finding true philosophy is a quest; (4) the quest leads to the discovery of true and stable existence revealed by the prophets and their vision of Christ; (5) accepting this as true and living accordingly constitute conversion to Christianity.

Like other young men from the empire's elite (recall the Neopythagoreans), Justin was in search of a usable philosophy of life. His first teacher was a Stoic, with whom he spent considerable study time, mostly on basics. An Aristotelian, who proved oversubtle and too much concerned about his fee, was next. Then followed a celebrated Pythagorean, who would not accept Justin as a student because he had not yet had adequate training in the liberal arts. Though crushed, Justin was finally accepted by a noted Platonist, with whom "he progressed and made the greatest improvements daily."[39]

Quite by accident, during a day out by the sea, Justin encountered an old man, who, it turned out, happened to be a well-educated Jewish Christian; a long dialogue ensued, the upshot of which was that philosophical reasoning, especially Justin's beloved (Middle) Platonism, could not yield the knowledge of what really exists and the happiness that flows therefrom. His aged interlocutor established in Justin's mind that an older wisdom alone would lead him to the truth he sought— reminiscent of Pseudo-Clement, only the prophets could yield the knowledge of the beginning and the end and witness to truth that exceeded all demonstration. The discussion ended as abruptly as it started: "and I saw him no more." Nonetheless, almost immediately, the decisive moment arrived:

> [A] fire was enkindled in my soul, and a passionate desire pos-
> sessed me for the prophets, and for those great men who are the
> friends of Christ. As I weighed his words within me I found that
> this alone was philosophy, philosophy safe and serviceable.[40]

Justin's account is literary, composed with an audience of philosophically minded Jews and Pagans in mind. Like convert testimonies then and now, it was written well after the fact, shaped by his subsequent experience and understanding, not to mention that of the church. Nonetheless, scholars accept his account as reflecting something of the actual process and experience—autobiographical in intent, if not in detail.[41]

The existence of an account distilled by subsequent experience is an advantage for the student of conversion in early Christianity, for the *Dialogue* account is in some ways paradigmatic, disclosing the content and method of the initial appeal to educated Pagans, as well as of pre-baptismal instruction. The first eight chapters suggest a syllabus of preaching and instruction, condensed, to be sure, but quite different from the two ways of the *Didache:* God, the divine reality behind a world of flux, as the unchanging creator (ch. 3); the soul as the created and mortal link between the divine and human (chs. 4–6); the scriptures, especially the prophets accredited by miracles, as font of knowledge about the beginning and end of things and the proclamation of Christ (ch. 7).

Within a comparatively short space of time, the syllabus had shifted from the preaching and teaching outline behind the gospels and epistles and the two ways to homilies on the Bible and to a declaratory creed; Justin's syllabus is an interim stage.[42]

Justin's search was long and it ended in baptism, about which he tells us nothing in the *Dialogue*. How long was it? A definite answer would simply mislead. The Pseudo-Clementine *Recognitions* would answer between three and twelve months. But however long, his experience inspired him to continue as a teacher and to charter what might be called "school," or scholastic Christianity, as a way of conversion.[43]

Justin went to Rome, where he opened a school in the 140s, attracted many a convert, produced a celebrated Christian teacher, Tatian (c. 150), disputed with other philosophers and their schools, and eventually was executed with six of his students (c. 165), having been fingered by an angry philosopher.[44]

Although Justin says nothing in the *Dialogue* about his own baptism, in his second and more famous work, *The First Apology,* using *philosophy* in the sense explained in the third chapter and in connection with Clement below, he describes the rite of entry as he knew it in Rome and had himself experienced it:

> As many as are persuaded and believe what we say is true and undertake to live accordingly are instructed to pray and to entreat God with fasting for the remission of sins, with us praying and fasting with them. Then we bring them where there is water, and they are born again in the same way in which we ourselves were. They then receive the washing with water in the name of the Father and Lord of all, and of our Savior, Jesus Christ, and of the Holy Spirit. . . .
>
> Moreover, after we have thus washed him who has been convinced and has assented to our teaching, we bring him to a

place where those whom we call brethren are assembled, to offer
prayers in common for ourselves, for the baptized person, and for
all others everywhere, that we, now that we have learned the truth,
may be found worthy by our actions to be esteemed good citizens
and observant of the commandments, so that we may attain everlasting salvation. Our prayers concluded, we greet one another
with a kiss. Then bread and a cup of wine mixed with water are
brought to the one presiding over the assembly; he takes them and
addresses praise and glory to the Father of the universe through
the name of Christ and of the Holy Spirit. . . . When he is finished
the prayers and thanksgivings, every one present expresses agreement by saying "Amen." . . . Those who are deacons distribute to
each some bread and some wine mixed with water . . . and take
them to those who are absent.[45]

Though we learn about the first eucharist in some detail and that
the name for baptism is illumination, the elements of the process have
a familiar ring: (1) extended preparation by preaching and teaching,
(2) fasting, (3) Trinitarian baptism, followed by (4) the celebration of
the eucharist for the newly illuminated.

The School at Alexandria: Clement

Although Justin may have chartered "school" Christianity in
Rome, its hub was Alexandria, the cultural capital of the empire.[46] By
180 a remarkable Sicilian, former Stoic philosopher, and convert to
Christianity named Pantaenus opened a school in Alexandria to teach
the Christian philosophy of life. Pagans and Christians, including catechumens, were among his students.

Pantaenus' most famous student was Clement, born of Pagan parents in Athens about 150. After Clement became a Christian, he sought
out well-known Christian teachers, the last being Pantaenus, whom he
eventually succeeded as teacher during the 190s. The mission of their
school was moral and spiritual formation—the general goal of philosophy and a vital goal of Christian conversion.

Clement left Alexandria when persecution broke out in the city
under Emperor Septimius Severus in 201 and died sometime after 215.
Under Clement's successor, Origen, Pantaenus' academy took on a
more formal relationship with the Alexandrian church as its school for
catechumens, an orientation that it may have had from the beginning—
but more of that in the next chapter.

Clement applied a classical approach to the conversion of the elite of the city. The first task was to interest them in a way of life that offered truth, goodness, and perfection; the second, to initiate them into the kind of moral and spiritual formation that would lead them to a perfection that combined both truth and goodness; and the third, to lead them to perfection, the goal of the Christian way. In effect, Pantaenus' academy in Clement's hands became a school of conversion, and his three extant major works contain his approach. They are textbooks, so to speak, fashioned in the lecture hall.

The first is the *Exhortation to the Greeks;* its title in Greek has a familiar word in it, *Protreptikos pros Hellenas.*[47] As we have seen (Chapter 3), the protreptic, generated by the sometimes intense competition between rival ways of life in antiquity, was an exhortation to follow a particular way of life, particularly rhetoric, philosophy, medicine, and law. The spokesman—a philosopher, for example—would give an opening lecture to potential disciples to urge them to adopt his way of thought and life. Cicero, as we noted, composed just such a work, the now lost *Hortensius,* which persuaded Augustine to adopt "different priorities and values," even altering the way he prayed.[48]

In Clement's Alexandria, the principal rivals to the Christian way of thought and life were the Pagan mystery cults; the Mysteries of Isis (Chapter 3) were especially appealing at the time. The term *mystery* is frequent in his writings; by it he means the rites of initiation in the mystery cults discussed in the second chapter. It is hardly a surprise, then, that he uses the term to refer to the rites of baptism.[49]

In the *Exhortation* he summons his audience to abandon the idols, their mystery religions, and other philosophers and be initiated into the true Christian mysteries through the rites of baptism.[50] Clement adheres to a syllabus of instruction, in which, as for Justin, the final element is that true doctrine is found in the prophets: They alone disclose that Christ is the true and great mystery of God and that he is to be found in the church, the new chosen people, with a new commandment and a new priesthood and temple.[51]

To those who signed up with him, Clement addressed a second work, the *Tutor (Paidogogos),* a work devoted to the day-to-day conduct of their new way of life.[52] At what point they were baptized and entered the ranks of the faithful is uncertain. If we think of the academy as a philosophical school, their initiation took place early in the second stage, perhaps at its beginning. To philosophize meant to turn from one's old ways to new ways of life. As the philosopher Seneca put it, the idea was not only to be reformed *(emendari)* but to be transformed *(transformari).*[53] Two surviving treatises by Clement based on baptismal homilies suggest that conversion was climaxed by baptism early in the course, as noted above.[54]

Clement addressed his third major work, *Stromata,* or *Carpets,* (a way philosophers discussed varied questions randomly), to advanced students, those who had reached the maturity or perfection promised in baptism *(teleios).*[55] In this collection of notes, ideas, and reflections, Clement draws heavily on both Platonic and Stoic philosophy. Among other things, he seeks to justify the study of philosophy and to establish the superiority of the Bible and its anteriority to Greek philosophy. It is clear that his teaching at this stage was one-to-one.

As we have seen earlier, in Clement's vision conversion was an extended journey in three stages: the first, reflected in the *Exhortation,* was faith; the second, reflected in the *Tutor,* was moral precepts and progress; the third, reflected in the *Carpets,* maturity or perfection. Unfortunately, nowhere does he disclose the rites of the baptismal mystery; like his mystery-cult competitors, he considered the sacred rites privileged information not to be disclosed to anyone else.[56]

III. Conclusion

From the moment of its birth among the Johannites, Christianity, like its Jewish mother, demanded conversion. The hinge was baptism, which, though it appears as a deceptively simple act in the New Testament, symbolized a difficult and demanding process with two phases: the preparatory stage that led to baptism and the ritual stage that centered on baptism and the eucharist.

Preparation

The first, preparation, led to the critical moment of personal decision and baptism. The New Testament tends to assume the initial stage and concentrate on the things about which the baptized have already been instructed.

We found the *Didache* a more helpful guide to a clearly articulated initial stage. The work demands a clear-cut choice, but not one made out of the blue. What preceded that choice was a hallowed form of Jewish moral instruction—the "two ways." In the course of instruction, the candidates were persuaded to choose between their old way of death and a new way of life, both clearly depicted.

The experiences of Clement of Rome in the Pseudo-Clementine *Recognitions,* Justin Martyr, and Clement of Alexandria added a new dimension. For Pseudo-Clement, the moment of decision arrived when the apostolic preaching, especially Peter's, established for him the truth of the history of salvation in Christ. For Justin, the privileged moment came when he found that Christianity alone was the safe and serviceable philosophy. For Clement of Alexandria, the moment approached when he came "to understand the good things which 'no human ear has heard nor human heart conceived' [1 Cor 2:9]"—the mystery of Christ.[57]

In the case of all three, the initial phase was intense. The approach and syllabus of instruction reflected the philosophy of the schools and the Jewish understanding of how God acts in history. Although Pseudo-Clement discarded philosophy, Justin and Clement found their philosophical quest fulfilled in Christianity—Justin, as the true philosophy, Clement, as the true mystery. But all three were converted to a new religious reality, the God of the Bible, or, more accurately, Jesus as God's definitive act in history. All three pioneered the "school" approach, one which laid the groundwork for the church's catechetical schools with their biblical and creedal curriculum.

Ritual

The second, the ritual stage, was critical, for the decision was not purely interior, entirely personal, or strictly rational. Pseudo-Clement's had to be ratified and enacted; he had to give in his name, hear the "mysteries," prove himself for three months, receive the anointing, be baptized, and receive the eucharist (*Recognitions* 3:67). Justin had to agree to live according to what he now knew, to experience the washing called illumination, and to celebrate with the community a eucharist specially designed for conversion (*I Apology* 61, 65). Clement is silent about what constituted his initiation into the mystery of Christ. But if what he required of his catechumens is any indication, at the end of Pantaenus' course for beginners, he fasted and was baptized according to rites similar to those of Pseudo-Clement and Justin.

For our purposes, however, the importance lies not in the details but in twin facts: there was no conversion without both preparation and baptism followed by eucharist. Preparation solidified conversion; prayer, fasting, baptism, and the eucharist focused, ratified, and enacted it. It was a process and, as such, thought to be the work of the Father, the Son, and the Spirit. Thus, it was in their name.

In these early centuries, some of the characteristics of authentic conversion identified at the outset of this study are clearly in evidence. We have just considered the centrality of decision. One of the characteristics all too easily neglected dominates the first two centuries: continual mutual interaction between candidate and the community that embodies the new religious reality. It is spelled out in detail during the two phases of the process we have just considered. The following chapters will spell out the interaction in more and dramatic detail.

Finally, the active search for a new identity, meaning, and purpose is nowhere better dramatized than in the lives and teaching of Pseudo-Clement, Justin, and Clement, not to mention their encounters with a new religious reality that satisfied their needs. The three looked until they found. Our search must turn to the third century.

NOTES

1. For an assessment of the research and evidence, see John P. Meier, *A Marginal Jew: Rethinking the Historical Jesus,* vol. 2 (Garden City, N.Y.: Doubleday [Anchor Bible Research Library], 1994) 19–56; Paul W. Hollenbach, "John the Baptizer," ANRW 19.1:851–75; Jerome Murphy-O'Connor, "John the Baptist: History and Hypothesis," *NTS* 36 (1990) 359–74; Adela Yarbro Collins, "The Origin of Christian Baptism," *SL* 19 (1989) 28–44; and Nathan Mitchell, "Baptism in the *Didache,*" in Clayton N. Jefford, ed., *The Didache in Context: Essays on Its Text, History, and Transmission* (Leiden and New York: E. J. Brill, 1995) 226–55, especially 232–35.

2. The disciples were Andrew and Philip, and probably Peter and Nathaniel. Meier reviews the research and the evidence in *A Marginal Jew,* 2:116–30. Two key early studies are Jean Thomas, *Le mouvement baptiste en Palestine et Syrie 150 av. J. C.–300 ap. J. C.* (Gembloux, J. Duculot [Dissertation, Louvain], 1965), followed by Walter Wink, *John the Baptist in the Gospel Tradition* (Cambridge: Cambridge University Press, 1968), especially 107–15. John, as Wink puts the consensus, "is the beginning of the gospel of Jesus Christ, and all of the Christian elaborations of it are but the theological expression of a historical fact, that through John's mediation Jesus perceived the nearness of the kingdom and his own relation to its coming" (113).

3. For John and Qumran, see Meier, *A Marginal Jew,* 2:23–27.

4. See Luke 7:18–23, Matthew 11:2–19, Acts 19:1–17, and the mild polemic in John for the ongoing life of the Johannites. Meier devotes a section of *A Marginal Jew* (2:116–30) to the question of Jesus as a disciple of John.

5. Meier reviews and assesses the historicity and meaning of Jesus' baptism by John, the sense in which he was a disciple of John, and the gospel traditions about John (Jesus and the early Christians on him) in *A Marginal Jew,* 2:100–233.

6. For the discussion about Jesus as convert, see Meier, *A Marginal Jew* 2:106–16, and Hollenbach, "The Conversion of Jesus: From Baptizer to Healer," ANRW II, 25.1:196–219. Meier holds that the baptism was the marker of the conversion of Jesus, though he observes that the historian cannot identify the stages. He takes up the question of Jesus' self-awareness of his sinfulness in receiving John's baptism (111); rejecting Hollenbach's position, he concludes that the historian cannot judge because there are no data.

7. Thus, Meier, *A Marginal Jew,* 2:109.

8. For a study of these verses, see Meier, *A Marginal Jew,* 2:118–22.

9. Thus, Hollenbach, "The Conversion of Jesus" 25.1:197–98. For the debate, see Meier, *A Marginal Jew,* 2:111–13.

10. See Meier, *A Marginal Jew,* 2:100–233.

11. The relationship and cooperation between John and Jesus is the subject of a contemporary debate. At one extreme are those who hold that Jesus saw John as the pivotal figure in the climax of salvation history; at the other, those who see Jesus turning his back on John and his ministry, substituting exorcism and healing for baptism. Meier holds it likely that "the practice of baptizing flowed like water from John through Jesus into the early church, with the ritual taking on different meanings at each stage of the process" (*A Marginal Jew,* 2:9).

12. Thus, Meier, *A Marginal Jew,* 2:9.

13. See ibid., 2:237–506.

14. Thus, Hollenbach, "The Conversion of Jesus," 25.1:196–219. Meier argues that Jesus' conversion is marked by his baptism at the hands of John (*A Marginal Jew,* 2:109), "the only external, historically verifiable marker of this pivotal 'turning around.'"

15. Hollenbach (n.1) holds to the double conversion. E. P. Sanders, however, holds that Jesus diverged from John's life-style and ministry, because of Jesus' association with have-nots ("tax collectors" and "sinners"), who had been created by the socioeconomic conditions in Israel. In particular, Sanders has in mind the fact that repentance required restitution, which John would have required but Jesus did not. As Murphy-O'Connor notes, given the precarious livelihood of so many, there was no margin for error, and restitution was often impossible. If a tenant farmer, for instance, had been dispossessed for debt, very likely he could only work as a herdsman and, as such, be

classed as a "sinner." See Murphy-O'Connor "John the Baptist: History and Hypothesis," 373; and E. P. Sanders, *Jesus and Judaism* (Philadelphia: Fortress Press, 1985) 174–211, cited by Murphy-O'Connor. Meier rejects the Hollenbach contention that Jesus broke with John's practice of baptism because of a conversion (see *A Marginal Jew,* 2:125–27).

16. John's gospel excepted (Jn 3:22–30; 4:1–3). For discussion, see Collins, "The Origin of Christian Baptism," 28–44, especially 36–37.

17. See Chapter 4 (Qumran and Proselyte Baptism); see also Collins, "The Origin of Christian Baptism," 31–35; B. E. Thiering, "Inner and Outer Cleansing at Qumran as a Background to New Testament Baptism [1 QS 3:6–9; 4:18–22]," *NTS* 26 (1979/1980) 266–77; her "Qumran Initiation and New Testament Baptism," *NTS* 27 (1980/1981) 620–23; and Meier, *A Marginal Jew,* 2:129. In Thiering's analysis, at Qumran there were two rites of entry: (1) a secondary rite—washing to forgive ritual impurity that resulted from sin and (2) the primary rite showing inner atonement and entry into the community, where the Spirit of Holiness resided. A Levite celebrated the first rite (lasting three days) to purify the community; a priest of high rank, the second rite, which did not involve washing. Collins does not think that the lustrations were initiatory, but she does not deal with Thiering's study, in view of which John's baptism might be considered the secondary rite, which signified desire for the primary rite. About proselyte baptism, the midrash *Sifré Numbers* is the first text to enumerate the three standard elements of proselyte conversion ritual unambiguously (circumcision, immersion, and sacrifice); it is generally dated in the second half of the third century. See Gary G. Porton, *The Stranger Within Your Gates: Converts and Conversion in Rabbinic Literature* (Chicago: University of Chicago Press [Chicago Studies in the History of Judaism, ed. William Scott Green], 1994) 51, 60–61.

18. For discussion, see Collins, "The Origin of Christian Baptism," 28–44, especially 37–41; and Petr Pokorný, "Christologie et baptême à l'époque du christianisme primitif," *NTS* 27 (1981) 368–80.

19. For the most recent précis and studies and for what follows, see Lars Hartman, "Baptism," *ABD* 1:583–94.

20. See Stuart G. Hall, "Stephen I of Rome and the Baptismal Controversy of 256," in Bernard Vogler, ed., *Miscellanea historiae ecclesiasticae VIII: Colloque de Strasbourg, Septembre 1983, sur L'institution et les pouvoirs dans les églises de l'antiquité à nous jours* (Bruxelles: Éditions Nauwelaerts, 1987) 78–82. For a briefer treatment, see his "Ministry, Worship, and Christian Life," in Ian Hazlett, ed., *Early Christianity: Origins and Evolution to A.D. 600* (Nashville: Abingdon Press, 1991) 101–5.

21. In speaking this way, Paul wrestles with an ancient problem: How can what happened in the past be actualized in the present? or, more specifically, How can the death and resurrection of the Jesus in history be applicable

to the present? In using his participative "in/into Christ" language, which pervades his authentic letters, Paul invokes a mode of thought characteristic of Greco-Roman religious thought at the root of ancient thinking about ritual—*mnesis/anamnesis:* ritual actualizes in the present what was accomplished in a paradigmatic act of the past, which it dramatizes symbolically. For an account of the history of religions' discussion of this question, see Collins, "The Origin of Christian Baptism," 41–42.

22. For discussion, see A. Benoit, *Le baptême au second siècle* (Paris, 1953).

23. These elements were identified by C. H. Dodd in *The Apostolic Preaching and Its Developments* (London: Hodder & Stoughton, 1963). For a recent discussion of them and a comparison with Paul's kerygma, see Calvin Roetzel, *The Letters of Paul: Conversations in Context,* 3rd ed. (Louisville: Westminster/John Knox, 1991) 72–79; he reconstructs a Pauline proclamation on 81. But see James I. H. McDonald, *Kerygma and Didache: The Articulation and Structure of the Earliest Christian Message* (Cambridge: Cambridge University Press, 1980); he discusses the principal forms of New Testament preaching and teaching: prophecy, popular preaching in the Greco-Roman world (*paraclesis* and homily), and *paraenesis* and *catechesis* in relation to tradition (*paradosis*).

24. For detailed discussion, see Kilian McDonnell and George T. Montague, *Christian Initiation and Baptism in the Holy Spirit: Evidence from the First Eight Centuries,* 2nd ed. (Collegeville: Liturgical Press [A Michael Glazier Book], 1994) 3–90.

25. See Chapter 4; see also Thiering, "Inner and Outer Cleansing at Qumran," 266–77, especially 274–77; and her "Qumran Initiation and New Testament Baptism," especially 623–31.

26. Montague lays out the discussion and debate well in McDonnell and Montague, *Christian Initiation,* 23–41; for bibliography, see 3, n. 1 passim.

27. Thiering, "Qumran Initiation and New Testament Baptism," 621–27; note 52 supplies relevant bibliography for the discussion.

28. McDonnell and Montague, *Christian Initiation,* 345–46, 360–63; the detailed study is in 299–338.

29. Ibid., especially 339–49, where McDonnell provides a concluding overall view of the evidence. Death and resurrection as a paradigm largely disappears, as already noted, in the second century (A. Benoit, *Le baptême*). In his *Stromata,* Clement of Alexandria hints at the death and resurrection paradigm (see "The School at Alexandria: Clement" later in this chapter). In his homilies on Exodus, Origen is the first patristic thinker of record to espouse the paradigm (see my *ECBC* 6:195–97). The fourth century, however, marks the paradigm's ascendancy (see Chapter 8).

30. Thus, F. L. Cross, *I Peter: A Paschal Liturgy* (London: Mowbray,

1994); Raymond E. Brown, *The Epistles of John* (Garden City, N.Y.: Doubleday [Anchor Bible Commentaries], 1982) 90; and Massey Hamilton Shepherd, *The Paschal Mystery and the Apocalypse* (London: Lutterworth [Ecumenical Studies in Worship 6], 1960). 1 Peter and 1 John are generally conceded to reflect homiletic material that might have baptism as their life setting; Revelation is shot through with liturgical fragments, as is Ephesians, especially chapters 4–6. In form and style, however, they are not baptismal homilies.

31. For the text, translation, studies, and what follows, see Jefford, *The Didache in Context*. About the dating, I follow the dating in Jefford; but note the caution with which Paul F. Bradshaw approaches the dating of Church Orders, as well as the range of dates scholars have proposed. See his *The Search for the Origins of Christian Worship: Sources and Methods for the Study of Early Liturgy* (Oxford: Oxford University Press, 1992) 80–110, especially 84–86.

32. For discussion of the community, see Mitchell, "Baptism in the *Didache*," especially 231–38. For a recent discussion of early Jewish Christianity, see George W. Buchanan, "Worship, Feasts, and Ceremonies in the Early Jewish Christian Church," *NTS* 26 (1980) 279–97, especially 280–81.

33. Thus, John P. Meier in Meier and Raymond E. Brown, eds., *Antioch and Rome: New Testament Cradles of Catholic Christianity* (New York: Paulist Press, 1983) 81–84.

34. The translation is that of Aelred Cody in Jefford, ed., *The Didache in Context*, 5, 8. I follow the Cody translation throughout. For similar material, see the *Community Rule* 1–5, in the Dead Sea Scrolls.

35. For what follows, see McDonald, *Kerygma and Didache*, 72, 85, 95–96.

36. Although not certain, it is extremely likely that the newly baptized went directly to the eucharist, which in the *Didache* is an anticipation of the eschatological meal with the risen Christ. Baptism, however, gave them entry to the meal, just as initiation gave the full-membership candidate entry to the "pure meal" at Qumran, for which, see Thiering, "Qumran Initiation and New Testament Baptism," 619–20. On the meal in the *Didache*, see John W. Riggs, "The Sacred Food in *Didache* 9–10," in Jefford, ed., *The Didache in Context*, 256–83, especially 273.

37. For discussion, see F. Stanley Jones, "The Pseudo-Clementine *Recognitions*: A History of Research," *The Second Century* 2 (1982) 1–33, 63–96, reprinted in *Studies in Early Christianity*, vol. 2, ed. Everett Ferguson (New York and London: Garland, 1993); and his *An Ancient Jewish Christian Source on the History of Christianity: Pseudo-Clementine Recognitions 1.27–71* (Atlanta: Scholars Press, 1995). The translation is that of M. R. Riddle, "Recognitions of Clement," ANF 8:75–211. Clement's situation:

1:1–8 (the history of salvation fills out the rest of the book); 3:31–32 (diligence in study and daily study); 3:67 (rite of baptism); 6:8–9 (necessity and practice of baptism); 10:1 (a year of probation); 10:72 (Clement's father's conversion).

38. *Dialogus cum Trypho Judaeo* 1:1–8 (PG 6:471–93; translation, Alexander Roberts et al., eds., ANF 1 [1908] 194–98). For discussion see Oskar Skarsaune, "The Conversion of Justin Martyr," *ST* 30 (1976) 53–73.

39. *Dial.* 1:2 (PG 6:480; ANF 1:195).

40. *Dial.* 1:8.2 (PG 6:492–93; ANF 1:198) and Skarsaune, "The Conversion of Justin Martyr," 57.

41. Ibid., 55, citing E. J. Goodenough, *The Theology of Justin Martyr* (1923; reprint, Amsterdam, 1968) 58.

42. For discussion, see J. N. D. Kelly, *Early Christian Creeds,* 3rd ed. (New York: David McKay Co., 1972) 70–76. He finds it very unlikely that Justin knew a declaratory creed but concludes that he provides the "earliest direct evidence" of relatively fixed creedal questions at baptism (75). For the biblical homilies, see below, Justin's description of baptism in Rome.

43. For the school tradition in early Christianity, see Patrick Henry, ed., *Schools of Thought in the Christian Tradition* (Philadelphia: Fortress Press, 1984), especially 15–48 (Alexandria and North Africa).

44. Herbert Musurillo, ed., *The Acts of the Christian Martyrs* (Oxford: Clarendon Press, 1972) 42–61. There are three recensions of the account, the middle seeming to have emanated from Justin's school.

45. *Apologia I pro Christianis* 61:2–12; 65:1–5 (Charles Munier, ed., *Saint Justin: Apologie pour les Chrétiens* [Fribourg: Éditions Universitaires, 1995] 112–14, 120; trans. Finn, *ECBC* 6:39–40). For discussion, see Cullen I. K. Story, "Justin's Apology I. 62–64: Its Importance for the Author's Treatment of Christian Baptism," *VC* 16 (1962) 172–78.

46. For discussion, see Robert L. Wilken, "Alexandria: A School for Training in Virtue," in Henry, ed., *Schools of Thought,* 15–30.

47. For protreptic, see above, Chapter 3 ("Neopythagoreanism"); Clement, *Protreptikos* 1:118–19 (Claude Mondésert, ed., *Clément d'Alexandrie: Le Protreptique: Introduction, Traduction, et Notes,* SC 2bis [1949], 187–89). Galen, for instance, composed a protreptic for medicine as a way of life (Mondésert, SC 2bis: 12–14).

48. Augustine, *Confessions* 3:4.7 (James J. O'Donnell, ed., *Augustine: Confessions* [Oxford: Clarendon Press, 1992] 1:25). See below, Chapter 9.

49. For discussion of Clement's use of *mysterion,* see Harry A. Echle, "Sacramental Initiation as a Christian Mystery-Initiation according to Clement of Alexandria," in Odo Casel, *Vom Christlichen Mysterium* (Düsseldorf: Patmos-Verlag, 1951) 54–61.

50. See Clement, *Protrep.* 12:118–23 (Mondésert, SC 2bis:187–93). For discussion, text, and translation, see Echle, "Sacramental Initiation," 57–60.

51. See his *Protrep.* 4:59.1–2; see also 7:7—9:88 (Mondésert, SC 2bis: 123, 143–56.

52. For the strategy of the *Tutor* as well as the text, see Henri-Irénée Marrou and Marguerite Harl, eds. *Clément d'Alexandrie: Le Pédagogue, Livre I,* SC 70 (1960) 17–22.

53. Seneca, *Epistles* 6:1, cited in Wilken, "Alexandria," 21.

54. Clement, *The Rich Man's Salvation* (G. W. Butterworth, ed. and trans., *Clement of Alexandria,* Loeb [1919] 270–366); *Exhortation to Endurance* (ibid., 370–77).

55. For an introduction to the text, see Claude Mondésert and Marcel Caster, eds., *Clément d'Alexandrie: Les Stromates: Stromate I,* SC 30 (1951) 5–41. The themes of its seven books are: philosophy, the sciences and Christian revelation, the antiquity and a priority of the Bible in relation to the Greeks; faith and the knowledge of God; faith and the other virtues; marriage, the martyr; perfection and the true Christian (gnostic); symbolism; true gnosis; and heresy.

56. For the theology of the mysteries and Clement's thinking, see Echle, "Sacramental Initiation," 59. The death-resurrection paradigm influenced Clement and Origen, in my view, because the mysteries were center stage in the city.

57. Clement, *Protrep.* 12:118.4 (Mondésert, SC 2bis:188).

Chapter 7

THE THIRD CENTURY

In the days of Alexander Severus [222–235 c.e.] there lived at
Rome a Greek freedman. As he was a clever craftsman his lot was
not hard. His body was secure, his belly full, his hands and brain
pleasantly busy. He lived amongst intelligent people and handsome objects, permitting himself such reasonable emotions as
were recommended by his master, Epicurus. . . . Into this existence burst suddenly a cranky fanatic, with a religion. To the
Greek it seemed that the breath of life had blown through the
grave imperial streets. Yet nothing in Rome was changed, save for
one immortal, or mortal, soul. The same waking eyes opened on
the same objects; yet all was changed; all was charged with meaning. New things existed. Everything mattered. In the vast equality
of religious emotion the Greek forgot his status and his nationality. His life became a miracle and an ecstasy. . . . [1]

The account bears all the earmarks of conversion. It could have
been to the synagogue or to the Isis mysteries or to the church. Let us
assume to the church and ask what exactly happened to make the
craftsman's life a miracle and an ecstasy. We can also assume that, as a
freedman of Epicurus, his name was also Epicurus. The previous chapter disclosed a pattern that partly answers how he became a Christian:
instruction, acceptance, prayer, fasting, baptism, and eucharist. The
third century adds clarity, if not uniformity, to the answer. Indeed, to
expect uniformity of practice from ancient cultures as diverse as Latin,
Greek, and Syriac is to look for a unicorn.

I. Rome: The Apostolic Tradition

The Text[2]

Since Epicurus' conversion was in Rome, the imperial capital is the place to start, for it is the place of a remarkable document that provides the clearest picture of Christian worship and liturgical practice in the first three centuries. The *Apostolic Tradition* was long known only as a title inscribed on the headless statue of a figure on a magisterial chair. Two scholars, working independently, recovered the work early this century. It is generally attributed to Hippolytus of Rome (d. c. 235 C.E.), who sits on the magisterial chair.

Although controversy continues to swirl over the author and his identity and over the origin, date, and provenance of the document, the prevailing opinion among scholars is that the work is a Church Order in the tradition of the *Didache* and was composed by a Roman priest for a community of Roman Christians around the first decade of the third century.[3] Like the *Didache,* which exhibits editorial seams, the *Apostolic Tradition* went through at least three editorial hands: the first, that of the compiler sometime between Justin and 200 C.E.; the second, sometime in the third century; the third, completing the final edition by 325 C.E.[4] Of the many chapters (forty-two), six (16–21) deal with initiation into the church and suggest our freedman's route.

Before Baptism

A. ENROLLMENT: THE FIRST CRISIS

Allowing for the work of our three editorial hands, which need not deter us from a sketch, the cranky fanatic who encountered Epicurus would likely have been an artisan himself and, perhaps, an older man, like Justin's seashore acquaintance. And Greek-speaking, perhaps, an immigrant from Antioch.

One encounter led to another until finally Epicurus determined to find out more formally about the Christian religion. His friend, now his sponsor, brought him to the teachers early in the morning, before the congregation arrived (ch. 15).

This early-morning visit was the first step in a careful and extended screening process dictated by the fact that the church was an illegal society in the empire; to be a Christian, or on the way to becoming one, was to be subject to prosecution and, if convicted, to execution.[5] The teachers asked the candidate a battery of questions about his social status: Was he a slave? free? married? single? demon-possessed? Then came some occupational questions: Was he engaged in the amphitheater and its spectacles? the theater? the circus? painting and sculpture? the military? Was he a civic magistrate or a military officer? The inquiry (in Greek the term is *krisis,* and in Latin, *judicium*) involved a searing decision: "Let him desist or be rejected" (16). Epicurus would have to agree that he would no longer either sculpt or paint idolatrous subjects (amulets and statues)—the usual way such artists made a living. Were he a teacher of children, he had to desist, unless he had no other way of earning a decent living. Not so the artist. It was a searing decision. His step set in motion conditions in which a crisis would engulf him. To proceed meant that his body would no longer be quite as secure, nor his belly as full, nor his hands and brain as pleasantly busy, nor would he continue to live with such ease among intelligent people and handsome objects.[6] But he could have been rejected out of hand, as were pimps, prostitutes, pederasts, magicians, astrologers, diviners, certain kinds of tailors, and all who intended to enlist in the legions (16).

B. INSTRUCTION

With his cranky sponsor attesting to the truth of his answers and the quality of his character, Epicurus passed the test. For the instructor, the issue was straightforward: should Epicurus be permitted to receive instruction—literally, "to hear the word"—which could not readily be assumed.

Instruction was oral, frequent, if not daily, and early, before going to work. The *Apostolic Tradition* only hints at the content, which appears to have been a blend of biblical commentary and doctrinal (creedal), liturgical, and moral instruction. Indeed, the very name of those who passed muster at the inquiry—"catechumens"—was derived from the act of receiving such instruction. Focusing on the Greek root of the word, *ech,* a celebrated teacher of the next century characterizes the catechumen as an echo chamber: "My discourse is called a *catechesis,* so that even when I am not here my words may echo *(en-eche)* in your minds."[7] That moral catechesis predominated is clear; the *Apostolic Tradition* cautions: "Let reformation of life be the test" whether a catechumen is ready to advance to baptism (17). The purpose of instruction was to reshape the catechumen's values, mode of life, and conduct; conduct was to mirror conviction.[8]

In any case, Epicurus was now a catechumen or hearer—in the ambiguous condition of being and not being a Christian. (Were he apprehended by the city's police, he would be considered a Christian.) He could be on the fringes of both society and church for an extended period—three years. If his character and conduct showed the evidence of conversion at work, however, the period could be shortened.

With the other catechumens, he would have attended frequent instruction and prayer (daily?) with, but apart from, the faithful. At dismissal, the teacher placed his hand over them, prayed, and sent them off to work. If the eucharist were to be celebrated, only the faithful could remain. Were Epicurus, the catechumen, arrested for being a Christian—the evidence indicates that it could easily happen—he would be saved, "for he has received baptism in his own blood" (19).

C. SECOND CRISIS: SCRUTINY

At the end of Epicurus' catechumenate stood a second searing decision, later called "scrutiny"; this time conduct rather than status was the issue.[9] Had he lived honestly? honored widows? visited the sick? done every kind of good work? In short, had his values, way of life, and conduct demonstrably changed? Again, his cranky friend had to speak for him.

Granted that he passed scrutiny, he was chosen for baptism and set apart from the other catechumens as one of the chosen, an *electus* (20). Daily instruction changed: he could now "hear the gospel" (20), and at the end of the instruction he was exorcised. As the day of baptism neared—the text only indicates "Sunday," but it might well have been Easter Sunday (20)—the bishop performed a solemn exorcism to determine whether he was "free of every alien spirit" (20). He set aside anyone who in his judgment had not heard the instructions "with faith, for it is not possible that the alien [Satan] hide himself forever" (20). The scrutiny was to determine the measurable extent of conversion, that is, whether Epicurus had truly changed his values and conduct.

D. IMMEDIATE PREPARATIONS (20)

There is reason to believe that some of the details in what follows have been added by the second and third editors, but again, that need not detain us.[10] On the Thursday before baptism—perhaps the third or fourth Thursday since he had become an *electus*—Epicurus and his fellow *electi* were instructed to bathe, and on Friday and Saturday, to fast. On Saturday night they assembled for a final exorcism by the bishop. As they knelt and prayed, he extended his hand over them, commanded every evil to flee from them for good, exhaled on their faces, signed the forehead, ears, and noses of each, and raised them from kneeling to standing. They then spent the entire night in vigil hearing the scriptures and homilies on the readings.

Baptism (*Apostolic Tradition* 21)

At cockcrow on Sunday, solemn baptism began with the blessing of the waters. The *electi* were ritually stripped. The bishop blessed the oils to be used: the "oil of exorcism" for the anointing about to be given and the "oil of thanksgiving" for the anointing after baptism. The oils were held by a deacon and a priest; the priest commanded Epicurus to say, "I renounce you, Satan, and all your service and all your works." A priest then anointed him with the oil of exorcism, saying, "May every spirit depart from you," and brought him to the bishop, who was standing close to the water. A deacon descended into the water with Epicurus, imposed his hand on his head, and asked him three creedal questions, indicating that at some point over the past few weeks those about to be baptized had been taught the creed:

> Do you believe in the Father Almighty? Do you believe in Christ Jesus the Son of God, who was born from the Holy Spirit and the Virgin Mary, was crucified under Pontius Pilate, died, [was buried], rose on the third day from the dead, ascended into the heavens, and sits at the right hand of the Father; and who will come to judge the living and the dead? Do you believe in the Holy Spirit and in the church and in the resurrection of the flesh?[11]

To each question Epicurus answered, "I believe," and after each was immersed[12] in the water. When Epicurus emerged, a priest anointed him with the oil of thanksgiving, saying, "I anoint you with holy oil in the name of Jesus Christ" (21). After Epicurus dried, he put on a white garment and entered the church with the other neophytes. When they were all assembled, the bishop imposed his hand over them and offered a prayer that spelled out the meaning of baptism:

Lord God, you who have made them worthy to receive the remission of sins through the bath of regeneration by the Holy Spirit, send into them your grace that they may serve you according to your will; for to you is glory, to the Father and the Son with the Holy Spirit, both now and for the ages of ages. Amen.[13]

The bishop then imposed his hand on Epicurus' head, poured oil on him, and said "I anoint you with holy oil in the Lord Father almighty and Christ Jesus and the Holy Spirit" (21). Finally, he signed him on the forehead, offered him a kiss of peace and welcome, and said: "The Lord be with you" (21). Now Epicurus could pray with the faithful as members of the same family.

Eucharist (*Apostolic Tradition* 21)

As the *Didache* and Justin led us to suspect, there was more. The neophytes celebrated their first eucharist, which included the eucharistic bread and three cups: a cup of water to symbolize the interior cleansing accomplished by baptism, a cup of milk and honey to symbolize their entry into the Promised Land, and a cup of wine to symbolize the very blood of the Christ who redeemed them. The text hints that there may have been special rites celebrated during the week following, centered around the eucharist and featuring homilies that underscored the meaning of baptism and the eucharist.

Although we hear nothing more about baptism and conversion in Rome for more than a century, there is every reason to think that the ritual process we have just considered became the norm by century's end.

Whatever its editorial history may be, the *Apostolic Tradition* prescribes an extended, exacting, and dramatic ritual process of conversion at Rome in the third century. Eventually the document would travel east to Greek-speaking Syria, Egypt, and Ethiopia to shape the catechumenate and baptismal rites in the eastern Mediterranean (West Syria and Egypt).

II. Alexandria

We left Alexandria at the end of the second century with an obscure rite of entry in formation, much as the Alexandrian church was taking on an identifiable face and form. Two figures stand out with the arrival of the third century: Demetrius, the bishop, and Origen, the teacher.

We first see them in the aftermath of a persecution under Septimius Severus (193–211 C.E.) designed to stamp out Jewish proselytism and Christian evangelism (201–203). It drove Clement from the city and took the life of Origen's father. But it also forced Demetrius to consolidate a church whose ranks were deeply shaken and whose diversity was striking. In the process, the bishop sought to bring catechetical instruction under closer control by appointing a very young Origen (eighteen) head of the catechetical school.

Origen

The pool of candidates was shallow because of the persecution; Origen happened to be Clement's best and brightest student. Serving in the post for more than two decades, Origen brought to the school the form, content, and rigor of his own Hellenistic education. He established the study and interpretation of the Bible as its ultimate mission, inaugurated an advanced course in Christianity as well as one for beginners, and set the school on a path that brought the church squarely into the Greco-Roman cultural and intellectual world.

As a result of a rift with Demetrius, Origen left the city about 230, at the height of his career. By 233 he had settled in Caesarea in Palestine, where he established a catechetical school along Alexandrian lines. Its curriculum included logic, physics, geometry, astronomy, and philosophy as the necessary preparation for the study of scripture. In both cities he proved a remarkably successful teacher, attracting numerous students—Jewish, Pagan, Gnostic, and Christian.

Origen's School in Caesarea

We have firsthand information about the school from a former student, Gregory, surnamed the Wonderworker, who brought Christianity to Anatolia (modern central Turkey). Born of a high-ranking Pagan family in Pontus on the Black Sea about 213, Gregory and his brother Athenodorus set out to complete their education in law at Beirut. As they were about to set off, their sister in Caesarea, the chief imperial city in Palestine, invited them to visit. They attended one of Origen's lectures and never got to Beirut. Gregory recounts why:

> Like some spark lighting upon our inmost soul, love was kindled
> and burst into flame within us—a love at once for the holy Word
> and toward this man, his friend and advocate. Deeply smitten with

this love, I was persuaded to give up all those objects or pursuits which seem so befitting to us and to others, even my favorite jurisprudence, my fatherland, and my friends. . . . And in my estimation there arose one object dear and worth desire: philosophy and that master of philosophy, this inspired man.[14]

Gregory and Athenodorus stayed for Origen's full course—five years (233–238)—becoming Christians sometime during the course. Like Justin and Clement, they had found the true philosophy.

About how the two brothers became Christians, Gregory is silent. Nor does Origen shed much light on the matter, because he treats the baptismal liturgy as he does the text of scripture: as a series of allegories about the Christian's journey to saving blessedness.

Conversion in Caesarea

According to his Caesarean homilies, delivered between 235 and 245, baptism and its preparations constitute the early stages of a long and dangerous journey to the Promised Land beyond the Jordan—the Red Sea and the Promised Land provide the route and setting, and baptism is the Exodus.

Indeed, water baptism opens onto three other baptisms: (1) the baptism of the Holy Spirit, which testifies to the acquisition of the state of blessedness and admits one to the Promised Land; (2) the baptism of fire in the Jordan, a remedial chastisement for those who fail to achieve blessedness by life's end; and (3) the baptism of blood (martyrdom), which transcends all other baptisms.[15]

Although the brothers' instruction was scholastic, it was not scholastic only. Like other catechumens, they would have attended two kinds of liturgical assemblies.[16] The first type was held daily (Sunday excepted) and consisted of a long, chanted biblical reading coupled with a homily on the text—Origen's *Homilies on Exodus* are an example. The second type took place on Sunday mornings (for the eucharist) and on Wednesday and Friday evenings (for communion services). At this second type of assembly, homilies were addressed to the catechumens and the faithful—Origen's *Homilies on Luke* are an example.

The catechumens admitted to the eucharistic assembly for these New Testament homilies were those immediately preparing for baptism—the chosen (*Apostolic Tradition*) or those about to be enlightened (Clement); they could hear the "word."

As for the significance of baptism, recent studies suggest that although Gregory and Athenodorus would have learned from Origen Paul's doctrine of baptism as participation in the death and resurrection of Christ (especially Rom 6:1–4), the more prominent paradigm for baptism in Alexandria and Caesarea was Christ's baptism in the Jordan.[17]

Catechumenate in Caesarea

The brothers' immediate preparations for baptism may well have begun with enrollment on Epiphany (January 6), after which they observed a forty-day fast in imitation of Christ's forty days in the wilderness. On Wednesdays and Fridays the bishop sent them and their fellow catechumens "bread purified by prayer" to signify their participation in the fellowship of the church.[18]

Close to the end of the forty days—mid-February, perhaps two days before baptism—they underwent a scrutiny to determine their readiness for baptism and to see whether they would be acceptable to the church.

The baptismal rites began with the anointing of those about to be enlightened in the name of the Father and of the Son and of the Holy Spirit.[19] Gregory and Athenodorus were baptized naked and immersed three times as they assented to three creedal questions about the Father, the Son, and the Holy Spirit—similar to those we saw at Epicurus' baptism in Rome. Though difficult to determine with certainty, it is possible that they were anointed after baptism as well as before, which might not have been the case had they been baptized in Alexandria.[20]

Beyond the suggestion that they dressed in white, little more detail can be added. Since their baptism did not take place on Sunday, their first eucharist awaited the following Sunday. Their continued instruction by homily and scholastic training may be assumed, since they were in Origen's school.

III. North Africa

Our next destination is Roman Africa. Its principal city was Carthage, now the northern suburbs of Tunis, capital of modern Tunisia.

Two Groups of Martyrs

North African Christianity emerges from the mists of its origins in two dramatic archival documents that underscore the jeopardy of

Christians in the empire. The first is *The Acts of the Scillitan Martyrs.*[21] Twelve Christians (nine men and three women) from Scillium (exact location unknown) were arrested on the grounds of jeopardizing the peace and order of the empire just by being Christians. Tried and convicted, they were beheaded on July 17, 180.

North African Christianity surfaces a second time twenty-three years later in an even more dramatic document, *The Martyrdom of Perpetua and Felicity.*[22] The work is an account of the trial and sufferings of a group of African Christians. Written in an apocalyptic mood reminiscent of the Book of Revelation, the work stands as a vivid witness to the youth, vitality, and hostile circumstances of the church in Roman Africa.

Vibia Perpetua, a twenty-two-year-old woman of a good Roman family from the city of Thuburbo Maior (a Roman garrison city south of Carthage) and mother of a two-year-old, was caught up in the net of persecution we already saw in Alexandria. Caught up with her was her slave, the pregnant Felicity, and four men, one of whom was a catechumen, Saturus. Perpetua was also a catechumen (as was her brother) at the time of her arrest; she was baptized in prison.

The seven were executed in 203 at a wild animal hunt *(venatio)* in a vast circus that lay on the south edge of the city.

Another Convert: Saturus

The other catechumen besides Perpetua was Saturus: she was baptized in prison with water; he was baptized in the circus with his blood.

To find out how he would have been baptized had he lived, we need to turn to the most celebrated North African Christian thinker and spokesman prior to Augustine of Hippo—Tertullian, who seems to have been the editor of the *Martyrdom of Perpetua and Felicity.*

The son of an officer in the Roman legions, a man of high education, a lawyer, and a gifted writer in both Greek and Latin, Tertullian converted to Christianity about 190.[23] Part of his literary legacy is the first formal treatise on baptism, the *Homily on Baptism,* our source for discovering how Saturus would have been baptized. The work is actually a series of homilies published as one, delivered about the time of Perpetua's death, and, though concerned with the ill instructed among the faithful, was intended for catechumens.[24]

A Gnostic Christian had come to Carthage to recruit for her sect. As part of her campaign, she argued that baptism was unnecessary because water is too trivial an element to have effects like rebirth attributed to it; besides, Pagan washings are far more impressive (and expensive). In the first part of his homily, Tertullian reviews the biblical significance and effect of water (chs. 1–6), the meaning of some of the rites (7–8), and Christ's use of water (9). In the second (10–20), he answers questions that faithful and catechumens alike raised about baptismal customs in Carthage: John's baptism, the validity of heretical baptism, baptism of blood, who can validly baptize, child and adult baptism, Easter and Pentecost baptism, and the preparations for baptism.[25] Although Tertullian's references to the details are allusive in the homily and in his other works, a sketch is possible.

Instruction

After an inquiry like that in the *Apostolic Tradition,* Saturus clearly would have received prebaptismal instruction that lasted over a considerable period, during which he would be considered a catechumen. Like the church in Rome, the Carthaginian church, with the Scillitan martyrs on its mind, could not countenance easy admission. Perhaps this is why Tertullian, though he reluctantly acknowledged the practice of baptizing children at Carthage, was all for delaying baptism until catechumens had proved themselves. He writes:

> That baptism ought not to be rashly given is known to those whose function it is [the bishop and clerics]. . . . For if [people] understand the obligations of baptism, they will fear more receiving than delaying: fully realized faith is assured of salvation."[26]

The syllabus, at least in part, was the Carthaginian creed, which Tertullian calls the "rule of faith" and about which he says:

> The Roman church, like that of Carthage, acknowledges one Lord God, the Creator of the universe, and Christ Jesus, of the virgin Mary, the Son of God the Creator, and the resurrection of the flesh: it combines the law and the prophets with the evangelical and apostolic writings: from them it imbibes its faith: that faith it seals with water, clothes with the Holy Spirit, feeds with the Eucharist, exhorts to martyrdom: in opposition to this constitution it accepts no one's person.[27]

Elsewhere, Tertullian enunciates the core principle of ancient thinking about ritual and conversion, a principle that would not have been neglected in Saturus' instructions:

> The flesh is the hinge of salvation *[caro salutis est cardo]*. . . . The flesh is washed that the soul may be made spotless: the flesh is anointed that the soul may be consecrated: the flesh is signed [with the cross] that the soul too may be protected: the flesh is overshadowed by the imposition of hands that the soul may be illuminated by the Spirit; the flesh feeds on the body and blood of Christ so that the soul as well may be replete with God.[28]

Baptism[29]

Had Saturus lived to be baptized, at the end of his catechumenate he would have undergone scrutiny—as in Epicurus' case, an inquiry into his character and conduct, coupled with the attestation of his sponsor.

In view of his martyrdom, there is no question that Saturus would have passed scrutiny and become an *ingressurus* ("one about to enter" the church). Associated with the rite was the renunciation of "the devil, his pomp [i.e., cultic processions], and his angels" in the presence of Optatus, then bishop of Carthage—a rite that Saturus would have repeated again before Optatus and the full congregation at baptism.

In the interim between scrutiny and baptism (three weeks?), he would have been enjoined to pray frequently, fast, kneel often, spend nights in vigils as if a soldier on watch, and confess his sins.

As the day approached, Saturus would have bathed as enjoined, perhaps in the vast "Baths of Antoninus" that lie (partially excavated) on the shoreline of the ancient city. He would have fasted for several days before baptism.

Although baptism was not confined by time or place, Tertullian witnesses to a preference for Easter or Pentecost. Since vigils were a prominent feature of North African Christian customs, Saturus' baptism would have taken place at night, as in Rome, and in a "house church"—very likely a converted Roman house *(domus)*.

Initiation began outside the house with a repetition of the renunciation of the devil. Perhaps Saturus would have entered the church building as Optatus was consecrating the water in a rectangular font.[30]

Accompanied by his sponsor and the other *ingressuri,* he would have been stripped, anointed, and immersed three times, each time responding "I believe" to the creedal questions concerning the Father, Son, and Spirit. Perhaps Tertullian was the instructor who had explained the meaning of the creed to which Saturus would have responded.

When the newly baptized (Tertullian calls them "novices," *novitioli*) came up from the font, they were urged to pray for special gifts:

> [F]rom the most sacred washing of the new birth, and when for the first time you spread out your hands with your brethren in your mother's house, ask of your Father, ask of your Lord, as a special gift, for an abundance of spiritual gifts [*charismatum,* 1 Cor 12:1–31].[31]

In between washing and praying with the faithful, Saturus and his fellow novices would have been anointed. Optatus would then have imposed his hands to symbolize the gift of the Holy Spirit, offering a prayer "inviting the Holy Spirit."[32]

Then, vested in a white garment, they would have received the welcoming kiss of peace. They also would have prayed the Lord's Prayer for the first time—Tertullian was the first to write a commentary on it. Finally home in his "mother's house" (Tertullian was also the first to call the church "mother") and surrounded with his new brothers and sisters, Saturus could truly have called God his Father.[33]

Eucharist and After

With the newly baptized, Saturus would then have celebrated his first eucharist in the midst of his new family. There would have been bread and two cups: one with milk and honey mixed to symbolize his newborn status (Tertullian calls it regular baby food), and one of wine to symbolize Christ's redemptive blood. After his initiation, Saturus would have abstained from the baths for a week. If later custom is any indication, he and his fellow newborns would have received homiletic instruction during the week on the meaning of the rites and their experience, and worn their white garments, to be laid aside on the Sunday following Easter.

The ritual process of Saturus' conversion would have been extended and demanding. In fact, he was baptized in his blood—conversion could be a deadly business.

IV. West Syria

Our next destination is a part of Syria where the culture, though Hellenistic, was deeply Semitic. The reason for our journey is a document recovered only in the middle of the last century. A Jewish Christian bishop composed it for a circle of churches that looked to him as their leader. *The Teaching of the Twelve Holy Apostles and Disciples of Our Savior*—the *Didascalia* ("Teaching"), for short—was composed in Greek during the first half of the third century, though it survives largely in Latin fragments and a full Syriac version.[34] A Church Order familiar with the *Didache,* the *Didascalia* provides detailed information about all aspects of an early Christian community's life.

The location of the community is not known, but it need not have been far from the ancient Roman frontier garrison town Dura Europos on the Euphrates (modern Iraq), the site of the earliest church building unearthed to date—a Roman house (complete with a rectangular baptistery and striking murals) converted to church use in the first half of the third century.[35]

In the *Didascalia*'s twenty-six chapters there are only scattered references to baptism and its preparations.[36] Those who seek baptism (1) are largely Pagans ("Gentiles" in the document); (2) have sponsors, (3) gradually become integrated into the community; (4) bear the name "hearer"; (5) receive oral instruction from deacon-teachers, though the bishop handles creedal instruction and biblical homilies; (6) undergo a twofold prebaptismal anointing; (7) are baptized by immersion in the name of the Trinity; (8) celebrate the eucharist; and (9) are the subjects of special instruction and attention after baptism.

The *Didascalia* makes a unique contribution to our picture of developing patterns in the process of conversion: the conversion of women. Although no personal names appear in the document, let us name one of the leading ladies Rhoda.

Rhoda was the matron in a "Gentile" household and encountered one of the many Christian women ordained as deacons. For convenience's sake, let us call the deacon Phoebe and recall that, as a woman, she could enter the women's quarters of the household and, as a deacon, she was charged with a mission to help with the practical things of domestic life, including the distribution of food and clothes, health care, comfort in grief, and prayer. Rhoda was intrigued, and the two talked about why Phoebe did what she did.

Like Epicurus and his cranky Christian friend, one encounter led to another. As a deacon (she might also have been in the order of widows), Phoebe could answer a variety of basic questions about the faith, but when Rhoda wanted to talk about beliefs, Phoebe brought her to the deacon-teachers (men). Presumably, they asked her some questions to get a picture of her status and situation. With the agreement of all concerned, Rhoda became a hearer—for how long we are not told, but we already know that in West Syria and Palestine it could range from three months to a year. The Didascalist's community was Gentile; the competition was Judaism, about which the author is both sensitive and deeply concerned.

At some point before baptism, the bishop would have instructed her in the creed of his churches, after which she would have had to make a decision. Eventually and in spite of personal struggle—no small crisis in her world, because she was wife, mother, and arbiter of the household—she determined to be baptized and was accepted.

She may have been baptized at Easter, the customary celebration of which was unusual. The community called Easter by its earliest name, *Pascha* (Passover) and kept vigil the night of 14 Nisan, the date of the Jewish Passover; with the dawn of 15 Nisan (3:00 A.M.) the members celebrated their Pasch. For this Easter custom they were considered *Quartodecimans* ("fourteenthers")—a custom that caused grave conflict because the majority of Christians celebrated Easter on the Sunday following 14 Nisan. If the community baptized on Easter, the celebration would have begun about dawn of 15 Nisan.

Rhoda would have fasted with Phoebe and the rest of the community all during what later came to be called "Holy Week"—the document is quite explicit about the "six days" and insistent that the fast meant a diet of bread, salt, and water, save for the last two days (Friday and Saturday) when there was complete abstinence: no food or drink.

The distinctive feature of Rhoda's baptism is that Phoebe would have gone down with her into the font especially to anoint her:

> In the first place, when women go down into the water, it is required that those who go down into the water shall be anointed by deacons with the oil of anointing. . . . But where there is a woman, and especially a [deacon], it is not right that women should be seen by men, but with laying on of hand anoint the head only. As of old time the priests and kings in Israel were anointed,

so in like manner, anoint the head of those who receive baptism, whether of men or of women. And afterwards, whether you yourself baptize or you command the deacons or presbyters to baptize—let a woman deacon [Phoebe], as we said before, anoint the women. But let a man recite over them the invocation of the divine names in the water. And when she who is being baptized has come up from the water let the woman deacon receive her, and teach and educate her in order that the unbreakable seal of baptism shall be (kept) in chastity and holiness. On this account we say that the ministry of a woman deacon is especially required and urgent.[37]

Rhoda would have then celebrated her first eucharist; at her side would have been Phoebe, in whose care she was then placed for further integration into the community.

The Gospel of Philip

Rhoda's community would not have been far from another unusual community, one responsible for the *Gospel of Philip*.[38] Found only in 1947 at Nag Hammadi in Egypt among the buried remains of a monastery library, the text is a collection of theological statements concerning sacraments and ethics in the form of dialogues, parables, aphorisms, biblical interpretation, doctrine, and Jesus' sayings. The principal source was a Gnostic Christian instruction on the rites of initiation and the ideal life of the initiated. The target audience was those to be initiated.

The author, a Syrian writing in the mid-third century, uses terminology quite different from what we have come to expect. His audiences are coming to be "free men and virgins" (chs. 55:27–28; 81:34ff.) and coming to know their true origin and destiny (64:9–12). When they enter the "mystery," they will be called the "perfect" because they will possess the "resurrection" and the "cross" (74:18–21).

In the meantime, their predicament is the result of Eve's separation from Adam—the differentiation of the sexes (68:22–26). In the baptismal rites, Christ will make them one (70:12–22).

As for the rites themselves, they are "types and images" of another reality that the candidates are unable to receive in any other way (67:10). We learn that there are five stages.[39] Instruction, which may have occupied considerable time, leads to baptism, which involves the first of three stages: baptism, chrism, and eucharist.

Naked, the candidates are immersed and anointed with warmed and perfumed oil in the name of the Trinity. They exchange a kiss with the initiated, put on white garments, and celebrate their first eucharist.

Two stages remain. About the fourth stage, redemption or ransom, the author tells us nothing but its name *(apolutrosis)*. The fifth stage, the marriage chamber *(nymphon)*, is the core of the mystery, where the Adam and Eve in the initiates are reunited and their alienation healed (70, 71, 72). It is at this point that the converts are truly free men and women, embarked on the ideal life of the spirit. They are the "perfect."

V. East Syria

Our last journey takes us to another circle of churches that produced a body of early Christian works called the "Thomas Literature": the *Gospel According to Thomas,* the *Book of Thomas the Contender,* the *Hymn of the Pearl,* and the *Acts of Judas Thomas.*

The *Acts of Judas Thomas*

The Thomas of the literature is a legendary figure, Didymus Judas Thomas, apostle of the east, credited with the conversion of India (the Indus Valley) as well as northern Mesopotamia and Persia (modern eastern Turkey, Iraq, and Iran). *Didymus* means "twin" in Greek; Judas was his personal name. As a variant of Jesus' name, it points to the fact that he was considered Jesus' twin brother.

The document of our immediate concern is the Syriac *Acts of Judas Thomas,* one of a set of apocryphal *Acts—of John, of Paul and Thecla, of Andrew,* and *of Peter*—some of which the author may have known.[40]

Composed in the third century, the *Acts of Judas Thomas* recounts the exploits of Judas Thomas in establishing Christianity in the Indus Valley. Patterned on Luke's Acts of the Apostles, the work revolves around five conversion stories about high officials at the royal Indian court. Composed in Edessa (modern Urfa in eastern Turkey), *Acts* appears to be based on two cycles of traditions about Thomas, one from South India and the other from Mesopotamia. Its importance for us is that the work reflects the early Syriac Christian understanding of conversion.[41] The potential convert discovers the power of Jesus embodied in Thomas, his twin, through a combination of miracle, message, instructions, the reception of baptism and the eucharist, and a commitment to celibacy (even for the married).

The Conversion of Mygdonia and Narkia

The account of the conversion of Mygdonia, the new bride of Karish, the king's nephew, is the pivot on which the other four conversion accounts turn (82–133).[42]

Thomas, we read, draws attention to himself as a healer and preacher of a "new religion." Curious about Thomas because he had healed the wife and daughter of the king's general, Mygdonia goes to see and hear the newcomer preach (82–105). Coming to believe that Judas Thomas is the very Jesus that he preached (89), Mygdonia is smitten by his message of humility, temperance, and continence. When she goes home, she refuses to eat and sleep with Karish. He dreams about Thomas, whom he sees as an eagle stealing away his dove. The next day is a repeat. Mygdonia spends the day with the apostle and again refuses to eat and sleep with Karish, who lies down next to her anyway.

Enraged at the loss of his dove, Karish accuses Thomas of sorcery and seduction, and the king has the apostle arrested. A trial follows, in every point like the trial of Jesus before Pilate, even to the scourging and imprisonment.

Karish goes home victoriously to reclaim his new bride, only to find her undone by mourning. A debate ensues (114–118), during which Karish reminds Mygdonia of all the pleasure they have had together and of his nobility, wealth, and standing. He even promises to arrange Thomas' release if he agrees to leave the country and she agrees to come back as his wife. Mygdonia replies that she now has in Jesus far more than Karish has to offer, Jesus "who abides alone for ever, with those souls that have taken refuge with him" (117).

Karish goes to sleep. Mygdonia slips out to bribe the jailers to let her see Thomas. She mistakes him for a noble and flees into the street terrified. When she slumps down in despair over her plight, Thomas suddenly appears to her and tells her of Jesus' presence as her refuge. She asks for baptism, which she calls "the sign of Jesus" (120).

Mygdonia then slips back into her house, awakens her slave, Narkia, and asks her to get a loaf of bread and wine mixed with water.

Thomas first anoints Mygdonia on the head, offering a prayer that stresses her healing:

Holy oil, which was given to us for unction, and hidden mystery of the cross, which is seen through it—You, the straightener of crooked limbs, You our Lord Jesus, life and health and remission of sins—let your power come and abide upon this oil, and let your holiness dwell in it. . . . Heal her of her old wounds, and wash away her sores, and strengthen her weakness. (121)[43]

Narkia anoints Mygdonia's body and puts a loincloth on her. Thomas then pours water over her in the name of the Trinity. After she dries herself and dresses, Thomas, we read, takes and breaks the eucharist and fills the cup, and lets Mygdonia partake of the table of the Messiah and of the cup of the Son of God. And he says to her: "Now . . . you have received the sign, and gained for yourself your life for ever and ever." (And a voice is heard from heaven which says: "Yes, Amen and Amen.") Narkia then asks for the "sign," joining her convert mistress in a life of celibacy and service.[44]

Derived from the five central accounts, with the Mygdonia account as the key, the ritual structure of the process exhibits the following elements: (1) preaching and teaching combined with miracles; (2) the struggle against powerful personal ties and obligations; (3) the decision to be baptized coupled with community approval; (4) ritual stripping; (5) anointing of the head in the sign of a cross; (6) anointing of the entire body; (7) a prayer calling Jesus and the Spirit of Holiness to effect the mystery; (8) immersion in the name of the Trinity; (9) reclothing in a white garment; and (10) the celebration of the eucharist coupled with a baptismal exhortation. One account (*Acts* 27) hints that the newly baptized were given lighted tapers, and another (46–50) associates exorcism with baptism as a preliminary.

VI. Conclusion

We have considered third-century texts and writers that represent conversion to Christianity across the Greco-Roman world and beyond. Baptism continues to be patterned primarily on Jesus' baptism in the Jordan (Egypt and Syria) and on his death and resurrection (Italy and North Africa); the Pentecost pattern of the descent of the Holy Spirit remains in the background, save in East Syria, where it is associated with anointing (see Mygdonia, above), a rite that shares the stage with immersion.

The characteristics of the conversion process that we identified in the earlier centuries continue in the third: preparation (remote and immediate), the rites of baptism, the eucharist, and postbaptismal biblical, moral, and doctrinal instruction. Yet they undergo extensive development. A careful screening process appears in Rome and Carthage. The period of instruction is extended and expanded by a syllabus that combines biblical and creedal instruction, at least in the urban centers (Rome, Carthage, Alexandria, Caesarea). In the West, exorcism dramatizes conversion as a struggle with Satan, and the renunciation of Satan personalizes the struggle for the candidates in rite and symbol. Prayer and fasting assume prominence in preparation for baptism—forty days in Egypt—to underscore discipline and training as integral to the process of conversion. And in East Syria, celibacy seems to have been required of some, if not all, converts.

Further, the rites that compose baptism are more richly articulated: Easter (with Pentecost) emerges as the most solemn day of baptism in the West; the water is consecrated; anointing stands with immersion as a focus of conversion; and the form of baptism takes a creedal shape.

Finally, the postbaptismal rites are elaborated with great variety: anointing, the white garment, the Lord's Prayer, the liturgical kiss, a baptismal candle, and a distinctive form of the eucharist (wine, water, and milk and honey).

As if to emphasize the unfinished character of baptismal conversion and integration into the community, a period of special attention to the newly baptized appears—a week in Italy and North Africa, perhaps a longer period in Syria *(Didascalia)*.

NOTES

1. Cited in Clive Bell, *Art* (New York: Capricorn Books, 1958) 163. Bell does not give a source, and subsequent attempts to identify it have failed. The reference may very well be an edited version of a historical account: the Greek freedman might be historical; the account as it stands, fictional.

2. Bernard Botte has reconstituted the text from a variety of later versions and translations. The original was Greek, on which the Latin and Sahidic versions depend, but there are other versions (Arabic and Ethiopian), and it has been embedded in other Church Orders (*The Testament of Our Lord, The Canons of Hippolytus,* and *The Apostolic Constitutions*). I follow Botte's *La*

Tradition Apostolique de Saint Hippolyte: Essai de Reconstitution, LQF 39 (1963), but see Botte's SC version, *Hippolyte de Rome: La Tradition Apostolique d'après les anciennes versions,* SC 11bis (1968). For English translations, see Geoffrey J. Cumming, ed., *Hippolytus: A Text for Students,* GLS 8 (1976); his edition, *Essays on Hippolytus,* GLS 15 (1978); Gregory Dix, *The "Apostolic Tradition" of Hippolytus,* rev. ed., ed. Henry Chadwick (London: SPCK, 1968); and my *ECBC* 6:46–51, which I follow in these pages. There is a commentary on the *Apostolic Tradition* (abbreviation *AT)* in preparation: Hermeneia Commentaries, Fortress Press, ed. Paul Bradshaw, Maxwell E. Johnson, L. Edmund Phillips, and Grant Sperry-White. See the work of the late G. G. Willis, *A History of the Early Roman Liturgy: To the Death of Pope Gregory the Great* (London: The Henry Bradshaw Society, 1994) 9–16, 117–18; he relies on Dix and Botte, rejecting J. Hanssens' opinion (*La Liturgie d'Hippolyte*) that it was an Alexandrian work intended as an ideal rather than an actual liturgy. Willis traces the rites of initiation from Hippolytus to the seventh century in his work (116–36).

3. For a recent study of the current state of research, see Georg Kretschmar, "Early Christian Liturgy in the Light of Contemporary Historical Research," *SL* 16:3–4 (1986–1987) 31–53, especially 31–33, 37–38, 41; for a current discussion, see Maxwell E. Johnson, "The Postchrismational Structure of *Apostolic Tradition* 21, The Witness of Ambrose of Milan, and a Tentative Hypothesis Regarding the Current Reform of Confirmation in the Roman Rite," *Worship* 70 (1996) 16–34; for another current discussion, see Paul F. Bradshaw, "Re-dating the *Apostolic Tradition:* Some Preliminary Steps," in *Festschrift for Aidan Kavanagh,* ed. J. Baldovin and N. Mitchell (Collegeville: Liturgical Press, forthcoming 1997); for a wide-ranging discussion of some of the issues, including the magisterial chair, see the papers from the conference held by the Institutum Patristicum Augustinianum at Rome in 1976: *Ricerche su Ippolito* (Rome: Institutum Patristicum "Augustinianum" [*Studia Ephemeridis "Augustinianum"* 13], 1977).

4. Maxwell E. Johnson and Paul F. Bradshaw, as cited in n. 3. See n. 10 below for the details.

5. See my "Ritual Process and the Survival of Early Christianity: A Study of the *Apostolic Tradition* of Hippolytus," *JRS* 3 (1989) 69–89, especially 70–72. The first emperor-initiated persecution was launched in 249, but social and legal hostility was escalating already at the end of the first century.

6. For baptism as a crisis, see Peter Cramer, *Baptism and Change in the Early Middle Ages: c. 200–c. 1150* (Cambridge: Cambridge University Press, 1993) 10.

7. John Chrysostom, *Baptismal Instruction* 12:1; PG 49:231; trans. Paul Harkins, *St. John Chrysostom: Baptismal Instructions,* ACW 51 (1963) 173. For discussion, see Leonel L. Mitchell, "The Development of Catechesis in the

Third and Fourth Centuries: From Hippolytus to Augustine," in J. Westerhoff and O. C. Edwards, eds., *A Faithful Church: Issues in the History of Catechesis* (Wilton: Morehouse-Barlow, 1981) 49–78, especially 49–53.

8. For a perceptive treatment, see Walter J. Burghardt, "Catechetics in the Early Church," *The Living Light* 1 (1964) 100–118.

9. *AT* 20 (Botte, LQF 39:42; Finn, *ECBC* 6:48–49) for what follows.

10. *AT* 21 (Botte, LQF 39:44–53; Finn, *ECBC* 6:49–50) for what follows. Bradshaw, in a forthcoming study cited by Johnson, proposes the following reconstruction as the first stage, arguing that the second stage contained the rites assigned to the bishop alone (postbaptismal prayer for grace with the imposition of hands, the episcopal anointing, the kiss, and the greeting, "The Lord be with you"). The final stage contained the more detailed instructions pertaining to presbyters and deacons (prebaptismal rites of the blessing of oils, renunciation, the anointing with "exorcised oil," and the presbyteral postbaptismal anointing). See Johnson, "The Postchrismational Structure of *Apostolic Tradition* 21," 2–3 (first stage, i.e., between Justin and 200 C.E.):

> At the time when the cock crows, first let prayer be made over the water. Let the water [be pure and] flowing [in the font or poured over it]. Let it be thus unless there is some necessity; if the necessity is permanent and urgent, use what water you can find. They shall take off their clothes. Baptize the little ones first. All those who can speak for themselves shall do so. As for those who cannot speak for themselves, their parents or someone from their family shall speak for them. Then baptize the men, and lastly the women, who shall have loosened all their hair, and laid down the gold and silver ornaments which they have on them. Let no one take any alien object down into the water.
>
> As he who is to be baptized is descending into the water, let him who baptizes him say thus [as he lays his hand on him], "Do you believe in God the Father omnipotent?" And let the one being baptized say, "I believe." And the giver shall baptize him once. And then he shall say: "Do you believe in Christ Jesus, the Son of God . . . ?" And when he has said, "I believe," he shall be baptized again. And he shall say again: "Do you believe in the Holy Spirit . . . ?" The he who is being baptized shall say, "I believe," and thus he shall be baptized a third time. And so each of them shall wipe themselves and put on their clothes, and then they shall enter into the church....And then they shall pray together with all the people: they do not pray with the faithful until they have carried out all these things. And when they have prayed, they shall give the kiss of peace. (See above, n. 2)

11. *AT* 21 (Botte, LQF 39:48–50; Finn, *ECBC* 6:49–50).

12. Where the font (stream, pool, public bath, or baptismal font) permitted (as here), immersion involved submerging the head of the baptizand. Archaeological evidence indicates that it was not always possible. When it was not, the baptizand often stood in water waist high, and the baptizer poured water over the head, often from a laver. As the *Didache* indicates, sometimes sprinkling (aspersion) was the only feasible way. Nonetheless, immersion was the norm, whether submersion or by laver, the better to signify baptism as death and rebirth/resurrection. For discussion, see Everett Ferguson, "Baptistery," *Encyclopedia of Early Christianity* (New York and London: Garland, 1990) 135–37; and Walter Bedard, *The Symbolism of the Baptismal Font in Early Christian Thought* (Washington, D.C.: Catholic University of America Press [Studies in Sacred Theology 45, series 2], 1951).

13. *AT* 21 (Botte, LQF 39:52; Finn, *ECBC* 6:50). This may be the result of the third editor (see above, n. 10).

14. *Panegyric to Origen* 6 (PG 10:1072B; A. Coxe, trans., ANF 6:28).

15. For discussion and texts, see my *ECBC* 6:194–95, and the homilies on Exodus, Joshua, and Luke (195–210); see also Cécile Blanc, "Le baptême d'après Origène," *SP* 11:2 (1972) 113–23.

16. See my *ECBC* 6:193, 195–216 for what follows and the supporting texts.

17. For what follows, see Maxwell E. Johnson, *Liturgy in Early Christian Egypt,* GLS (forthcoming) MS pp. 7–17, cited with the kind permission of the author; and Paul F. Bradshaw, "Baptismal Practice in the Alexandrian Tradition: Eastern or Western," in Bradshaw, ed., *Essays in Early Eastern Initiation,* GLS 56 (1988) 5–17.

18. Ibid., 10. There appear to be no parallels outside of Egypt.

19. See Thomas Halton, "Baptism as Illumination," *Irish Theological Quarterly* 32 (1965) 28–41.

20. Origen, *Homilies on Romans* 5:8 (PG 14:1038C); *Homilies on Leviticus* 6:5 (PG 12:472D), cited in Bradshaw, "Baptismal Practice in the Alexandrian Tradition," 15. See also, Johnson, *Liturgy in Early Christian Egypt,* MS pp. 11–12.

21. For the text and discussion, see H. Musurillo, *The Acts of the Christian Martyrs* (Oxford: Clarendon Press, 1972) xxii–xxiii, 86–89; in lvii–lxii, he reviews the bases in Roman law for their prosecution.

22. Ibid., xxv–xxvii, 106–31.

23. For Tertullian and his works, see Timothy D. Barnes, *Tertullian: A Historical and Literary Study* (Oxford: Clarendon Press, 1971).

24. For the text and a helpful introduction, see Ernest Evans, ed., *Tertullian's Homily on Baptism* (London: SPCK, 1964); and my translation in *ECBC* 5:118–28.

25. Tertullian, *On Baptism (De bapt.)* 18 (Evans, 38; Finn, *ECBC* 6:127).

26. Ibid. (Evans, 36–37).

27. Tertullian, *On the Prescription of Heretics (De praescr. haer.)* 36 (Evans, xxiv). See also *On the Veiling of Virgins* 1 (PL 2:889AB).

28. *On the Resurrection of the Flesh* 8 (PL 2:806), cited in Evans, xxv.

29. Tertullian, *On the Chaplet (De cor.)* 3 (PL 2:79: a brief description of baptism—not complete). For amplification, see *On Prescription (De praescr. haer.)* 36 (PL 2:49: creedal questions); *Against Marcion (Adv. Mar.)* 1:14 (PL 2:262: anointing, milk and honey, eucharistic bread and wine); *On the Resurrection of the Flesh (De res. carn.)* 8 (PL 2:806: anointing, signing with the cross, the body and blood of Christ); *On Baptism (De bapt.)* 4, 6, 7, 19, 20: consecration of the waters (4), Trinitarian formula (6), postbaptismal anointing (7), Easter and Pentecost baptism, any time, place, hour suitable (19), prebaptismal prayer, fasting, vigils, confession of sins, postbaptismal eucharist (20); see also Evans, *Tertullian's Homily on Baptism,* xxiii–xxvii.

30. For discussion, see S. Anita Stauffer, *On Baptismal Fonts: Ancient and Modern* (Bramcote, Nottingham: Grove Books [Grove Renewal of Worship Studies 29–30], 1994) 15–18. The earliest (third century) are rectangular, likely patterned after the Roman baths.

31. *On Baptism* 20 (Evans, 43). For discussion of the passage, see Kilian McDonnell and George T. Montague, *Christian Initiation and Baptism in the Holy Spirit: Evidence from the First Eight Centuries,* 2nd ed. (Collegeville: Liturgical Press [A Michael Glazier Book], 1994) 108–15. This is the first time that the baptismal gift of the Spirit is described outside the New Testament in its manifestations *(charismata).*

32. *On Baptism* 7–8 (Evans, 16).

33. *On Prayer,* CSEL 20, 180–200. The homily was directed to catechumens and delivered at about the same time as the baptismal homily.

34. For text, see Arthur Vööbus, ed., *The "Didascalia Apostolorum" in Syriac,* CSCO 401, 408 (1979) vol. 1, chs. 1–10; vol. 2, chs. 11–26. For the translation, see ibid., CSCO 402, 407 (1979); see also the introduction in 402 for discussion, especially 55–67. R. Hugh Connolly has translated it also, *"Didascalia Apostolorum": The Syriac Version Translated and Accompanied by the Verona Latin Fragments* (Oxford: Clarendon Press, 1929), with a valuable discussion, especially lxvii–lvi. A recent English translation is Sebastian Brock, *The Liturgical Portions of the "Didascalia,"* GLS 29 (1982). See also my *ECBC* 5:38–41.

35. For discussion of the stages of early Christian building history, see L. Michael White, *Building God's House in the Roman World: Architectural Adaptation among Pagans, Jews, and Christians* (Baltimore: Johns Hopkins

University Press [American Schools of Oriental Research], 1990) 1–25; and other Dura entries.

36. See especially *Didascalia* 9 (100, 104: deaconesses as the counterpart of the Holy Spirit; bishop as teacher and baptizer); 10 (112–14: on Pagans coming to the church, hearers, repentance); 12 (130–31: orientation and arrangement of the church building; 133: bishop as preacher of scripture); 13 (136: Pagans as Gentiles; Jews as "the People"); 14–15 (141–54: duty and conduct of widows); 16 (155–62: deacons and deaconesses; women's baptism); 19 (172: the Lord's Prayer); 20 (179–80: a creedal fragment; 183: Gentile's sins forgiven in baptism); and 21 (184–200: Paschaltide, especially 198–99 on fasting, vigil, resurrection). Note: the page references are to Vööbus, CSCO 401, 408 (the translation, in which he gives the text pages).

37. *Didascalia* 16 (Vööbus, CSCO 407:172–74; CSCO 408:156–57).

38. For text and translation, see Wesley W. Isenberg, "The Gospel According to Philip," in *Nag Hammadi Codex II, 2–7,* vol. 1, ed. Bentley Layton (Leiden: E. J. Brill [Nag Hammadi Studies 20, ed. James M. Robinson], 1989) 142–215. For discussion, see his introduction (132–39), and for its cultic aspects, see Jorunn Jacobsen Buckley, "A Cult-Mystery in *The Gospel of Philip,*" *JBL* 99 (1980) 569–81.

39. For discussion, see Isenberg, "The Gospel According to Philip," 136–37; and my *ECBC* 5:120–27.

40. The Syriac text is that of William Wright, ed., *Apocryphal Acts of the Apostles* (London, 1871); the translation and commentary are that of A. F. J. Klijn, *The Acts of Thomas: Introduction, Text, and Commentary* (Leiden: E. J. Brill [Supplements to the New Testament, ed. W. C. van Unnik, 5], 1962). See also my *ECBC* 5: 129–41. For the most recent account of the work and bibliography, see Harold Attridge, "Thomas, Acts of," *ABD* 6:531–34.

41. See Robert Murray, "The Characteristics of Early Syriac Christianity," in Nina Garsoian et al., eds., *East Byzantium: Syria and Armenia in the Formative Period* (Washington, D.C.: Dumbarton Oaks, 1982) 3–16; Klijn, *The Acts of Thomas,* 38–60 (includes baptism and the eucharist).

42. *Acts* 82–133 (Wright, 256–59; Klijn, 108–33); the Greek text is *Acta Thomae* 82–133 (Richard A. Lipsius et al., eds., *Acta Apostolorum Apocrypha*, vol. 2, pt. 2 [Hildesheim: Georg Olms, 1959] 197–240): the exploit is the ninth and tenth in the Greek version.

43. *Acts* 121 (Wright, 257; Klijn, 130). Note the emphasis on the anointing.

44. Ibid.

Chapter 8

THE FOURTH CENTURY:
CONVERSION IN JERUSALEM

I. Introduction

The fourth century changed everything. Baptism in blood disappeared: the church moved out of the catacombs into the forum, a move that came from the top down. The movers were three emperors: Galerius (305–312 C.E.) and Constantine (324–337 C.E.), who enacted edicts of toleration for Christianity (311 and 313, respectively), and Theodosius I (379–396 C.E.), who established Catholic Christianity as the religion of the empire (381).

Predictably, the move had enormous consequences for conversion. From a cult to be shunned, the church became an institution to be embraced, but not overnight.

Assume that the city of Rome numbered about seven hundred thousand people in the year 250. No more than twenty thousand were Christians—close to 3 percent.[1] At the end of the third century, after almost forty years of comparative civic peace for Christians, the number may well have doubled and the percentage grown to 5 percent— forty to fifty thousand. Empirewide the percentages were likely the same. The numbers of Christians? Perhaps as many as one and a half million, mostly city dwellers.

The Diocletian persecution (303–311) slowed conversions—jeopardy has a way about it—but the Constantinian settlement accelerated them; whereas before it had been a burden to be a Christian, now it was a boon. Nonetheless, in the smaller towns of the empire, like Gaza in Palestine, where Paganism was entrenched, Pagans did not rush to the church. At the end of the century (395) there were only two hundred and eighty Christians in Gaza (the total population may have been ten to fifteen thousand), to which we must add seventy-eight male converts, thirty-five women, nine boys and five girls, and by year's end thirty-five more converts, making a total of four hundred and forty-two Gazan Christians.[2]

In the great metropolitan centers—Rome, Carthage, Alexandria, and Antioch—the percentages were far higher. The ambitious and upwardly mobile tended to live in the great cities. In Antioch, which boasted a population of some three hundred thousand, almost half were Christian, although John Chrysostom (c. 385) complained that there were only about one hundred thousand Catholics.[3] By the century's end, the plagues and famine that bedeviled the eastern Mediterranean may have reduced the population, both Christian and non-Christian.

Whatever the actual figures, one fact is clear: from an obscure sect of Palestinian Jews, Christianity became the religious foundation of the empire in less than four hundred years and assumed majority status in the fifth century. Conversion was the key to its survival before Constantine and to its supremacy after him.

Pre-Constantinian animosity ensured that Christians would be small, tightly knit, and intense clusters of people on the fringes of society. The catechumenate of the second and third centuries—especially in Rome, Carthage, and Alexandria—developed in the shadow of imperial social and legal hostility. As we have seen, Justin and his disciples were tried, convicted, and executed because they were Christians; Origen lost his Christian father to the executioner; and Perpetua, Felicity, and their companions were catechumens when the Romans arrested and imprisoned them. To be in the church was to be in jeopardy. The church's response was a catechumenate that served as an effective system of screening and training. The result was a demanding and extended ritual process—a rite of passage—that would separate inquirers from a way of life and a set of familiar relations sanctioned by Roman law, custom, and convention and introduce them to a new way of life in a new family that contravened law, custom, and convention.[4]

The fourth century presented Christians with an entirely different problem. Social and legal jeopardy had forced the church to guard the gates and to screen entrants rigorously. Imperial establishment now threatened to open the gates to a flood of people who, for a hundred different reasons, wanted entrance. The problem was how to keep the floodgates in place so that the flood would not wash away the faith of the first three centuries. For the solution, we need to turn to the catechumenate in two of the empire's major cities: one, the religious capital of the empire, the other, the administrative capital of the Western empire. Our focus in this chapter is Jerusalem and its distinctive liturgy of conversion, and in the next, Milan and its distinguished convert, Augustine.

II. Holy Land, Holy City

Almost from the outset of the fourth century, the eyes of Christians turned to Palestine and its holy places; Jerusalem was the holiest of holy places. Constantine hardly had acceded to the imperial throne when the first pilgrim arrived from the West.[5]

For the first three centuries, the "pilgrims" were primarily Roman legions sent to quell Jewish uprisings against Rome. The first Roman pilgrimage, in 66–73 C.E., led to the siege of Jerusalem, the destruction of the second temple, the fall of Masada, and the dispersion of Jews and Jewish Christians around the Mediterranean and east to Persia. The second (115–117) started in Libya and spread to Egypt, decimating the large Jewish community in Alexandria and in the towns and villages up the Nile and changing the composition of Egyptian Christian communities. The third (132–135), the Bar Kokhba revolt, led to the destruction of the old city, to its renaming as Aelia Capitolina, and to the interdiction of Jews entering the city under pain of death.[6]

Until the interdict, the church in Jerusalem (as in Palestine) was predominantly Jewish, and its center was a small church "on the spot where the disciples went up to the upper room" on Zion after the ascension (Acts 1:13). The church was known as the "Mother of all Churches."[7] The Upper Room church remained the center after the interdict, but those who frequented it were now Gentiles, as were its bishops—at least according to the historian Eusebius, who records the succession of the city's bishops.[8]

Christians of note, including Origen (c. 230 C.E.) and a Cappadocian pilgrim, visited the church occasionally. The city remained the center of Palestinian Christianity, but the church at Caesarea, Rome's provincial headquarters and the site of Origen's catechetical school, exercised jurisdiction over the Jerusalem church.

A New Jerusalem

Nowhere was the Constantinian impact on Christianity more strikingly visible than in Jerusalem. Pilgrims and permanent residents, especially ascetic Westerners like Jerome and friends, came in numbers.[9] Constantine's mother, Helena, reportedly found the cross of Christ. Constantine built a striking basilica on Golgotha, called the Martyrium, to commemorate Christ's death.[10] A second church followed—a rotunda built over the tomb from which Christ was thought to have risen, appropriately called the Anastasis ("resurrection"). In between the two was a garden court, at the east corner of which stood the cross that marked the spot of Christ's death and, behind it, a chapel. The court fronted on the Anastasis to the west and on the baptistery, which stood close to the Anastasis on its right (south).

Constantine built other ecclesiastical buildings in the Holy City as well: the Church of the Eleona on the Mount of Olives, commemorating the agony of Jesus and his arrest in the garden of Gethsemane, and the Imbomon ("hillock"), a place for teaching that commemorated Jesus' ascension. By 350 a new church, the Upper Church, replaced the old Church of the Upper Room on Mount Zion, and by century's end a church commemorating Christ's ascension stood on the Imbomon. Outside the city, he built the Lazarium (the Church of Lazarus) in Bethany and the Church of the Nativity in Bethlehem.

Except for the ruins of the second temple, Jerusalem had been transformed from the Pagan city of Emperor Hadrian to the city of the birth, death, and resurrection of Jesus—the Christian Holy City.[11]

This transformation also signaled something more: now place and sight entered into the constitution of Christian faith. To be on Golgotha, to see the tomb, to go to the Imbomon, to stand in the Upper Church was to enact the faith. As comparative religionists and anthropologists put it, Jerusalem for Christians became the axis upon which the world turned *(axis mundi)*, the navel of the universe *(omphalos)*.[12] The church of the catacombs was now the church not only of the forum or the empire, but of the world.

The Jerusalem Church

How many people lived in fourth-century Jerusalem is impossible to say. On the threshold of the fifth century, at least, the majority were Christians. Chief among them was the bishop—for us Bishop Cyril.

Like the high priest of old, who alone could enter the holy of holies in the temple, he alone could go into the holiest places, Christ's tomb on Golgotha being the new holy of holies.

Gathered around the bishop as his councilors, the crown and senate of the church, were the presbyters. They preached and taught, read the scriptures, led prayers and the psalmody, received the formal registration of the catechumens, and exorcised. Often the bishop sent them out to teach and celebrate the eucharist in the towns and villages too remote for the people to come regularly to Jerusalem. The hierarchy also included men and women deacons and an archdeacon.

Among the faithful, three ranks existed: countless ascetics (both men and women), the faithful, and the catechumens. It was a Greek-speaking community, though Palestinian Aramaic—and some Latin—could also be heard on the streets and in church.

Catechumens[13]

The catechumens appear to have been numerous and of two kinds: those who had been inscribed in the register of catechumens and those who had been accepted for baptism, in short, the beginners and the advanced. Given the favored position of the church in the empire, it was an obvious advantage to be even a beginner: catechumens were considered Christians by aspiration and anticipation, if not by initiation. As such they were expected to participate in the preparatory part of the eucharist—the prayers, biblical readings, and homily, called the "Mass of the Catechumens" in the West, the "Assembly" *(synaxis)* in the East, and the "Liturgy of the Word" in recent times. In addition, as we will see, they shared in the numerous liturgical celebrations at the holy places throughout the year.

But they stood on the fringes of the church and even had a special place assigned them in the church building apart from the faithful. In short, they were "hearers":

> You were called catechumens, while the word echoed around you: hearing hope but not seeing it, hearing the mysteries but not understanding them, hearing the scriptures but not plumbing their depths.[14]

Almost all were Gentiles and Pagans. Some were simply curious hearers; some were courting a potential spouse; some were trying to please someone (a slave, the master; a friend, a friend); some were children of Christians; some sought social advantage and economic gain; some simply wanted to belong somewhere.[15]

Whatever the reason that brought them to have their names inscribed, the work of the catechumenate was to change the faithless *(apistos)* into faithful *(pistos),* however long that might take.[16] In short, the status of catechumen was the church's response to the pressure of numbers; it could give people a threshold status without opening the floodgates. People would be catechumens until they (and the church) were ready for advanced status.

Delayed Baptism

There was a problem: catechumens kept putting off the decision to be baptized.[17] Part of the reason was that as catechumens they were considered members of the church; why go all the way and thereby get entangled in Christian discipline and demands? Part was also the severity of the public penitential system for grave postbaptismal sin; there was only one chance for reconciliation, and the way was daunting. Catechumens were afraid that they could not live the kind of life that baptism demanded—a feeling reinforced by the constant reminder that there was only one baptism, as Cyril put it, lest they think that "though I failed once, I will set it right the second time."[18]

So widespread was the custom of delayed baptism that the leading figures of the fourth-century church, almost all of whom were raised in Christian homes as catechumens, were baptized as adults. The common parental response, especially for their sons, was that they should wait until they had settled down to home and career.

Yet the common response led to a common complaint: too many catechumens delayed baptism until they were on their deathbeds. John Chrysostom decried the custom because, he argued, the majesty and meaning of baptism was lost on the candidate: the tumult and confusion, fear and fever, lament and wailing rendered the symbol of eternal life the symptom of impending death.[19]

Perhaps the most striking example of delayed baptism was Constantine. Although he sat among the bishops in councils and considered himself the "bishop of those outside," he was not inscribed as a catechumen until he was in his final illness and not baptized until just before his death on Pentecost 337.[20]

III. Lent and Jerusalem

Some catechumens did not delay; they actively sought baptism. For those, the church of the fourth century adapted an institution already in place by the year 330—the forty-day fast in preparation for Easter.[21] The "forty days" quickly became a technical term to denote the prepaschal season: in Greek, *tesserakoste,* in Latin, *quadragesima,* in English, Lent. Paradoxically, in Jerusalem they were known as the "Feasts" *(eortae)* because the fast days were punctuated by dramatic liturgical celebrations at the holy places—feast days.[22]

The Jerusalem church felt two pressing needs with regard to catechumens: the need to accommodate those who wanted baptism and the need to prepare them with some of the rigor of previous centuries. The Jerusalem church authorities (very likely, Bishop Cyril) incorporated the catechetical and ritual preparation for baptizands into the ascetic preparation for Easter. The ascetic and the catechetical coincided admirably, for both preparations sought to renew the community: the ascetic to replenish the community's fervor, the baptismal to replenish its numbers.

Social scientists have long realized that rites of initiation are remarkably effective in replenishing the bonds that knit a community together—bonds continually in jeopardy from backsliding. As anthropologist Victor Turner puts it, such rites help people to realize their condition and to "'burn out' or 'wash away' the accumulated sins and sunderings of daily life."[23] The community was annually rejuvenated (like the community at Qumran, which we considered in the fourth chapter).

Lent quickly spread across the ancient Christian world, but it was no more dramatically observed than in Jerusalem. Two remarkable people allow us to see the process of conversion there through their eyes—Jerusalem's Bishop Cyril and the Western pilgrim Egeria.

IV. A Guide and a Commentator

Cyril (350–387)[24]

Cyril left behind an invaluable liturgical legacy: the earliest complete set of extant baptismal instructions in ancient Christianity. They include eighteen[25] instructions primarily on the articles of the Jerusalem baptismal creed, delivered about 351, and five homilies on the rites of initiation, delivered some thirty years later.

Born about 315 in Jerusalem, Cyril was ordained a deacon about 330 and a priest by 343; he was consecrated bishop of Jerusalem in 350/351. The doctrinal turbulence of the Arian controversy three times occasioned his exile (357, 362, 370?). With the death of Emperor Valens in 378, he returned to his see for good. All told, he was bishop of the Holy City for almost forty years; he died in 387.

Cyril's legacy was more than the earliest complete set of baptismal instructions. During his episcopate, the golden age of Christian ritual process (liturgy) dawned in Jerusalem. Such are the qualifications of our commentator.

Egeria[26]

Egeria, our eyewitness, was a Latin-speaking woman, most likely from Gaul (Arles?), who made a pilgrimage to Jerusalem and the biblical sites of the ancient Near East from 381 to 384. In her travels Egeria went east to Edessa and Nisibis, north to upper Syria, and south to Egypt. But Jerusalem was her home base.

Her legacy, discovered only at the end of the last century (1888), is a diary composed for a circle of ascetic laywomen back home. Often she is depicted as a nun writing for her sisters at home, but this is far from certain.

Regrettably, the *Diary* is not complete; as much as a third appears to be missing. But it is clear that her aim was to visit the holy places in the ancient Near East wherever they were. As it turns out, the holy places were inhabited by holy people—monks and other ascetics—who were almost as much the object of her visits as the holy places. Half of what remains of the *Diary,* however, is devoted to her liturgical pilgrimage in and around the Holy City.

With the Bible as guidebook to the sites, Palestinian Christians had developed the liturgical year *in situ.* Continually, Egeria remarks about how scriptural account, biblical site, and liturgical rite conspire to reenact a sacred event narrated in the Bible. In the feasts of Epiphany, Lent, Easter, and Pentecost she saw the Bible relived in a remarkable drama, and she continually remarks on the aptness of site, lection, and prayer.

Pentecost is an example. Egeria describes clergy, ascetics, laity, and catechumens processing up Mount Zion to the Upper Church (it replaced the Upper Room church) to relive the account in Acts, when the apostles and Jesus' mother and family gathered for prayer, and a roar "like the rush of a violent wind" filled the entire house and a divided "tongue of fire rested on each of them" (Acts 1:13–14; 2:2–3).

The *Diary,* coupled with Cyril's baptismal instructions, puts in the hands of the student of conversion a guided tour and running commentary on the making of a Christian in late-fourth-century Jerusalem.

V. The Lenten Catechumenate

Enrollment

Lenten preparation for baptism began on Epiphany (January 6), the feast of the Nativity of Christ. Those who sought baptism assembled in the Martyrium. Egeria describes what happened:

> When the priest has noted down everyone's name, then on the following day, the first day of Lent, [Cyril's] chair *[cathedra]* is placed in the center of the . . . Martyrium, the priests *[presbyteri]* sit in chairs on both sides, and all the clergy stand nearby. One by one the candidates are led forward, such that the men come with their godfathers *[patribus]* and women with their godmothers *[matribus]*.
>
> Then [Cyril] questions individually the neighbors of the one who has come up, inquiring, "Does this person lead a good life?" He seeks out in the person all the serious human vices. If the person proves guiltless in all these matters . . . he notes down the name in his own hand. If, however, the person is accused of anything, [Cyril] orders him to go out and says: "Let him amend his life, and when he has done so, let him then approach the baptismal font." He makes the same inquiry of both men and women. If, however, someone is a stranger, he cannot easily receive baptism, unless he has witnesses who know him.[27]

Those whose names Cyril writes down are no longer catechumens; they are now *photizomenoi* (those about to be enlightened) or *baptizomenoi* (baptizands—those about to be baptized). Beginning the next day, they fast for the next eight weeks, Monday through Friday. Egeria makes it clear that the rigor of people's fasting varies according to the norms of strength and health.[28] Some of the Jerusalem Christians eat nothing during the week (they are known as *hebdomidarii,* "Week Keepers"); others eat twice a week; and still others, once a day (much as in Islam today during Ramadan). Perhaps some of the baptizands adopt the more austere fasts, but in the main they eat what is necessary for health and strength—a bland meal of gruel and water each day.

Exorcism[29]

At dawn on Monday the community assembles in the Anastasis to sing and recite morning prayer (Egeria, 24). The baptizands then process across the court to the Martyrium, where the priests wait to exorcise them. (In an attempt to preserve the personal contact of the earlier communities, each baptizand had an exorcist.)

Lying prone with their faces veiled, the baptizands, shielded from every distraction, are very much alone with themselves. In a loud and commanding voice, the exorcist invokes Christ, curses Satan, and hisses at his baptizand. The rite is an ordeal that seeks to evoke in the baptizands a sense of the power of evil and to elicit confession of sins (we are not told in what form). The daily repetition of exorcism seeks to force the evil spirit to give way to the Holy Spirit. The intended effect is gradual withdrawal from the power of their culture and their past—a therapeutic rite.

The Curriculum: Bible and Creed

Once exorcised, the baptizands—both men and women—sit in a circle around Cyril in the Martyrium with their sponsors standing behind and the faithful also sitting nearby. Cyril's first instruction is called a *procatechesis*. In it he sets out the work of the coming weeks, indicates what he expects of them, assures them of his constant concern for their progress, and holds out the prospect of their entry into the "mystery" of baptism.[30]

From beginning to end, morning prayer, exorcism, and instruction take three hours—6:00 A.M. to 9:00 A.M. (Egeria, 46).

Beginning on Tuesday just after exorcism and for four successive weeks, Cyril selectively reads and comments on the Bible. Unfortunately, none of his biblical homilies (Egeria calls them *catecheses*, 46:2) are extant, but examples from both East and West abound. The closest in time and geography are those of John Chrysostom on Genesis delivered at Antioch (Lent, 386).[31] Chrysostom's are largely moral exhortation (*paraenesis* is the usual term); Cyril's concentrate on the key figures and events of the Bible's history of salvation, each passage, according to Egeria, explained first literally and then spiritually

(46). The emphasis is moral reformation through depicting God's acts in history, especially as they affect the life, character, and deeds of the biblical heroes.

Confiding the Creed

On Monday of the fifth week, the curriculum changes from Bible to creed, which recapitulates under ten headings, or articles, the essentials of Christian belief. But first Cyril delivers three instructions on the origin, nature, and necessity of baptism. Then, in a fourth, he delivers an overall view of the contents of the creed and confides it to them orally, article by article, in a rite he calls *paradoseôs pistin* and the Latins call *traditio symboli*—confiding the creed.[32]

With the help of godparents, family, and friends—not to mention Cyril—the baptizands attempt to commit the creed to memory and to understand its meaning. Over the next two weeks Cyril explores each article of the creed in detail, using the same method as with the Bible—first literal then spiritual. When he comes to the articles about the birth of Jesus from Mary and about his passion, death, and resurrection, it is not lost on the baptizands that prayer, exorcism, and instruction are taking place in close proximity to Bethlehem, Golgotha, Jesus' tomb, the Mount of Olives, Gethsemane, and the mount of the ascension, the places made holy by Jesus' actual presence.

Holy Week[33]

A. LAZARUS SATURDAY

On Saturday of the seventh week, the end is in sight. At ten o'clock in the morning everyone processes to the Church of Lazarus in Bethany—the place where Jesus raised Lazarus from the dead (Jn 11:38–44)—with a stop at the place Jesus met Lazarus' sister Mary (Jn 11:20). A chapel marks the spot.

When the procession gets to the Lazarium (about two miles outside the city), the people spill out over the surrounding fields—the church could not hold them. Carefully chosen readings about Lazarus (Jn 11:45) and hymns about the raising of Lazarus hold their attention. Finally, a priest ascends an elevated spot and intones, "When Jesus came into Bethany six days before the Pasch" (Jn 12:1) to announce the beginning of "Great Week." Egeria notes that in six days Jesus would be arrested (29:6).

On Sunday at cockcrow, the eucharist is celebrated in the Martyrium. At about 9:00 A.M., the baptizands come to the basilica, where Cyril's chair has been set in the apse. One by one they come with their godparents to Cyril. The baptizands, in their proper turn, each recite to Cyril the creed that he had confided and explained to them over the past two weeks (46:5–6), and he comments that they are still only "hearers" of the creed because only baptism will bring them knowledge of the "higher mystery" *(misterii altioris)*.[34]

At 1:00 P.M. everyone, including baptizands, again assembles at the Church of the Eleona on the Mount of Olives, where Jesus was arrested. At three o'clock they move to the Imbomon, the mount of the ascension. At five o'clock, the account of Jesus' triumphal entry into Jerusalem is read (Mt 21:6–11). The crowd, including children with palms in their hands, form a long procession to reenact the entry. Cyril trails the procession, which ends at the Martyrium. Evening prayer (vespers) is celebrated, a prayer is offered at the monument of the cross, and the people go home.

C. HOLY WEEK

The next three days are crammed with dramatic liturgy, generally on the appropriate biblical site. As Great Week's drama unfolds, excitement intensifies as Thursday evening comes. Three eucharists are celebrated to commemorate the Last Supper, the final one in the Upper Church on Mount Zion, the site of the original supper.[35]

Although the baptizands are not allowed to attend the eucharists, they break their fast in honor of the Last Supper and bathe, commemorating Jesus' washing of his disciples' feet.

The entire focus on Friday is the crucifixion, dramatized by the veneration of the cross, which lies on the altar of the Martyrium.[36] Dispersed among the crowds, the baptizands file by to venerate.

At three o'clock in the afternoon, the people congregate in the courtyard before the monument that marks the place where the cross was found. Cyril sits before the monument, a cross, while the passion is read, followed by other New Testament readings interspersed with appropriate psalms. The rite lasts for three hours, the inspiration for the modern Three Hours devotions.

D. SATURDAY VIGIL[37]

The moment for which the baptizands have long and rigorously prepared begins Saturday evening with the lamplighting *(lucenare)* in the Martyrium. The paschal vigil has arrived. Faithful, godparents, friends and family, and those to be baptized assemble in the Martyrium.

The heart of the vigil is twelve readings from the Bible on carefully chosen themes to illuminate the meaning of baptism.[38] For the faithful, it is a review and reminder; for the baptizands, it is a new experience designed to enhance their expectation. Psalm 117 (118) is chanted, and the baptizands respond by saying, "This is the day which the Lord has made." Prayer and kneeling follow each reading, save for the last, when the baptizands are led out of the Martyrium.

The first reading is the entire creation account (Gn 1–3:24). Just as the Spirit hovered over the waters at the original creation, so now the same Spirit hovers over the baptismal waters to create anew. The account of Adam and Eve in the Garden of Eden forms part of the reading because baptism will wash away the baptizands' sins (Adam's and their own) and return them to paradise.

The next reading is about the binding of Isaac (Gn 22:2–18). The account addresses how sin was taken away: the baptizands see in Abraham the Father, and in Isaac, with the wood of his own sacrifice on his back, the crucified Son.

The Passover reading follows, as if to reinforce the Abraham-Isaac typology (Ex 12:1–2): it recalls Jesus as the Lamb of God (Jn 1:29–34), the Passover sacrifice (1 Cor 5:6–8). Jonah (1:1—4:11) is then read to hint at the end—the prophet's three days in the "great fish" prefigure Jesus' three days in the tomb (Mt 12:38–42).

The image of the Red Sea (14:1—15:21) is a central image for baptism: through the waters of baptism the baptizands, like the Israelites, escape the evil that has pursued them for so long. They are on their way to the Promised Land.

The next reading is closer to home: Isaiah's prophetic promise to Jerusalem (Is 60:1–13). Surrounded by night's shadows, yet sitting in a radiant church at the heart of a transformed Jerusalem, the baptizands hear the prophet rehearse the often sad story of their city. In spite of it all, they hear, the city is to rise up in splendor: "Your light has come. . . . Upon you the Lord shines" (Is 60:1–2). They know that they are identified as those about to be illuminated *(photizomenoi)* and, in the morning, to be the newly illuminated.

The readings are interwoven, so that what has been said one way is then said another. The creation account is revisited in God's answer to Job from the whirlwind—actually a series of questions—recapitulating the creation story (38:2–28). The next reading, the assumption of Elijah (2 Kgs 2:1–22), recalls Jonah, who emerges from the belly of the great fish after three days to symbolize resurrection. Given the baptizands' familiarity with the Imbomon, they easily understand what the account prefigures: Jesus' ascension and with it the promise of their own.

As the accounts are woven together and the night advances toward first light, the last four readings emphasize the final destiny of the baptizands' journey to conversion. The ninth reading is from Jeremiah's vision of the new covenant, into which they are about to enter (Jer 31:31–34); the tenth is about Joshua leading Israel into the Promised Land (1:1–9), where they too are headed; and the eleventh is about Ezekiel, who prophesied over the dry bones. When the bones had joined together, Ezekiel summoned the spirit, as Cyril will shortly do, and "they came alive and stood upright" (37:1–14).

The final reading is from the Book of Daniel. Perhaps it is designed to compliment the baptizands on the steadfastness of their conversion thus far and to assure them in the days ahead. The account is about the three youths cast into the furnace because they refused to worship the king's statue (3:1–90). However much the firemen stoke the furnace, the youths walk "about in the flames singing to God and blessing the Lord" (3:24). For songs and blessings, the baptizands have the psalms they had learned in the catechumenate; in spite of the heat of adversity's furnace, they too can sing to God and bless the Lord.

Baptism[39]

With the Daniel reading, the baptizands are led from the Martyrium across the garden court to the cross before which Cyril sat the day before. From there they go to the baptistery next to the Anastasis, a building that contained four rooms: a vestibule running across the front, two side rooms for disrobing and anointing (one for men, one for women), and the baptistery proper.

None of the baptizands know in any detail what is going to take place or what it means. Everything is bound by the discipline of the secret, which ensures that the experience comes first and the explanation only later—during the week following Easter, and then annually for a lifetime. Cyril will give them an initial explanation of the rites and their meaning for five of the seven days that follow Easter, which will be discussed shortly.

A. RENUNCIATION AND ALLEGIANCE

In the dark vestibule, the baptizands, one by one, face the west, stretch forth a hand, and renounce Satan, his works, his pomps, and his service. In doing so, they, perhaps, hiss at the west (exsufflation), the land of darkness and evil. Up to this time, the exorcists had acted on them as if they were passive recipients. Now they stand on their own two feet (often on goatskin, to symbolize the wretchedness of their fallen condition) and in their own voices break their ancient pact with Satan.

They are then free to turn to the east—the land of the rising sun, the direction of paradise, and the place of the baptismal font, now illuminated. They make a new pact with a simple profession: "I believe in the Father, and in the Son, and in the Holy Spirit, and in one baptism of repentance."[40]

B. ANOINTING

The baptizands are then led to their respective anointing rooms, where they are anointed with olive oil from head to toe for the last drama of the struggle with Satan.

C. IMMERSION

Newly anointed and naked, they join in procession to the baptismal font—as Cyril puts it: "Just as Christ was carried from the cross to the tomb."[41] They are not allowed to forget where they are: on Golgotha, across from the place of the crucifixion, and near the tomb in the Anastasis. Each baptizand enters the pool and is immersed three times.

There is no record of the words said—perhaps none were—but Cyril makes dramatically clear the significance of the rite:

> What a strange and astonishing situation! We did not really die, we were not really buried, we did not really hang from a cross and rise again. All this he did gratuitously for us [on this very site], so that we might share his sufferings by imitating them, and gain salvation in actuality. . . . So in order that we may realize that Christ endured all his sufferings for us and our salvation actually and not in make

believe, and that we share in his pains, Paul cried out the literal truth: "If we have been planted together with him in a death like his death, we shall certainly be planted together with him in a resurrection like his" [Rom 6:5—part of the reading for the homily].[42]

Long before Cyril, Tertullian had characterized the ancient conviction about the power of ritual: "Flesh is the hinge of salvation *(caro est cardo)*";[43] Cyril emphasizes its mimetic power and effect: the baptizands individually enact in rite and symbol the hallowed events of crucifixion and resurrection in the very place of their happening and, as Cyril sees it, participate in what the events accomplished.[44] The ritual is their assurance.

D. POSTBAPTISMAL ANOINTING

After they come up from the font, the newly baptized are anointed with aromatic oil *(myron/chrisma)* first on the forehead that they may be without pride, then on the ears that they may hear the divine mysteries, then on the nostrils that they may know the sweet savor of Christ, and finally on the chest that they may have the armor of Christ against assaults of the devil.[45]

The imposition of hands immediately follows. Although Cyril insists that the anointing reenacts Christ's baptism in the Jordan, it especially signifies the descent of the Spirit.

Now, at long last, the newly baptized can say, as in the *Gospel of Philip*, "I am a Christian," for they are "anointed ones *(christoi)*."

The Far Side of Baptism

A. THE WHITE GARMENT, THE LORD'S PRAYER, AND THE EUCHARIST

The newly baptized put on white garments and process to the tomb from which Christ rose, to the Anastasis, symbolizing their resurrection. Then they process to the Martyrium where, with the faithful, they celebrate their first eucharist.

They are both baffled and silent; the eucharist is unfamiliar. Only later in the following week will they be instructed about the rite and its meaning.

B. EASTER WEEK

Each day during the week following, the newly baptized (Cyril calls them "newly illuminated"; Egeria, "infants," 38:1) assemble in their white garments with the faithful for a variety of rites, about which

Cyril does not speak and Egeria is far from clear, save that they celebrate the "eight days of Easter till a late hour" (38:2). The heart of the
celebrations is the daily eucharist, during which Cyril explains the rites
that they had experienced during the vigil and Easter dawn.

His homilies are called "Mystagogical Catecheses." Cyril seeks to
initiate the newly baptized into the deep-buried significance of the rites
by interweaving biblical account and symbol with ritual enactment, the
site of the rite, and the images of Palestinian culture. The task of the
mystagogue was to help the newly initiated reflect on the meaning of
the rites they had experienced; Cyril's are the earliest Christian mystagogical instructions we have.

Ever since the time and work of Clement of Alexandria (d. c.
215 C.E.), the mystery cults had left their mark on Christian thinking
and practice. As Cyril's understanding of Christian initiation indicates,
the early church was much influenced by the cults and the high opinion
the ancients had about their rites.

Cicero praised Greece for them:

> Your Athens was the source of many great and wonderful benefits
> to the human race, but I think that none is greater than those mys-
> teries which refined our uncouth rustic lives and made us humane
> and gentle.[46]

Aelius Aristides (c. 120–181 C.E.), the rhetorician whose *Sacred
Teachings* is a unique account of Pagan religious experience, hailed the
celebrated Eleusinian mysteries:

> The effect of the festival is not only immediate pleasure or release
> from past misfortunes, but with regard to death they have fairer
> hopes that they will enjoy a happier existence and not lie in the
> darkness and mud that are in store for the uninitiated.[47]

And Egeria often remarks about how moved the participants were: their
shouts, laments, and ululations could be heard all across the city (36:3;
37:7; 34).

VI. Conclusion

Nowhere in antiquity—Pagan, Jewish, or Christian—do we have a
clearer and more dramatic picture of conversion as a ritual process than

in Egeria's *Diary* and Cyril's baptismal homilies. The Jerusalemites, baptizands and baptized, confirmed in word and deed the anthropological axiom: "People express in ritual what moves them most."[48]

The Lenten catechumenate in Jerusalem created a new world for the baptizands. Its center was Jerusalem—not the earthly Jerusalem of old, but the transformed Jerusalem with its numerous holy places, an icon through which the heavenly Jerusalem could be glimpsed. As if on an axis, their new world revolved around the holy in a universe otherwise perceived as dark, evil, and in the power of Satan.

Their new world offered a new experience of space and time. Going to the cross in the courtyard or to the Martyrium, the baptizands were going to the crucifixion; going to the Lazarium in Bethany, to the resurrection of Lazarus; going to Bethlehem, to the birth of Jesus; going to the Anastasis, to his resurrection; going to the Imbomon, to his ascension. And going, they were cumulatively sharing, we read, in what those events had achieved: birth, death, resurrection, and ascension—transformation. What the baptizands enacted in ritual, according to Cyril, they achieved in reality in the here and now, and in full and permanent measure then, at the end of life.

The Lenten catechumenate is a striking example of what contemporary research has identified as encapsulation, a procedure developed to teach something new, especially a new set of values and way of life.[49] Encapsulation has three aspects: the physical, the social, and the ideological.

Physical encapsulation occurs when people—in our case, potential converts—are separated from their usual contacts and way of life. A monastery or even a classroom are examples. The catechumens at Jerusalem were separated from their daily horarium, usual haunts, and customary food and drink. The Lenten liturgy gave them a new horarium, haunts, and food and drink. They moved into the world of the holy, and even their dress—the penitential tunic—was different.

A new set of contacts and relationships encapsulated them socially. The baptizands' personal contacts were restricted to Cyril, their godparents, the exorcists, the other baptizands, and the faithful. Marital intercourse was not permitted. The baths and the society of the baths were out of bounds (except for Thursday of Great Week). One can only guess at the social impact of their conversion, since neither Cyril nor Egeria speak about the baptizands' families, employers, or social networks. It is clear, however, that they were in an extended rite of passage from their former communities into a new community that held out the promise of a new family and social network for them.

But most of all the baptizands were encapsulated ideologically. They had been given a new worldview, including a new code of values and conduct, a view inculcated cognitively and performatively. For seven of the eight weeks, the cognitive predominated. Cyril taught the models of belief and practice from his chair daily: the syllabus called for the history of salvation from creation to the Promised Land and the ten articles of the creed.

In the eighth week, ritual took over. What the baptizands had learned, they now enacted at the Lazarium, the Eleona, the Church of the Nativity, the Martyrium, the Anastasis. Finally, in the baptistery they died to an old self and way of life in an old Jerusalem and rose to a new self and way of life in the new Jerusalem. As one contemporary researcher puts it, "Ritual action is a means by which its participants discover who they are in the world and 'how it is' with the world."[50]

Such was the nature of the ritual process of conversion in fourth-century Jerusalem.

NOTES

1. For the reasons, see R. M. Grant, "The Christian Population of the Roman Empire," in R. M. Grant, ed., *Early Christianity and Society: Seven Studies* (New York: Harper & Row, 1977) 1–12, especially 7.

2. Ibid. 10. His source is H. Grégoire and M. A. Kugener, *Marc le Diacre: Vie de Porphyre* (Paris, 1930); see also A. H. M. Jones, *Cities of the Eastern Roman Provinces* (Oxford: Oxford University Press, 1937) 502–40, especially 534.

3. Chrysostom, *Homilies on Matthew* 85:3–4 (PG 58:761–64).

4. For discussion, see my "Ritual Process and the Survival of Early Christianity: A Study of the *Apostolic Tradition* of Hippolytus," *JRS* 3 (1989) 69–72.

5. *Itinerarium Burdigalense* (P. Geyer and O. Cuntz, eds., CCL 175; John Wilkinson, trans., *Egeria's Travels* [London: SPCK, 1971] 163). See Francine Cardman, "Fourth Century Jerusalem: Religious Geography and Christian Tradition," in *Schools of Thought in the Christian Tradition,* ed. Patrick Henry (Philadelphia: Fortress Press, 1984) 49–64, especially 51–52: Melito of Sardis, Justin Martyr, the Pilgrim from Bordeaux, and Origen are mentioned. But see also a study that brings together the scholarship, recent

and older, on the Jerusalem church and its most celebrated bishop, Cyril of Jerusalem: Alexis J. Doval, *The Authorship of the Mystagogic Catecheses Attributed to St. Cyril of Jerusalem* (Dissertation, Oxford University, Faculty of Theology, 1992), especially 18–38.

6. For the account, see Eusebius, *Historia ecclesiastica* 6:1–4 (G. Bardy, ed., *Eusèbe de Césarée: Histoire ecclésiastique, livres I–IV,* SC 31 [1978], 165–66).

7. Epiphanius, *Treatise on Weights and Measures* 54C, cited in Wilkinson, *Egeria's Travels,* 38; on the "Mother of all Churches," see Cardman, "Fourth Century Jerusalem," 52.

8. Eusebius, *Hist. eccl.* 4:5 (Bardy, SC 31:163–64); in the next (4:6), he describes the siege, interdiction, destruction, and renaming (SC 31: 165–66). But see Robert L. Wilken, *The Land Called Holy* (New Haven: Yale University Press, 1992) 81–85.

9. See Wilken, *The Land Called Holy,* 109–22; Susanna Elm, "Perceptions of Jerusalem Pilgrimage as Reflected in Two Early Sources on Female Pilgrimage (3d and 4th Centuries)," *SP* 20 (1989) 219–23; Cardman, "Fourth Century Jerusalem," especially 54–64; and Doval, *"Mystagogic Catecheses,"* 33–38.

10. For a brief account of the church building history in and around Jerusalem in the fourth and fifth centuries, see John F. Baldovin, *Liturgy in Ancient Jerusalem,* GLS 57 (1989). For an extended discussion, see Wilkinson, *Egeria's Travels,* 36–53. For a recent account of the location of the baptistery and for extensive drawings of all three buildings, see Alexis J. Doval, "The Location and Structure of the Baptistery in the *Mystagogic Catecheses* of Cyril of Jerusalem," *SP* 26 (1993) 1–13. At the end of the study he wonders (with no attempt to answer) whether it was built by Constantine.

11. Doval cautions that the rebirth and growth of the Christian community in the city did not mean complete Christianization—there was still a large non-Christian population, and it remained an urban center with a diverse population (*"Mystagogic Catecheses,"* 34–35).

12. See Wilken, *The Land Called Holy,* 108–25; and Cardman, "Fourth Century Jerusalem," especially 53–55 and n. 9, for a valuable select bibliography.

13. See Doval, *"Mystagogic Catecheses,"* 38–48, for a summary of the scholarship.

14. Cyril, *Procatechesis* 6 (PG 33:344).

15. See Cyril, *Procat.* 4–5 (PG 33:340–44).

16. Cyril, *Procat.* 6 (PG 33:345).

17. Thus Cyril's *Procat.* (PG 33:332–65): it is a protreptic for baptism. See also Chrysostom, *Baptismal Instruction* 1 (Antoine Wenger, *Jean Chrysostome: Huit catéchèses baptismales,* SC 50 [1957]). For the West,

see William Harmless, *Augustine and the Catechumenate* (Collegeville: Liturgical Press [A Pueblo Book], 1995) 244–50.

18. Cyril, *Procat.* 7 (PG 33:345). For the reasons, see my *The Liturgy of Baptism in the Baptismal Instructions of St. John Chrysostom,* SCA 15 (1967) 27–30; and J. A. Jungmann, *The Early Liturgy: To the Time of Gregory the Great,* trans. F. Brunner (South Bend: University of Notre Dame Press [Liturgical Studies 6], 1959) 240–52. On the penitential system, see Robert Taft, "Penance in Contemporary Scholarship," *SL* 18 (1988) 2–22, especially 2–9. Only in the third century does a penitential rite appear. It was once-in-a-lifetime severe penance for grave postbaptismal crimes (apostasy, murder, and adultery); the rite included accusation (or self-accusation), admission of guilt, community prayer, a lengthy period of penance, and reconciliation through the bishop. In the sixth-century West it began to wane; in the East it first appears in a letter from Fimilian of Caesarea to Cyprian of Carthage, and by the end of the fourth century begins to lose its hold. See also Paul De Clerck, "Pénitence seconde et conversion quotidienne aux IIIème et IVème siècles," *SP* 20 (1989) 352–74, especially 360–65, on the second penance.

19. Chrysostom, *Bapt. Instr.* 9:9 (PG 49:224–25).

20. See Edward J. Yarnold, "The Baptism of Constantine," *SP* 26 (1993) 95–101. In the fifth century the account of his baptism was sanitized because it was an Arian, Eusebius of Nicomedia, who baptized him. The new account, which appears in the *Liber Pontificalis,* had him baptized at the Lateran shortly after the battle at the Milvian Bridge in 311; a monument marks the spot outside the Basilica of St. John Lateran.

21. The fast appears in the second festal letter of Athanasius (330) announcing the date of Easter and the beginning of the fast. For discussion of origins and development, see Thomas J. Talley, *The Origins of the Liturgical Year* (New York: Pueblo Books, 1986) 168–74.

22. Egeria, *Itinerarium* 27:1 (Pierre Maraval, ed., *Égérie: Journal de voyage [Itinéraire] et Valerius du Bierzo: Lettre sur la B^se Égérie,* SC 296 [1982] 258). See Doval, *"Mystagogic Catecheses,"* 48–58, for summary of the evolution of Lent and the catechetical program.

23. Victor Turner, *The Ritual Process: Structure and Antistructure* (Chicago: Aldine Press, 1969) 185. See also my "Ritual Process and the Survival of Early Christianity: A Study of the *Apostolic Tradition* of Hippolytus," 69–89, especially 78–79.

24. The texts for Cyril are in PG 33:331–1064; for the most recent edition of the *Mystagogic Catecheses,* see August Piédagnel, *Cyrille de Jérusalem: Catéchèses mystagogiques,* SC 126 (1966). The first nineteen are translated in William Telfer, ed., *Cyril of Jerusalem and Nemesius of Emesa* (Philadelphia: Westminster Press [Library of Christian Classics 4], 1955); all are translated in LNPF 7:1–143. For the instructions on the rites (the

Mystagogic Catecheses), see Edward J. Yarnold, *The Awe-Inspiring Rites of Initiation: The Origins of the R.C.I.A.,* 2nd ed. (Collegeville: Liturgical Press, 1994). For a recent study of the rites, see Baldovin, *Liturgy in Ancient Jerusalem,* GLS 57:11–44. Of critical importance is Doval, *"Mystagogic Catecheses."* For Cyril as a mystagogue, see Enrico Mazza, "Mystagogie: Pensée liturgique d'aujourd'hui et liturgie ancienne," in A. M. Triacca and A. Pistoia, eds., *Conférences Saint-Serge XXXIXᵉ semaine d'études liturgiques* (Rome: Edizioni Liturgiche [Ephemerides Liturgicae Subsidia] 1993) 203–26. And for Cyril and the mysteries, see Edward J.Yarnold, "Baptism and the Pagan Mysteries in the Fourth Century," *Heythrop Journal* 13 (1972) 247–67, especially 259–63.

25. There are two disputed issues about the preparatory instructions: (1) the number of the instructions and (2) the days when they were delivered. It is possible that the eighteenth instruction on the creed is in fact two instructions, but not necessarily. Further, the way in which the instructions have been distributed in Lent is difficult to reconcile with what Egeria describes. The distribution that commends itself best is that the instructions on the creed were delivered Monday through Saturday during weeks five, six, and seven of Lent. For discussion of the problems and proposed solution, see Maxwell E. Johnson, "Reconciling Cyril and Egeria on the Catechetical Process in Fourth-Century Jerusalem," in Paul F. Bradshaw, ed., *Essays in Early Eastern Initiation,* GLS 56:18–30, especially 28–29.

26. For the texts and translations, see Maraval, SC 296; the letter is edited and translated by Manuel C. Díaz y Díaz. For English translations, see Wilkinson, *Egeria's Travels;* and George E. Gingras, ed., *Egeria: Diary of a Pilgrimage* (New York: Paulist Press [ACW 38], 1970). For a detailed study, see Wilkinson, *Egeria's Travels,* 3–88; and the introductions in Maraval and Gingras. For Egeria's identity, see Hagith Sivan, "Who Was Egeria? Piety and Pilgrimage in the Age of Gratian," *HTR* 81 (1988) 59–72, especially 71–72; and his "Holy Land Pilgrimage and Western Audiences: Reflections on Egeria and Her Circle," *Classical Quarterly* 38 (1988) 528–35. For a study of the contrast between Cyril and Eusebius on the Holy City, see P. W. L. Walker, "Eusebius, Cyril, and the Holy Places," *SP* 20 (1989) 306–14; Walker notes that it is an outline of his thesis, *Fourth Century Christian Attitudes to Jerusalem and the Holy Land: A Comparison of Eusebius of Caesarea and Cyril of Jerusalem* (Dissertation, Cambridge University, 1987). Again, of critical importance is Doval, *"Mystagogic Catecheses"*: Egeria is a primary witness in his attempt to identify Cyril as the author of the mystagogic catecheses.

27. Egeria, *Itin.* 45:1–20 (Maraval, SC 296:304–6; Gingras, ACW 38: 122–23).

28. Egeria, *Itin.* 27:9–28:4 (Maraval, SC 296:264–66).

29. Egeria, *Itin.* 46:1 (Maraval, SC 296:306); Cyril, *Procat.* 1:3; *Cat.* 1:1, 5; 2:19–20 (PG 33:336–37; 369, 376–77; 408) for what follows.

30. Cyril, *Procat.* (PG 33:332–66).

31. Chrysostom, *Hom. on Gen.* 9 (PG 54:581–63). There are two series on Genesis (consisting of nine and sixty-seven homilies), which, together, constitute a commentary on the entire book.

32. Cyril, *Cat.* 4 (PG 33:457B).

33. Cyril, *Cat.* 14:10 (PG 33:836–37); Egeria, *Itin.* 30:1 (Maraval, SC 296:270, *septimana maior*). For Egeria on Holy Week in Jerusalem, see 30:1–38:2 (SC 296:270–92); Wilkinson, *Egeria's Travels,* 73–76; and Baldovin, *Liturgy in Ancient Jerusalem,* 39–41.

34. Egeria, *Itin.* 46:6 (Maraval, SC 296:312).

35. Baldovin, *Liturgy in Ancient Jerusalem,* 40.

36. Egeria, *Itin.* 37:2 (Maraval, SC 296:286).

37. For discussion, see Thomas J. Talley, *The Origins of the Liturgical Year,* 47–54. Egeria says little.

38. For baptismal typology, see Jean Daniélou, *The Bible and the Liturgy* (Notre Dame: University of Notre Dame Press [Liturgical Studies], 1956); and his *From Shadows to Reality: Studies in Biblical Typology,* trans. Wulstan Hibberd (London: Burns and Oates; Westminster, Md.: Newman Press, 1960). The types not familiar to the catechetical tradition, though specific to Jerusalem, are Isaiah's promise to Jerusalem and Ezekiel's dry bones; Daniel's three young men in the furnace is not one of the traditional baptismal types.

39. The chief witness is Cyril, *Mystagogic Catecheses* (PG 33: 1065–93); see A. Piédagnel, *Cyrille de Jérusalem.* For a brief treatment, see Baldovin, *Liturgy in Ancient Jerusalem,* GLS 57:15–20. The most recent translation is that of Yarnold, *The Awe-Inspiring Rites,* 70–97.

40. Cyril, *Myst. cat.* 1:9 (Piédagnel, SC 126:98). See Cyril, *Cat.* 18:22 (PG 33:1044): the phrase about one repentance does not appear in any other fourth-century creed.

41. Cyril, *Myst. cat.* 2:4 (Piédagnel, SC 126:110).

42. Cyril, *Myst. cat.* 20:5,7 (PG 33:1081, 1084; Yarnold, *The Awe-Inspiring Rites,* 78–79).

43. See Chapter 7: Tertullian, *On the Resurrection of the Flesh* 8 (PL 2:806).

44. For discussion, see my *ECBC* 5:8–10. I have compared the thinking and explanations of Cyril, Chrysostom, and Theodore of Mopsuestia in my "Baptismal Death and Resurrection: A Study in Fourth Century Eastern Baptismal Theology," *Worship* 43 (1969) 175–89. For the Christian mysteries in Jerusalem and the Pagan mysteries, see Yarnold, *The Awe-Inspiring Rites,* 59–66.

45. Cyril, *Myst. cat.* 3:4 (Piédagnel, SC 126:126).

46. Cicero, *De legibus* 2:36, cited in Yarnold, *The Awe-Inspiring Rites,* 63.

47. Aristides, *Eleusinios* 259, cited in Yarnold, *The Awe-Inspiring Rites,* 63.

48. Monica Wilson, "Nyakyusa Ritual and Symbolism," *American Anthropologist* 56 (1954) 230.

49. For the role of encapsulation in the conversion characteristic of interaction with the new religious reality, see Lewis R. Rambo, *Understanding Religious Conversion* (New Haven: Yale University Press, 1993) 103–8.

50. Theodore W. Jennings, "On Ritual Knowledge," *Journal of Religion* 62 (1982) 113, cited in Rambo, *Understanding Religious Conversion,* 114.

Chapter 9

THE FOURTH CENTURY: CONVERSION IN MILAN

I. Introduction

The Holy City was the most striking example of the church's move from catacombs to forum, but all the major cities of the empire experienced transformations: Byzantium became New Rome; old Rome became the city of the pope; Antioch, the location of the famed Golden Church; Nicaea and Ephesus, the sites of major ecumenical councils; Edessa, the religious capital of the Syriac world.

In addition, the catechumenate and baptismal rites in Jerusalem can be found around and beyond the Mediterranean in great variety. To see the variety, Egeria might take us north to Antioch, where we would find four accounts of catechumenate and baptism, two of them in sets of baptismal instructions recovered only in this century (1932 and 1957). One comes from the most celebrated preacher in the Greek East, John Chrysostom; the other comes from the most revered bishop in Eastern Christendom, Theodore of Mopsuestia.[1] The other two are Church Orders: *The Testament of the Lord,* compiled about the middle of the fourth century, and the *Apostolic Constitutions,* compiled shortly before 380—both deeply indebted to the *Apostolic Tradition.*[2]

Egeria might also take us south to Egypt, where we would find three more accounts. One is an adaptation of Hippolytus: *The Canons of Hippolytus.*[3] The second, which exists in Coptic, Arabic, and Ethiopian, was known as the *Egyptian Church Order* until two scholars working independently at the beginning of this century showed that the original document on which the versions depended was the *Apostolic*

Tradition.[4] The third, the *Sacramentary of Sarapion,* was compiled about 350 by Sarapion, bishop of Thmuis in Egypt; it contains thirty prayers, seven of which concern baptism.[5]

Egeria could also take us east to Edessa (modern Urfa in eastern Turkey) to see Syriac-speaking Christianity with its distinctive ascetic, literary, ritual, and theological characteristics.[6] Two celebrated Syriac Christian holy men could guide us through the conversion process: the first, a Persian sage, Aphrahat, whose *Demonstrations,* written in the mid-fourth century, provides fleeting glances; the second, a Syrian, Ephrem the Deacon of Edessa, lays out the rich symbolism of the rites in didactic hymns and chanted homilies.[7]

In Syria we would find adult baptism the norm. Combining the Jordan and Pentecost patterns, the baptismal ritual reenacted in rite and symbol Christ's baptism in the Jordan and emphasized baptism as rebirth through the descent of the Holy Spirit. A distinctive feature of the conversion process in East Syria was that catechumens determined to lead celibate lives in the service of the church made their ascetic commitment in baptism. They were known as the "Daughters and Sons of the Covenant"; Aphrahat and Ephrem were both Sons of the Covenant.

Studying conversion in Syria and in Egypt would add local color and distinctive details, but the enterprise would not change in any substantial way what we already know of the extended ritual process that refashioned the lives, values, and conduct of catechumens, baptizands, and the newly baptized.

Rather than more knowledge of the process, we need a convert who wrote about the experience, the autobiography of a convert. For that we must go west to Milan, the administrative capital of the Western Roman Empire, to meet a bishop, Ambrose, and his most celebrated convert, Augustine, whose conversion story, the *Confessions,* shaped all subsequent Western thinking about conversion.

II. Ambrose

The fourth century witnessed doctrinal turmoil that embroiled not only Cyril of Jerusalem—he was exiled three times—but also Christian emperors, leaders, thinkers, and lay people from west Gaul all the way to East Syria. The cause of the turmoil was a divisive question: In what sense is Christ, the son of God, divine? The answer was given in 325 at the Council of Nicaea: as son of God, Christ is what his Father is, divine in nature; Son and Father are consubstantial.

The answer provoked more tumult than the question had, pitting anti-Nicene Christians, customarily called Arians, and Nicene Christians against each other, sometimes violently (as religious controversy is wont to do even today).

Stepping into the middle of the controversy in Milan was Ambrose, the forty-year-old governor *(consularis)* of the province.[8] The year was 374 (the fall); the place, the New Basilica (Milan's cathedral);[9] the occasion, the death of the Arian bishop Auxentius; the reason, the restoration of order among the Milanese Christians in an uproar about who should succeed Auxentius. Things were about to turn violent.

Ambrose, a closet Nicene Christian, left the basilica as the reluctant bishop-elect of Milan. There were problems about the election that focused on two questions: (1) He was still a catechumen, was he not, and not even a petitioner *(competens)* for baptism? and (2) Was the election valid?

The first was answered with dispatch. Within the month Ambrose decided to accept the election, put himself in the hands of the man he would come to call his father, Simplicianus, for instruction (as Augustine later would), and was baptized on November 30, 374. With imperial approval, a week later he was consecrated bishop. Thus, Ambrose was no longer just a catechumen. Further, the emperor's consent coupled with the presence of provincial bishops at the election—whatever the irregularities—made the consecration valid.

Although Ambrose's conversion from catechumen to bishop was telescoped into weeks, with no reference to liturgical season and Lenten catechumenate, two facts justified the haste: (1) with Auxentius dead, Christians in the basilica insistently chanted their demand, "Ambrose for bishop," and (2) long-standing tradition sanctioned the primacy of circumstance, character, and conduct in determining when to baptize.[10]

Further, born and raised in a Christian household, Ambrose had long been initiated into the catechumenate with the rites then customary in Gaul (Trier, where he was born): a priest had imposed his hand on his forehead, traced the sign of the cross on it, and given him salt to taste.[11] From then on, his initiation into the Christian way was through day-to-day immersion in the Christianity of his home and city (Trier and Rome), including regular attendance at church. As we have seen in Jerusalem, immersion in the baptismal font could wait until the fires of youth had become home fires.

To be sure, the details of his upbringing are lost to us, but the stormy twenty-four years after his consecration as bishop would prove the mettle of the convert-bishop as he attempted to juggle the roles of diplomat, leader, and pastor. He did so deftly, if sometimes defiantly, where emperors were concerned.

III. Augustine, Catechumen

Our major interests, however, are Ambrose, the bishop, and Augustine, the catechumen, who himself would become the bishop of Hippo (modern Bône, Algeria), eventually replacing Ambrose as the leading Latin churchman of the West.

The Biography of a Convert[12]

A. THE EARLY YEARS (354–370)

Augustine was born in 354 in Thagaste (modern Souk Ahras, Algeria) to a pagan father, Patricius, and a Catholic mother, Monica. Like many other fourth-century converts (including Ambrose), he started life as a catechumen. His mother raised him as an attentive Catholic Christian. He regularly attended that part of the eucharist devoted to biblical readings and a homily—he came to call it the "Mass of the Catechumens"—and shared with his mother a variety of popular North African Catholic devotions. He prayed regularly; he reports that he drank in the name of Christ with his mother's milk, and even begged for baptism as a very sick youngster. In short, he grew up a devout Catholic, though his mother delayed his baptism, divining that he was and would be a handful.

In school Augustine proved a gifted child—one driven hard by parents ambitious for his career. Respectable property owners but far from affluent, they scraped together enough money to send him at fifteen to study at the university town of Madauros (369–370), the town of Apuleius and the *Metamorphoses*.

Strapped finances forced Augustine to drop out the next year, during which his parents scraped up more funds, this time to send him to Carthage to study rhetoric.

B. CARTHAGE (371–374)

The next year, 371, Augustine went to Carthage to complete his education, as it turned out, in more ways than one. Carthage, he recalls, was "the cauldron of illicit loves [that] leapt and boiled around me."[13] But ingrained habit prompted him to maintain Catholic religious practice, especially to attend the Mass of the Catechumens, where, it seems, he saw, met, and fell in love with the young woman with whom he would live for fifteen years, the mother of his son Adeodatus. We never learn her name.

In his rhetoric curriculum, Augustine also learned about philosophy in a work we have already met, Cicero's *Hortensius*. The work, now lost, was the orator's exhortation to lead a philosophical way of life demanding the single-minded pursuit of wisdom—a protreptic. The encounter had a lasting impact; the *Hortensius* altered his approach to God in prayer, gave him new values and priorities, and instilled in him ardor for the pursuit of wisdom for its own sake, wherever it might lead.

Although he speaks as if the encounter were the beginning of his conversion—"I began to arise and return to you"[14]—he means that Cicero had taught him about the love of a wisdom infinitely beyond the narrow confines of his ambition for honor and distinction.

The rhetoric courses quickly persuaded the eighteen-year-old student that the literary quality of the Old Latin version of the Bible and its God were no match for the classical literature and the hero-world he was studying (and mastering at the top of his class). Even so, his rearing as a catechumen had left its mark: he missed the name of Christ in his rhetoric books, a name he had drunk in with his mother's milk, a name so deeply part of him that no book "however well written or polished or true, could . . . entirely grip me."[15]

Paradoxically, while he was turning away from God in the classroom and on the streets of Carthage, he was also turning toward him: his discovery of divine wisdom was the first conscious movement of his return. His second conscious movement was sheer happenstance: he "blundered into" *(incidi)* a group of Manichaean Christians,[16] who had finely bound and decorated books from which they educed fascinating truths, which appealed to Augustine's fertile and hungry mind, a mind restive with what he considered the infantile follies of his Catholic Christianity.[17] Part of the attraction of Manichaeism was the requirement that adherents understand what they believed, a demand that fit perfectly with Augustine's dedication to the rational pursuit of truth.

At this point, now nineteen, Augustine began to slip his Catholic moorings. He frequented both the Manichaean and the Catholic liturgies and enrolled eventually as a "hearer" (*auditor,* catechumen) among the Manichees.[18] To many, his new allegiance and status precluded continued affiliation with the church: the doctrinal differences were sharp and the hostility bitter between the two—he took the Manichaean side in the feud. Nonetheless, there is some reason to think that he retained the status of catechumen in both, leading a double religious life.[19] In any case, Augustine eventually came to understand that the steps he took away from church paradoxically were steps back to it.

C. FROM CARTHAGE TO HOME AND BACK (375–383)

By the end of his rhetoric course (374), the newly minted rhetorician had decided to return to Thagaste to open a school of grammar and rhetoric. He returned an ardent Manichee—so much to his mother's horror that she would not let him live at home. But Thagaste quickly lost its savor, for his best friend died that year.

Devastated, Augustine returned to Carthage to continue his career in rhetoric with striking success. He made many friends, even the proconsul of Africa, Vindicianus (379–382); he read widely in Aristotle and the philosophers; he acquired a mastery of mathematics; and he published a well-received book, *On the Beautiful and the Fitting* (380 or 381).

In spite of what seemed unbroken success, by 383 disenchantment began to settle in. His ardor for the Manichees was cooling because, while they held out the promise of acquiring the fullness of truth for their adherents, they seemed to withhold it—perhaps, because he was not one of the perfect.

As a result, unanswered questions mounted. He pinned his hope for answers on the visit of a Manichaean bishop in 382. The bishop, Faustus, was their leading thinker and apologist. Although an able and disarming speaker and a person of candor and engaging personality, Faustus proved a grave disappointment to Augustine. He could not answer the questions the young intellectual had stored up, and he lacked the wide-ranging quality of liberal learning that Augustine expected. Instead they talked about literature that interested the bishop—parlor games in the place of penetrating analysis.

In addition to his intellectual and religious frustration, the rowdyism of his students in Carthage proved unendurably frustrating. By fall 383, he had had enough and set sail for Rome, encouraged by those who advised him that rowdyism did not characterize Roman students.[20]

D. ROME AND MILAN (384–385): PHILOSOPHY

Augustine was initially enchanted by the city, whose elegance and excellence were the center of his rhetorical education and teaching. But disenchantment quickly heated up the disillusion that had set in at Carthage. He fell gravely ill on arrival. Upon recovery, he discovered a sharp, if nonrowdy, student practice: they clubbed together and transferred to another teacher just as the fee (one gold *solidus*) came due. Besides, difficulties with Manichaean teaching mounted. The nub of the problem was the doctrine that God and evil are irreconcilable material substances.[21]

His winter of discontent—and it was winter when it set in completely—opened his mind to the school of Academics, for whom, he writes, everything is a matter of doubt and truth lay "beyond human capacity."[22] Little wonder that a besieged Augustine fell into a funk of skepticism and felt religiously adrift. But his connections saved the day. The Manichees and a friendly and powerful city prefect, Symmachus, helped him secure appointment to the municipal chair of rhetoric in Milan. He moved there in early autumn 384.

E. MILAN (385–387)

The excitement of a new (and exalted) beginning, coupled with membership in the city's circle of intellectuals, enthralled him. Some of the circle were Christians, including Ambrose, on whom he paid a courtesy call. The bishop received him warmly and with grace.

Through the circle, he discovered the Neoplatonist philosophers Plotinus and Porphyry, whose books disabused him of his Manichaean materialism: they showed him that God, as spirit, is the incorruptible, infinite, and eternal creator of all that exists, and that evil, far from being a substance, is the absence or privation of being. In addition, he learned from his Neoplatonist mentors that the divine self was buried deep within him, awaiting only discovery, a discovery that he sought by introspection:

> By the Platonic books I was admonished to return into myself. . . .
> I entered and saw with my soul's eye. . . . When I first came to
> know you, you raised me up to make me see that what I saw is
> Being, and that I who saw am not yet Being.[23]

The impact of the Neoplatonists on Augustine poses a difficult question: Was he converted to Neoplatonism at this point?[24] He had turned away from skepticism and from Manichaeism; he was captivated by the sense of elevation that his assent to God as "Being" gave him; he committed himself to a life of contemplation and philosophical exploration with a circle of like-minded friends; and he was astonished "to discover that I was already loving you, not a phantom surrogate for you."[25]

Augustine was certain that the Platonists had the true idea of God, and he agreed with them that a mediator who combined Being and not-yet-Being—creator and creature—was necessary for people to be united with God in a stable union. The problem was that the Neoplatonic mediators were creatures *(daimones)* and, in Augustine's view, inadequate to the task—the mediator needed a true divinity and a true humanity.[26] In their books he missed the human face of God; for that he would have to turn to other books—the scriptures, the very books, however crude their Latin, that had first formed in his mind such an image.[27]

F. AMBROSE AND THE RESUMED CATECHUMENATE (385–386)

While Augustine was reading the Neoplatonists he was listening to Ambrose, through whose gifted interpretation of the Bible Augustine learned a new way of reading scripture.[28]

In the process of rehabilitating the Bible in Augustine's mind, Ambrosian rhetoric rehabilitated the church for him as well. He resumed his old ways—attending the Mass of the Catechumens and, though with no desire other than the charm of Ambrosian rhetoric, found that "together with the words which I was enjoying, the subject matter . . . came to make an entry into my mind and so for the time being [I decided] to be a catechumen in the Catholic Church. . . . "[29] Even though he admits to a faith rough and hesitant,[30] he was no longer a Manichee or a Neoplatonist.

The rest of the events that led to Augustine's conversion happened within the context of his resumed catechumenate. Every Sunday Augustine heard Ambrose preach, and gradually he came to see from a more sophisticated perspective the religion of his birth:

I was being turned around [convertebar]. And I was glad, my
God, that your one Church, the body of your only Son in which
Christ's name was put on me as an infant, did not hold infantile
follies.[31]

G. THE SUMMER OF 386

Thus far Augustine had made his tortuous journey along the ritual
paths of the church of his birth, which, in spite of his long detour into
Manichaeism, had stamped their mark on him. The last leg of his journey now began, not to find more certainty, but "to be more stable in
you."[32]

In the summer of 386, Augustine, as Ambrose once had done,
put himself in the hands of Simplicianus, himself a convert from
Paganism and now an aged and venerable priest. Among other things,
Simplicianus recounted for him the conversion of the celebrated
Neoplatonist philosopher Marius Victorinus in Rome some thirty years
before (c. 355). Augustine, who knew the philosopher's work, could
not miss the parallels in his own life. Shortly thereafter (July 386),
Augustine was invited to stay at a villa in Milan. There he heard several
more conversion stories, including that of the Egyptian Antony, the
architect of desert monasticism, and of two court officials (fellow
North Africans) who were baptized and immediately adopted the
ascetic life. Again, he saw the parallels.

He was also studying the letters of Paul, who painted the human
face of God in deft and strong strokes for him, and whose conversion
suggested still further parallels (2 Cor 12:1–10).[33]

The internal tension mounted. One early-August day in the villa's
garden the tension became unbearable. He writes: "I heard a voice from
the nearby house chanting as if it might be a boy or a girl . . . , 'Pick up
and read, pick up and read.' . . . "[34] He immediately did so—Paul's letters were at hand—and found long sought relief in Paul's words about
putting off ambition, putting on the Lord Jesus, and making no provi-
sion for the lusts of the flesh (Rom 13:13–14). He neither wished nor
needed to read further: "At once, with the last words of the sentence, it
was as if a light of relief from all anxiety flooded into my heart. All the
shadows of doubt were dispelled."[35] Then and there he made up his
mind about his career ambitions: he would give them up; about marriage: he would not marry; about the church: he would accept its rule of
faith.

Augustine speaks about the garden experience as his conversion—"You converted me to yourself" *(convertisti enim me ad te)*[36]—and has been taken at his word ever since. But the *Confessions* is the autobiography of a conversion in progress. It lays out the full story of his conversion—from birth to baptism—as he came to understand and see it unfold a decade later. The garden at Milan represents the moment of decision. Thirty-two years lay behind the garden; before he would be a convert even more decisive events lay ahead.

H. CASSICIACUM

With his decision in hand and in spite of a serious infection in his lungs, Augustine fulfilled his commitment to his students; there were only twenty days to the end-of-term vacation (August 22–October 15). Accompanied by his mother, son, brother, two nephews, and a circle of friends, he went to a fellow professor's country estate at Cassiciacum (Como, north of Milan) for the vacation—as he put it, "untutored in your steadfast love, a catechumen on holiday at a country villa . . . ,"[37] where he would remain until January.

As he recovered his health, Augustine solidified his determination to act. He wrote Ambrose about his intention to be baptized and requested some biblical reading suggestions. He resigned his chair of rhetoric. He held extended discussions with his circle about the possibility of arriving at truth, the happy life and the knowledge of God, providence and the problem of evil, the quest for God, and the immortality of the soul, discussions that he later published.[38] And he made up his mind to go back to Milan.

IV. The Lenten Catechumenate: Milan

When the group returned to Milan, Augustine, Adeodatus, and Alypius submitted their names for baptism. The trio were accepted, enrolled, became "competents" *(competentes simul,* "those who seek baptism together"), and began their Lenten catechumenate. Augustine leaves little record of either the Lenten catechumenate or the rites of baptism in the *Confessions.* Ambrose's legacy, together with echoes from Augustine's life in Hippo, however, permits a reconstruction of both: a set of mystagogical instructions like Cyril's, a homily on the creed, and homilies on the Hebrew Bible.[39]

A. ENROLLMENT AND THE FAST

Lent starts for the trio on the day after Epiphany (387) with a dramatic rite that enacted their new status. John 9:6–7 is read:

> When [Jesus] had said this, he spat on the ground and made mud with the saliva and spread the mud on the man's eyes, saying to him, "Go wash in the pool of Siloam (which means Sent)." Then he went and washed and came back able to see.

Ambrose smears mud on the competents' eyes to signify that baptism, like the pool of Siloam, will open their eyes to the mysteries and life of faith and that the rite of enrollment disposes them for the "eye-opening work" of the rites and instruction to come in the next few weeks.

As elsewhere in the fourth-century East and West, the Lenten fast obligates them, and perhaps they actually hear Ambrose preach his extant homily on fasting:

> We are athletes, we strive, as it were, in a spiritual stadium. . . . Even an athlete's diet is given him, discipline is demanded, continence is observed. And you have given [in] your name for the contest of Christ, you have signed for the competition for the crown. . . . [40]

Ascetics and athletics were two sides of the same coin; for both, the regimen was demanding. The rest of the homily indicates that meat, wine, and the baths were out, that continence even for the married was in, and that hunger was the constant sign and reminder of compliance. Very likely the trio ate only once a day, but not before three o'clock in the afternoon.

B. INSTRUCTION

Ambrose's cathedral—the very one from which he had emerged a reluctant bishop-elect—had been built about 350, commanding Milan's forum. The length of a football field and nearly half a field wide, it could accommodate three thousand. Ambrose seems to have added the separate octagonal baptistery near the apse at the eastern end, to which Augustine and the others came twice a day for instruction.[41]

Ambrose's curriculum for Lenten instruction is impossible to reconstruct with any certainty. Nonetheless, his biblical homilies are a reliable index, for he devoted his extant homilies to the Hebrew Bible, emphasizing "daily moral discourse" on the history of the patriarchs, the Book of Proverbs, and such, because they provided a combination of examples and precepts that made it possible for the competents to follow the road of the "forefathers."[42] Whether Augustine actually heard Ambrose's homilies *On the Six Days of Creation, On Elijah and Fasting,* and possibly *On Abraham, Book I,* as some think, is less important than the fact that Ambrose's commentaries on the Hebrew Bible were the kind of moral discourse he heard.[43]

Unlike Jerusalem, no course of creedal instructions in Milan is evident, nor does Ambrose provide details about instruction and its accompanying rites. His biographer, Paulinus, however, says that they were part of a liturgical service held twice daily (at 9:00 A.M. and 3:00 P.M.) Monday through Friday, one that also included readings, psalms, and Ambrose's homilies.[44]

C. SCRUTINIES

Also unlike Jerusalem, exorcism did not accompany instruction, yet the rite was both prominent and dramatic: the bishop calls it the mysteries of the scrutinies, celebrated in vigils on the third, fourth, and fifth Saturdays of Lent.[45]

The rite consisted of a solemn exorcism and a physical exam to see whether there were any signs (psychosomatic or physical) that Satan still clung to the competents. Leprosy and other scabrous sores, like venereal disease, were a bad sign.[46]

Although Ambrose and Augustine say little about the rite, there is one extant description that suggests what it was like. Its author is Quodvultdeus, Augustine's younger contemporary and the last pre-Vandal archbishop of Carthage (437–439 C.E.):

> From concealment you were each presented before the entire church, where, with your head—once erect in pride and malice—bowed, you were standing barefoot on goat skin; in this way the proud devil was rooted out of you, while the humble and most noble Christ was invoked over you. All of you were thus humble of demeanor and humbly you were pleading by prayer, chanting psalms [especially Ps 138 (139)], and saying: "Probe me, Lord, and know my heart" [Ps 138:3]. He has probed, he has weighed, he has touched the hearts of his servants with fear of him; by his power he has caused the devil to flee, and he has freed his servant from the devil's dominion. Here the poor are not treated one way,

the rich another, the master one way, the slave another: for "there is one entrance for all into life" [Wis 7:6]; and if it is thus in this fragile and mortal life how much the better will it be for that immortal and everlasting life.[47]

The rite was a physical and psychological ordeal conducted in a darkened church. The competents wore penitential tunics, fasted, and were subjected to the raucous voices of the exorcists. The rite was what some contemporary researchers consider deconstructive and others, degradation ceremonies.[48] Whatever the term, they are rituals designed to break down destructive old patterns of behavior and make the subject more malleable in the shaping of new patterns. Historically, the rite represented something of the rigorous screening process in the *Apostolic Tradition* two centuries earlier, when the church was still in the catacombs.

To pass the scrutinies was to win community approbation for baptism. About 380, Ambrose's neighbor, Bishop Zeno of Verona, for whom the rite was just such a test, listed typical reactions: turning pale, bulging eyes, gnashing of teeth, foaming at the mouth, shaking, and weeping.[49] Such behavior (or evident sores and rashes) marked a baptizand out for rejection; he or she was still indwelt by Satan and not ready for baptism.

Like the other competents, Augustine, Adeodatus, and Alypius experienced three scrutinies, and Augustine may have brought the rite back with him to North Africa.

D. THE CREED[50]

As Easter approaches, the drama intensifies. On the last Sunday before Easter (Palm Sunday in Jerusalem), just after the dismissal of the catechumens, Ambrose leads his competents to the baptistery for a special rite we saw in Jerusalem, the confiding of the creed *(traditio symboli)*. Identical with Rome's, the creed at Milan consisted of twelve articles, with each one attributed to one of the twelve apostles: the eminently memorizable Apostles' Creed.

The competents sign themselves; Ambrose recites the creed alone, then bishop and competents recite it together. He repeats it a third time, article by article, adding a brief explanation of each article. At the end, he warns his hearers that the creed is not to be written down, save on the fleshly tablets of their memories, and that its recitation by heart will be required of them in a week. He finishes by asking them to recite the creed silently to themselves.

The four repetitions were designed to get distinguished thirty-three-year-old professors and seven-year-old children alike started on internalizing the creed. One can safely imagine Augustine, Adeodatus, and Alypius discussing the articles and coaching each other, perhaps with Monica as referee.

E. HOLY WEEK[51]

Both Ambrose and Augustine are silent about Holy Week in Milan, but customs in Augustine's Hippo depict the drama and its intensity (and probably many of the details).

Although the last three days, the paschal triduum, were central in Hippo, Holy Week and Easter Week were days of high holiday across the empire, Milan included.[52] People flocked to the city from far and wide, especially the friends, family, and sponsors of the competents. Monica and Augustine's Christian friends would have been much in evidence.

On Wednesday the liturgy turns toward the passion of Christ, with the lessons devoted to the lamentations of Jeremiah (Jer 9) and to Matthew's account of the unknown woman who anointed Jesus for his burial (Mt 26:1–13); the psalm of the day was Psalm 21 (22): "My God, my God, why have you forsaken me? . . . "

On Thursday the competents break their fast in honor of the Last Supper, and, much to everyone's relief, they go to Milan's public baths for long-overdue bathing. The symbolic reason in Hippo was Jesus' washing the disciples' feet at the Last Supper (Jn 13:1–11; Lk 22: 24–27);[53] the immediately obvious one was hygiene: the baptismal waters would wash away the competents' sins without the slightest residue, but not eight weeks of grime.

Friday centers around Jesus' death and burial, highlighted by the reading of Matthew's passion account and by Ambrose's homily on the passion.

The stage is set for Saturday; the focus is the expectation of resurrection, both the buried Christ's and the competents'. Like Friday, Saturday is a day of strict fast for everyone. And—just perhaps—the kinds of lament and ululation heard in Jerusalem also echo in the streets of Milan.

At dusk Saturday afternoon the next-to-last act of the drama begins. The lamps in the cathedral are lit—in Hippo the populace light them all over the city as well, including the paschal candle.[55] Augustine, Adeodatus, Alypius, the competents, the catechumens, and the baptized assemble for the vigil of the resurrection in the Ambrosian cathedral. If the Milanese vigil was like the vigil in Hippo,[56] it consisted of readings and brief commentaries about the key events of the biblical history of salvation, ranging from the creation account in the Book of Genesis to the awesome account in the Book of Daniel of the three young men who preferred a fiery death to apostasy (Dn 3:1–30). Appropriate psalms are interspersed to reinforce the readings.

At some point, perhaps at first light, one by one Augustine and the others climb a platform before Ambrose to recite the creed by heart, and, the bishop hopes, from the heart. Perhaps the cathedral echoes with Augustine's name as it had almost three decades before in Rome when that other distinguished professor of rhetoric and philosophy, Marius Victorinus, performed the same rite. Augustine records the occasion:

> Finally the hour came for him to make his profession of faith which is expressed in a set form. At Rome these words were memorized and recited from an elevated place before the baptized believers by those who want to come to your grace [baptism]. . . . When he mounted the steps to affirm the confession of faith, there was a murmur of delighted talk as all the people who knew him spoke his name to one another. And who there did not know him? A suppressed shout came from the lips of all as they rejoiced, "Victorinus, Victorinus!" . . . [57]

V. Baptism at Milan

We are now able to see the Milanese baptismal liturgy in a clearer light, for with cockcrow dawn is breaking, and we have Ambrose as our guide.[58]

Baptism

A. THE OPENING: EPHPHATHA

At the end of the vigil, the competents assemble at the door to Ambrose's new baptistery for the first rite, *ephphatha*. The rite recalls both their enrollment at the beginning of Lent and the gospel account about the deaf mute whom Jesus healed by putting his fingers into his ears (Mk 7:33-34). Jesus touched his tongue with saliva and, sighing, said, "*Ephphatha,* that is, 'be opened.'"

Ambrose touches Augustine's ears and nostrils to open his mind to understand the rites and his experience of them, and to unblock the channels of conduct so that they may exude, he says, the odor of goodness. Perhaps it especially touches Augustine, whose mind had been closed for so long and whose conduct, in particular his sexual drive, defied channeling.

B. THE ANOINTING

Next Augustine enters the baptistery proper (Ambrose considers it the "Holy of Holies"),[59] where he ritually removes his clothes. A priest anoints him from head to toe with olive oil to strengthen him, we read, in the last stages of the struggle finally to free himself from the grip of his world's powerful seductions. It is a poignant moment for him to remember his overriding ambition for a high imperial post and an advantageous marriage. Perhaps Ambrose's words bring back the memory of his agony in the garden at Milan, which he later sees under the twin images of Adam and Eve in the garden of Eden and Christ in the garden of Gethsemane (Mk 14:32–42).

C. RENUNCIATION AND PROFESSION

Thus prepared, a naked and glistening Augustine stands upright, facing west, and hears two questions.[60] "Do you renounce the devil and his works?" "Do you renounce the world and its pleasures?" To both he answers, "I do renounce them." His renunciation brings to fruition the determination he formed in the garden to resign his rhetoric chair, reject marriage, and seek baptism. He saw them in his later life as Satan's works and the spirit of the world and its pleasures, the bonds that held him.

Augustine then turns to the east, where the baptismal font stands and the land of resurrection lies. He pledges allegiance to Christ, possibly in the form of a shortened creed like the one at Jerusalem, a rite that likely evokes for him his discovery of the human face of God in the Catholic Christ.[61]

D. CONSECRATION OF THE WATERS

Attention then focuses on the baptismal font—rectangular like a Roman sarcophagus, perhaps with pillars at the corners and a marble baldachin.[62] Ambrose now consecrates its waters in the name of the Father and of the Son and of the Holy Spirit. He hints that the consecrating prayer also emphasizes the death and burial of both Christ and the candidate. The waters signify a tomb, as at Jerusalem, and Ambrose traces the sign of the cross over the waters and, perhaps, plunges a cross (his shepherd's staff?) into them. The Pauline baptismal pattern has clearly come front and center, a pattern that speaks to Augustine of his long, anguished journey to the font.

E. IMMERSION

Augustine then enters and stands waist-deep in the font. Baptism is by triple immersion, and the form is interrogatory. Three questions are put to him: "Do you believe in God the Father?" "Do you believe in our Lord Jesus Christ and in his cross?" "Do you believe also in the Holy Spirit?" Each time he answers, "I believe," he is immersed. He then comes up the stairs of the font. His conversion, if not finished, is complete at last. The old Augustine has died and been buried; the new one has risen to life regenerated. Later he will call his newly baptized in Hippo "infants."

F. ANOINTING AND FOOT WASHING

But the drama is not over. When Augustine emerges from the font, a priest awaits to anoint him with chrism (perfumed oil) on the forehead with the words, "God the Father All Powerful, who has given you new birth through water and the Holy Spirit and has forgiven your sins, he is the one who anoints you for eternal life."[63]

After all are anointed, the Milanese liturgy celebrates a striking rite. A deacon reads from the Last Supper account the words about Jesus tying a towel around his waist, washing, and then drying the feet of the disciples (Jn 13:1–11). Ambrose does the same for the newly anointed, with help from the priests. The point is far from lost on Augustine: the "disquiet of [his] past life" has vanished, completely washed away.[64]

G. THE WHITE GARMENT AND THE SEALING

Augustine dries, puts on a new linen garment, and takes his place in the white-robed line before Ambrose. Ambrose anoints him on the forehead with the sign of the cross in the name of the Trinity, thereby stamping him as their possession and strengthening him with the fullness of the Holy Spirit.[65]

After Baptism

A. THE EUCHARIST

Processing from the baptistery to the cathedral now jammed with the faithful, the newly baptized chant Psalm 22 (23) with its rich baptismal allusions:

> The Lord is my shepherd, I shall not want; he makes me lie down in green pastures. He leads me beside still waters; he restores my soul. . . . Even though I walk through the valley of the shadow of death, I fear no evil; for you are with me. . . . You prepare a table before me . . . ; you anoint my head with oil, my cup overflows.

The eucharistic table stands before them, a table to which they have never before been invited. The faithful give them the kiss of peace and welcome as newborn members of the family. They then stand in silence, baffled—bemused spectators who know nothing of what takes place at the Mass of the Faithful or what it is about. For the first time they hear the Lord's Prayer prayed; Ambrose will rehearse it with them, as he had the creed, during the week ahead.[66]

They receive the bread first and then the traditional three cups: one of wine, one of water, and one of milk and honey. The bread and wine symbolize the nourishing death of Christ; the water, the water of baptism seeping into their inmost selves; the milk and honey, the Promised Land that overflowed with milk and honey. Augustine has reached his destination. But his conversion is not quite complete.

B. EASTER WEEK

The newly baptized have yet to learn the meaning of the rites. As Cyril did in Jerusalem, Ambrose explains their rich symbolism in mystagogical instructions during the week following Easter baptism.

Part of his legacy is six such instructions. On Monday, Tuesday, and Wednesday he retraces the competents' steps from *ephphatha* through the final anointing, explaining the significance of each rite in detail, cross-weaving rite, biblical symbols, and native custom. On Friday and Saturday Ambrose leads them through the eucharist. He weaves together the elements of bread and wine with the biblical writings, especially the Song of Songs, the Psalms, and the Gospel of John. In the process, he twice confides to them the Lord's Prayer. Now, as never before, they can properly call God their Father.

The homilies were preached between 380 and 390, taken down by notaries in their high-speed shorthand, and may actually have been those heard by Augustine, Adeodatus, and Alypius in the company of Monica; Ambrose published an edited version, *On the Mysteries,* about 390.[67]

Finis

Now the task of the trio is to sustain the momentum of their conversions throughout their lives. Adeodatus' is short: he dies within two years. Alypius' is far longer; he serves as bishop of Thagaste, his hometown. Augustine's is the longest, forty-three years: four as a contemplative philosopher in the midst of his circle, and thirty-nine as priest, assistant bishop, and bishop of the primatial see of Numidia and leading churchman of the West.

VI. Conclusion

Although Augustine says nothing about the baptismal rites themselves in the *Confessions,* he clearly understood that baptism, not his experience in the garden in Milan, established his conversion and regeneration.[68] Nonetheless, he records his emotions about the rites: his anxiety about the past is banished; his delight in what has been done in and for him is immeasurable; and the hymns and chants of Ambrose's liturgy make him weep. He concludes, "And it was good for me to have that experience."[69] Just the year before, Ambrose had arranged the chant and initiated the hymns that evoked the tears, but they welled up from the ritual experience of the reality distilled into his heart, his conversion.[70]

Although this is not the customary way of reading the *Confessions,* the work documents that Augustine's conversion happened within the ancient ritual process known as the catechumenate. It began with his inscription in the catechumenate in 354 and culminated in the mysteries of baptismal initiation on Easter 387. His home and family, his education, his mistress, Adeodatus, the Platonic books, the Manichees, Ambrose's homilies, the garden in Milan, Monica's incessant pressure—they were part of the process, currents in a sea change about which Augustine might say, "It is not a lie but a mystery" *(non est mendacium sed mysterium).*

The journey took thirty-three years from start to finish. Easter Week 387 constituted the climax of Augustine's moving journey through his complex social, cultural, and religious world. During the journey he (1) faced an extended identity crisis that lasted for fifteen years, (2) launched an intensely active search in Carthage, Rome, and Milan for a new identity, meaning, and purpose, (3) encountered anew in Ambrose's Milan the religious reality of a Catholic Christianity that engaged his emotional, intellectual, and cognitive needs, (4) initiated and sustained the continual interaction with Ambrose and his community that led to his becoming a competent and, finally, one of the baptized, (5) made a definitive choice between his previous way of thought and life symbolized by his overwhelming sexual appetite and a new way characterized by ascetic Christianity, and (6) underwent a remarkable transformation from a professor of rhetoric with high ambitions for marriage, status, and wealth to a bishop who turned his back on marriage, on every symbol of prestige, and on wealth: the former Milanese dignitary moved alone among his poor townspeople in their simple dress.

The catechumenate in Milan and its most famous convert depict in dramatic detail the indispensability of ritual for conversion in an ancient convert's long and sometimes harrowing journey.

NOTES

1. Chrysostom, *Catecheses* 1–8 (Antoine Wenger, ed., *Jean Chrysostome: Huit catéchèses baptismales,* SC 50 [1957]; Theodore, *Catecheses* (R. Tonneau and R. Devreesse, eds., *Les homélies catéchétiques de Théodore de Mopsueste* (Vatican City: Biblioteca Apostolica Vaticana [Studi e Testi 145], 1949). For translations, see Edward J. Yarnold, *The Awe-Inspiring Rites of Initiation: The Origins of the R.C.I.A.,* 2nd ed. (Collegeville: Liturgical Press, 1994) 150–64 (Chrysostom), 165–250 (Theodore). For the translation and Syriac text of Theodore's eleven creedal instructions, see A. Mingana, ed., *Commentary of Theodore of Mopsuestia on the Nicene Creed* (Cambridge: Woodbrooke Studies 5, 1932).

2. Both works have complex histories and textual traditions. For the most recent discussion and translations, see Grant Sperry-White, *The*

Testamentum Domini, GLS 66 (1991); and W. Jardine Grisbrooke, *The Liturgical Portions of the Apostolic Constitutions,* GLS 61 (1990).

3. For texts, translation, and discussion, see Paul F. Bradshaw, ed., and Carol Bebawi, trans., *The Canons of Hippolytus,* GLS 50 (1987). It is extant only in Arabic and dated between 336 and 340.

4. The scholars are E. Schwarz, *Über die pseudoapostolischen Kirchenordnungen* (Strasbourg, 1910); and R. Hugh Connolly, *The So-Called Egyptian Church Order and Derived Documents* (Cambridge: Cambridge University Press [Texts for Students 8, vol. 4], 1916). See also Chapter 7, "The *Apostolic Tradition* of Hippolytus."

5. For recent discussions, translations, and texts, see R. J. S. Barrett-Lennard, trans., *The Sacramentary of Sarapion of Thmuis,* GLS 25 (1993); and Maxwell E. Johnson, *The Prayers of Sarapion of Thmuis* (Dissertation, University of Notre Dame, 1992). Johnson provides a text and translation, together with a valuable introduction to the text, its problems, modern scholarship, and commentaries. The baptismal prayers are 7–11 (Johnson's commentary, 111–14, text and translation, 56–62), to which should be added prayers over the baptismal oils, 15–16 (text and translation, 69–73, commentary, 105–8).

6. See Robert Murray, "The Characteristics of Early Syriac Christianity," in Nina Garsoian et al., eds., *East of Byzantium: Syria and Armenia in the Formative Period* (Washington, D.C.: Dumbarton Oaks, 1982) 3–16; his *Symbols of Church and Kingdom* (Cambridge: Cambridge University Press, 1975); and Sebastian Brock, *The Holy Spirit in the Syrian Baptismal Tradition* (Poona, India: Anita Printers [The Syrian Church Series 9, ed. Jacob Vellian], 1979).

7. For Aphrahat (text and discussion), see J. Parisot, ed., *Aphraatis Sapientis Persae, Patrologia Syriaca,* vols. 1–2 (Paris: Firmin-Didot et Socii, 1907); and E. J. Duncan, *Baptism and the Demonstrations of Aphraates, the Persian Sage,* SCA 8 (1948). For Ephrem (text), see Edmund Beck, ed., *Hymns on Faith,* CSCO 154–155 (1955); *Hymns Against Heresies,* CSCO 169–170 (1957); *Hymns on Paradise, Against Julian,* CSCO 174–175 (1957); *Hymns on Epiphany,* CSCO 186–187 (1959); *Hymns on the Church,* CSCO 198–199 (1960); *Hymns on Virginity,* CSCO 223–224 (1962); and *Nisibene Hymns,* CSCO 218–219, 240–241 (1960–1962). I give a brief introduction to Syriac Christianity and have collected the relevant translated texts for both Aphrahat and Ephrem in my *ECBC* 5:134–69. The didactic hymns are known as *madrashe,* and the metrical homilies, *memre.*

8. For what follows, see F. Homes Dudden, *The Life and Times of St. Ambrose,* vol. 1 (Oxford: Clarendon Press, 1935); Angelo Paredi, *Saint Ambrose: His Life and His Times,* trans. M. Joseph Costelloe (South Bend: University of Notre Dame Press, 1964); and Neil B. McLynn, *Ambrose of*

Milan: Church and Court in a Christian Capital (Berkeley: University of California Press, 1994).

9. For a valuable account of the church, built about 350 to replace the old cathedral *(basilica vetus)*, see Richard Krautheimer, *Three Capitals: Topography and Politics* (Berkeley: University of California Press, 1983) 69–92, especially 73–79. Ambrose was behind the erection of numerous churches in Milan and is reputed to have built the octagonal baptistery of the new cathedral, eventually dedicated to Saint Thecla.

10. See *The Apostolic Tradition of Hippolytus* 17 (Bernard Botte, ed., *La Tradition Apostolique de Saint Hippolyte: Essai de Reconstitution*, LQF (1963) 39:38; Paulinus, *Vita Ambrosii* 6, cited in Paredi, *St. Ambrose,* 119; and Rufinus, *Historia ecclesiastica* 11:11, cited in McLynn, *Ambrose,* 3.

11. Thus, Paredi, *St. Ambrose,* 11.

12. For the most recent text of the *Confessions* see James J. O'Donnell, ed., *Augustine: Confessions,* 3 vols. (Oxford: Clarendon Press, 1992): the first volume contains the introduction and text; the other two, commentary. For a recent translation, see Henry Chadwick, trans., *St. Augustine: Confessions* (New York: Oxford University Press, 1991). For two biographical studies of Augustine's conversion, see John J. O'Meara, *The Young Augustine: The Growth of St. Augustine's Mind up to His Conversion* (London: Longmans, Green and Co., 1954); and Peter Brown, *Augustine of Hippo: A Biography* (Berkeley: University of California Press, 1967), especially 28–181. For the catechumenate in Augustine's North Africa, see William Harmless, *Augustine and the Catechumenate* (Collegeville: Liturgical Press [A Pueblo Book], 1995); Harmless provides an insightful view of Augustine's understanding of the catechumenate, some of which he brought with him from Milan and his own catechumenate.

13. *Conf.* 3:1.1 (O'Donnell, 1:23; Chadwick, 35).

14. *Conf.* 3:4.7 (O'Donnell, 1:25): *surgere coeperam ut ad te redirem.*

15. *Conf.* 3:4.8 (O'Donnell, 1:26): *et hoc solum me in tanta flagrantia refrangebat, quod nomen Christi non erat ibi . . . in ipso adhuc lacte matris tenerum cor meum pie biberat et alte retinebat, et quidquid sine hoc nomine fuisset, quamvis litteratum et expolitum et viridicum, non me totum rapiebat.*

16. *Conf.* 3:6.10 (O'Donnell, 1:26).

17. *Conf.* 6:4.5 (O'Donnell, 1:61): *infantiles nugas.* For discussion of Augustine's encounter with Manichaeism at this point in his life, see Colin Starnes, *Augustine's Conversion: A Guide to the Argument of Confessions I–IX* (Waterloo: Wilfrid Laurier University Press, 1990) 72–92: books 3:10–18 to 4:2.3 concern this Manichaean part of Augustine's life. See also Brown, *Augustine of Hippo,* 46–60.

18. Augustine, *De duabus animarum* 11: for discussion of Augustine's

"conversion" to the Manichees and their criticisms of Catholic Christianity, see O'Meara, *The Young Augustine*, 80–83.

19. For discussion, see Leo Ferrari, "Young Augustine: Both Catholic and Manichee," *Augustinian Studies* 26 (1995) 109–28.

20. *Conf.* 5:8.14 (O'Donnell, 1:52): *et ideo placebat ire ubi talia non fieri omnes.* . . .

21. *Conf.* 5:10.19 (O'Donnell, 1:54): *et quoniam cum de deo meo cogitare vellem, cogitare nisi moles corporum non noveram (neque enim videbatur mihi esse quicquam quod tale non esset) et maxima et prope sola causa erat inevitabilis erroris mei.*

22. *Conf.* 5:10.19 (O'Donnell, 1:54): *quod de omnibus dubitandum esse censuerant nec aliquid veri ab homine comprehendi posse decreverant.*

23. *Conf.* 7:10.16 (O'Donnell, 1:89–90; Chadwick, 123).

24. For the question and the debate, see O'Donnell 1: xxiii–xli, especially n. 53, xxxvi; O'Meara, *The Young Augustine,* 131–55, especially 141–42; Brown, *Augustine of Hippo,* 101–14; and Robert J. O'Connell, *St. Augustine's Confessions: The Odyssey of Soul* (Cambridge: Harvard University Press, 1969).

25. *Conf.* 7:17.23 (O'Donnell, 1:84): *Et mirabar quod iam te amabam, non pro te phantasma* . . . ; "phantom surrogate" is Chadwick's rendering (127). The reference is to the Manichaean vision of God, for which, see O'Donnell, 2:180. It had no reality content. For instance, O'Donnell notes that he distinguishes between his image of his father, whom he often saw, and his uncle, whom he never saw: *aliter enim cogito patrem meum quem saepe vidi, aliter avum quem numquam vidi. horum primum phantasia est, alterum phantasma.* The image of his uncle had no reality content—*phantasma.*

26. See *Conf.* 7:20.26; see also the discussion in Starnes, *Augustine's Conversion,* 194–99.

27. See *Conf.* 7:20.26, 7:21.27; see also Starnes, *Augustine's Conversion,* 194–99.

28. For a recent treatment of Ambrose as preacher, see Harmless, *Augustine and the Catechumenate,* 80–90.

29. *Statui ergo tamdiu esse catechumenus in catholica ecclesia.* . . . (Augustine, *Conf.* 5:14.24 [O'Donnell, 1:57]). See Ferrari, "Young Augustine," 108–28; on 111 he translates *esse* as "remain," as does Starnes (*Augustine's Conversion*, 132). Neither author thinks Augustine ever left the church. I have followed Henry Chadwick's translation ("to be," *Confessions,* 89) because I think that Augustine may have left the church.

30. *Conf.* 7:5.7 (O'Donnell, 1:77).

31. *Conf.* 6:5.5 (O'Donnell, 1:70–71; Chadwick [altered], 94).

32. *Conf.* 8:1.1 (O'Donnell, 1:88): *nec certior de te sed stabilior in te.*

33. These verses describe Paul's visions, caught up into the third

heaven. The parallel in Augustine's life is his mystical ascent to God, when he saw God as Being and himself as nonbeing.

34. *Conf.* 8:12.29 (O'Donnell, 1:101; see O'Donnell, 3:59–61, for the baptismal parallels): *et ecce audio vocem de vicina domo cum cantu dicentis et crebro repetentis, quasi pueri an puellae, nescio: "tole, lege."*

35. *Conf.* 8:12.29 (O'Donnell, 1:101; Chadwick: 153).

36. *Conf.* 8:12.30 (O'Donnell, 1:102).

37. *Conf.* 9:4.8 (O'Donnell, 1:106): *rudis in germano amore tuo, catechumenus in villa (cum catechumeno Allypio feriatus . . .).*

38. *Contra Academicos, De beata vita, De ordine,* and *Sylloquia* (PL 32: 905–58; 959–76; 977–1020; 869–904).

39. Ambrose, *De sacramentis, De mysteriis, Explanatio symboli ad competentes* (Bernard Botte, ed., *Ambroise de Milan: des sacramentis, des mysteriis, l'explication du symbole,* SC 25bis (1961) 98–100. For an English translation of the homilies *De sac.,* see Yarnold, *The Awe-Inspiring Rites,* 100–149; *De myst.* is the edited version of *De sac.* The biblical homilies are listed below, nn. 40, 43; and *Explan. symb.,* below, n. 45.

40. *De Helia et jejunio I* 21:79 (PL 14:725–26; M. J. A. Buck, trans., *S. Ambrosii: De Helia et Ieiunio* [Washington, D.C.: Catholic University of America Press (Patristic Studies 19), 1929] 103–5).

41. See Krautheimer, *Three Capitals,* 68–92, especially 73–77. Ambrose is at least responsible for the inscription, if not for the building. For the frequency and the service, see below and Harmless, *Augustine and the Catechumenate,* 94.

42. *De myst.* 1:1 (Botte, SC 25bis:156).

43. *Hexaemeron* (PL 14:123–274), 386–90; *De Abraham Liber I* (PL 14:417–54); some date the former between 386 and 390, and the latter, 382. For discussion and the works clearly addressed to Lenten catechumens, see Maria Grazia Mara, "Ambrose of Milan, Ambrosiaster, and Nicetas," in A. Di Berardino, ed., *Patrology,* vol. 4, trans. Placid Solari (Westminster, Md.: Christian Classics, 1986) 153–65; and Harmless, *Augustine and the Catechumenate,* 94–95. *De Helia et jejunio* (PL 14:697–728), delivered in Lent, dates from about 377–390 (Harmless says 387–390).

44. Paulinus, *Vita Sancti Ambrosii* 28, cited in Harmless, *Augustine and the Catechumenate,* 94 and n. 68.

45. Ambrose, *Explanatio symboli ad competentes* 1:1 (Botte, SC 25bis: 46); he uses the plural: *mysteria . . . scrutaminum.* For Rome, see John the Deacon (c. 500): *Epistula ad Senarium* 2 (A. Wilmart, ed., *Analecta Reginensia* [Vatican City: Biblioteca Apostolica Vaticana (Studi e Testi 59), 1933] 171). For a detailed study tracing the development of the scrutinies in the West, see A. Dondeyne, "La discipline des scrutins dans l'Église latine

avant Charlemagne," *Revue d'Histoire Écclesiastique* 28 (1932) 5–33, especially 26–30 (Milan): he concludes to three scrutinies.

46. For discussion, see my "It Happened One Saturday Night: Ritual and Conversion in Augustine's North Africa," *JAAR* 58 (1990) 596–97. Augustine may have brought the scrutinies to North Africa from Milan.

47. Quodvultdeus, *De symbolo* I (CCL 60:305). For discussion, see my "It Happened One Saturday Night," 594–99; I have revised the translation published there but have not altered its substance. See Augustine's sermon 116, delivered on the occasion of the rite in Hippo; see also Suzanne Poque, ed., *Augustin d'Hippone: Sermons pour la Pâque*, SC 116 (1966) 26–33.

48. See Lewis R. Rambo, *Understanding Religious Conversion* (New Haven: Yale University Press, 1993) 116–18; and my "It Happened One Saturday Night," 599–608.

49. Zeno, *Tractatus* 1:16.3 (PL 11:374), cited in Yarnold, *The Awe-Inspiring Rites*, 11, n. 47.

50. Ambrose, *Expl. symb.* (Botte, SC 25[bis]:46–59). For translation, see R. H. Connolly, *Explanatio Symboli ad Initiandos: A Work of St. Ambrose* (Cambridge: Cambridge University Press [Texts and Studies 10], 1952). Harmless (*Augustine and the Catechumenate*, 96 and n. 77), citing Ambrose, *Ep.* 20:4, holds that the rite was the Sunday before Easter (Palm Sunday in Jerusalem).

51. For a discussion of the Holy Week liturgy, see Poque, *Augustin d'Hippone*, 69–77; and Benedictus Busch, "De initiatione christiana secundum sanctum Augustinum," *Ephemerides Liturgicae Analecta* 52 (1938) 446–49.

52. See Harmless, *Augustine and the Catechumenate*, 302.

53. See Busch, "De initiatione," 447; and my "It Happened One Saturday Night," 593, n. 16.

54. For Augustine's fifteen vigil homilies, see Poque, *Augustin d'Hippone*, 31–33, 73–78. The custom of the paschal candle and its blessing had taken hold in the West by Augustine's time.

55. For discussion, see my "It Happened One Saturday Night," n. 17. Augustine composed a metrical eulogy of the candle in *De civitate Dei* 15:22.

56. Harmless, *Augustine and the Catechumenate*, 303–7.

57. Augustine, *Conf.* 8:2.5 (O'Donnell, 1:90; Chadwick, 136–37). It is possible that Victorinus' *redditio* took place at Rome's Easter vigil rather than on Palm Sunday; there is no indication of the hour in Augustine.

58. For the texts, see Ambrose, *De sac.* and *De myst.* (Botte, SC 25[bis]: 60–193; for the translation, see Yarnold, *The Awe-Inspiring Rites*, 100–149: he translates *De sac.* 1–5 but leaves out 6, which is on the Lord's Prayer; for which, see R. H. Connolly, *Explanatio Symboli ad Initiandos*). See also Johannes Quasten, "Baptismal Creed and Baptismal Act in St. Ambrose's *De*

mysteriis and *De sacramentis,*" in *Mélanges Joseph de Ghellinck* (Gembloux: Éditions J. Duculot [Museum Lessianum Section Historique 13], 1951) 223–34; Orrin T. Wheeler, *Baptism According to St. Ambrose* (Dissertation, Woodstock, 1958); L. L. Mitchell, "Ambrosian Baptismal Rites," *SL* 1 (1962) 241–53; Edward J. Yarnold, "The Ceremonies of Initiation in the *De Sacramentis* and the *De Mysteriis* of S. Ambrose," *SP* 10 (1967) 453–63; Yarnold, "Did St. Ambrose Know the *Mystagogic Catecheses* of St. Cyril of Jerusalem?" *SP* 12:1 (1975) 184–89; Hugh J. Riley, *Christian Initiation: A Comparative Study of the Interpretation of the Baptismal Liturgy in the Mystagogical Writings of Cyril of Jerusalem, John Chrysostom, Theodore of Mopsuestia, and Ambrose of Milan,* SCA 17 (1974) 27–31 passim; and Harmless, *Augustine and the Catechumenate,* 98–104 (Milan), 302–13 (Hippo).

59. Ambrose, *De sac.* 4:1 (Botte, SC 25[bis]:102).

60. Ambrose, *De sac.* 1:2.5 (Botte, SC 25[bis]:62): his turning west is implied in *De myst.* 5 (Botte, SC 25[bis]: 138).

61. Ambrose, *De sac.* 1:8 (Botte, SC 25[bis]:64): Ambrose's play on words, *fides* as act of belief and as content, implies some form of profession, though I doubt a profession of the full creed. For the custom in the East, see my *The Liturgy of Baptism in the Baptismal Instructions of St. John Chrysostom,* SCA 15 (1967) 108–10.

62. See above, n. 41: Krautheimer, *Three Capitals,* 73–77.

63. Ambrose, *De sac.* 2:24 (Botte, SC 25[bis]:88).

64. Ambrose, *De sac.* 3:4 (Botte, SC 25[bis]:92) for the rite; and Augustine, *Conf.* 9:6.14 (O'Donnell, 1:109) for his sense of relief: *et baptizati sumus et fugit a nobis sollicitudo vitae praeteritae.*

65. Ambrose, *De sac.* 3:8, 6:6 (Botte, SC 25[bis]:96, 140); *De myst.* 42 (Botte, SC 25[bis]: 178). For discussion, see Yarnold, *Awe-Inspiring Rites,* 34–38.

66. See *De sac.* 5:4.18–30, 6:5.24 (Botte, SC 25[bis]:150–52). The rite was known as the confiding of the Lord's Prayer *(traditio orationis dominicae).*

67. I have not made extensive use of *De myst.* because *De sac.* is closer to what Augustine might actually have heard; the text for the former is in Botte, SC 25[bis], with the translation in R. J. Deferrari, trans., *St. Ambrose: Theological and Dogmatic Works,* FC 44 (1963) 3–28 *(On the Mysteries)* and 319–28 *(On the Sacraments).*

68. *Conf.* 9:3.6 (O'Donnell, 1:104): about Alypius and Nebridius, Augustine speaks about their conversion and regeneration *per baptismum tuum ipsum.*

69. Augustine, *Conf.* 9:6.14 (O'Donnell, 1:109).

70. The occasion for Ambrose's innovations in chant and the introduction of the hymns was the Empress Justina's (mother of Valentinian II)

attempt in 386 on the Sunday before Easter to confiscate for her Arian
Christians the "New Basilica"—Ambrose's cathedral. Ambrose introduced
the chant and the hymns to sustain his besieged congregation, which included
Monica. For the occasion and the texts, see A. S. Walpole, ed., *Early Latin
Hymns* (Hildesheim: Georg Olms, 1966) 16–114. Walpole lists twelve hymns
as authentic; others list only four—those for which Augustine is the authority.
F. Homes Dudden treats Ambrose, his chant, and his hymns in *The Life and
Times of St. Ambrose* (Oxford: Clarendon Press, 1935) 1:293–97.

CONCLUSION

We have ranged across the Mediterranean world from Gaul to Persia, across a thousand years, and across the religions of Greece and Rome in an attempt to understand and interpret conversion in antiquity. To do so, we have made extensive use of history, ancient documents and archaeology, and relevant contemporary research on conversion.

The evidence shows conclusively that conversion in Greco-Roman Paganism, second-temple and rabbinic Judaism, and early Christianity was an extended process interlaced with oral instruction and ritual. Sometimes the process led to a transforming commitment to the religion of one's birth; sometimes it led to leaving one's natal religion for a new religion. Both types of conversion, however, entailed carefully articulated ritual processes, attested to divinity as the initiator, and disclosed transformation as the effect. But the evidence yields far more than a general conclusion. A set of specific conclusions related to the characteristics identified in the literature of contemporary research will suggest how much more.

I. Toward a Definition

Although the term *religious conversion* seems to have as many meanings today as the number of people employing it, change is a characteristic common to all meanings, ancient and modern.[1]

When the term entered our cultural bloodstream in late antiquity, however, the change in question had two identifiable characteristics. The classical world of Greece and Rome shaped one; *conversion* meant a change in the way a person understood, valued, and lived in her or his world. The emphasis was on the cognitive—a change of mind, a new way of seeing—and led to a religious world of contemplation and mysticism. The biblical world of ancient Israel and Judaism shaped the other. Conversion meant a person's change from a life of infidelity to one of fidelity to God which involved repentance, return, and reconciliation. The emphasis was on the personal; it meant a change in the way a person lived and for whom—a change of being—that led to conduct based on God's will. The views were not contradictory; both involved a change that went to the root of a person's being—radical change. As a result, the convert thought of the old way of life as wrong and the new one as right. And both views affirmed that deity is the ultimate author of the change, be it Isis, ray-shooting Lord Mandulis, Yahweh, or Christ.

When the classical view met the biblical in the Greek and Latin Bibles, the two characteristics merged. Conversion meant a change in the way one (1) understands and values God and his world, (2) lives in it according to his will, and (3) experiences repentance, return, and reconciliation in the process.

No definition, however, captures the full meaning of conversion because it is an experience rooted in an extended and complex process that has religious, social, and psychological dimensions—a deeply personal event.[2] In Augustine's view, conversion is like falling in love. "You stimulate a person to take pleasure in praising you," we read, "because you have made us for yourself, and our hearts are restless until they rest in you."[3] Augustine was not thereby dispensed from drawing a set of conclusions about the process, and neither are we.

II. Cultural Crisis and Social Setting

As a corrective to seeing conversion primarily in its psychological and internal dimensions, as William James and Arthur Darby Nock did early in the century, contemporary research emphasizes the psychosocial by exploring the impact of social setting on a potential convert, that is, an individual's economic, social, cultural, and religious worlds.

Crisis

To explore the Greco-Roman social setting is far beyond the scope of this study. Nonetheless, a surprising image continually surfaces: crisis. The Greco-Roman world was a world in crisis, initiated when Alexander the Great's policy of Hellenism spread through his conquests (336–323 B.C.E.) and those of his successors. Rome's domination of the Mediterranean world accentuated the crisis, which climaxed in the barbarian invasions (250–550 C.E.) in the West.

A. JUDAISM

Although the crisis touched every aspect of the Greco-Roman world, the crisis that has concerned this study is cultural, which is to say, religious. *Hellenismos* (Hellenism), the Greek word for Greek culture—language, thought, mythology, images, and religion[4]—did more than just touch Palestinian Judaism; it ignited the Maccabean revolt against Hellenistic Syrian domination. Brought to a head in the revolt, the crisis was one of identity: Who is a Jew?

This question brought related questions in its train—whether a Gentile could become a Jew and who is the true Jew. The answer to the first is a straightforward yes. At least by the second century B.C.E., second-temple Judaism had developed a rite of conversion, which the rabbis subsequently clarified and normalized. Conversion to Judaism involved (1) the conviction that Yahweh is the one true God, (2) the commitment to observe the detailed code of conduct revealed in the Torah, (3) the rites of circumcision and a ritual bath of atonement, and (4) formal membership in the covenanted community of Israel.

The reform and separation movements of the period answered the second question: Who is the true Jew? The Pharisees, who stood at one extreme, answered that the true Jew is the one who renders himself, his family, and his home a dwelling for God's spirit of holiness by observing the temple purity laws. At the other extreme, the sectaries of Qumran answered that only the one who enters the community of the new covenant at Qumran, which alone bears Yahweh's spirit of holiness, is the true Jew. In the middle stood the Johannites, who answered that those who reject their sinful past and agree to live justly according to the Torah are the true Jews.

Christians modified the Johannite answer. The true Jews are those who reject their sinful past and agree to live according to the Torah as fulfilled and redefined by the life, death, and resurrection of Jesus. By the mid-first century, Christians were already speaking of a new creation, a new Israel of the circumcised in heart, and a new covenant of the spirit that invalidated the old (2 Cor 3:3–18).

B. PAGANISM

For Pagans, the crisis followed a different route. The heavy imperial hand of Rome lay on everyday life, needs, and aspirations. Civic religion, with its formality, began to pall; votive religion, with its responsiveness to the individual, commanded the attention of educated and uneducated alike. Many sought the help and solace they needed in healing cults, like that of Asclepius, and in mystery cults, like those of Mithra and Isis. Some sought the answer to their quest for a better here and hereafter in philosophical schools, like that of the Neopythagoreans. Some converted to Judaism. And as the second century C.E. turned into the third, fourth and fifth, more and more Greco-Roman Pagans became Christians.

III. Crisis in Personal Identity

Cultural crisis inevitably expresses itself in personal disorientation and in a crisis of personal identity.[5] Sometimes this crisis is the result of a dramatic experience; more often, however, it is the result of less dramatic but important things piling up. The crisis calls into question a person's fundamental convictions and orientation to life.

Unlike the amount of autobiographical evidence in our era, the evidence from antiquity is slender. Only Augustine of Hippo left us an extended autobiographical account. Nonetheless, other data underscore the fact that the crisis was a wrenching personal experience never to be forgotten. The rabbinic ritual of conversion, Apuleius' *Metamorphoses,* early Christian Church Order books (*Didache, Didascalia Apostolorum,* and *Apostolic Tradition*), and the baptismal catecheses of Cyril of Jerusalem and Ambrose of Milan confirm what we learn in autobiographical detail from Justin and Augustine.

Personal Crisis: An Autobiographical View

For Justin, the experience was triggered by his long-standing hunger for the knowledge of "that which really exists," accentuated by frustration with philosophical schools and teachers too elementary for him (Stoic), too concerned about their fee (Aristotelian), or too dismissive of his liberal education (Neopythagorean). In only the Platonic did he make progress, but even there he could not lay his hands on the truth.

For Augustine, the crisis was a series of searing questions:

> Who made me? Was it not my God, not only good but the Good
> itself: How is it then, that I can will to will the bad and will not to
> will the good? Is it so that I can be justly punished? Who put this
> in me and grafted in the shoot of bitterness . . . ?[6]

He had all the wrong answers and exclaimed, "I was brought down to
that hell of error."[7] Thus began the search for order, meaning, and purpose in life.

IV. The Quest[8]

A human world, that is, a world of order, meaning, and purpose, is
constructed by human action often called "world-building." The difficulty in doing so lies in keeping this socially constructed world going;
it is a world that requires continual building. For individuals, building a
world in which they can live is a long and exhausting quest. When
Justin's social world began to unravel, the crisis drove him to search for
a school of philosophy that met his needs. When Augustine realized the
depth of his errors, although devastated, he continued building what he
started in Carthage by embracing Neoplatonism, resuming his catechumenate, and seeking baptism. When Lucius discovered how wretched
the life of a man turned beast was, he ran until he slumped on the beach
exhausted. When a Jew sought entry into the community at Qumran, he
embarked on a four-year probation. For the aspirant who wanted to be a
Neopythagorean, the quest was almost doubled in length.

All of these converts are emblematic of the ancient quest for
order, meaning, and purpose in life. For the most part, the questers
in our study are nameless and faceless God-fearers, initiands of the
cults, probationers in the schools of philosophy, and catechumens
and baptizands in the church. Together with familiar names and
faces—Augustine, Justin, Lucius, Epicurus, Perpetua, Saturus, and
others—they searched beyond the borders of the world into which they
were born for a new world into which they could be reborn, a sacred
world. Their motives are largely unknown to us, but their destination is
clear, a world under the canopy of the sacred. The Isis cult,
Neopythagoreanism, Judaism, and Christianity represented the new
religious realities that beckoned, offering what an ancient hymn called
"pleasant coolness in the heat."[9]

V. The Encounter: A New Religious Reality

Like moderns, the ancients were uncertain about the definition of religion.[10] For Cicero, religion and ritual are two sides of the same coin, and a religious person is one who studiously retraces inherited ritual.[11] For Augustine, religion is "that which advances the love and veneration of a certain superior nature [people] call divine," and religious people are those who strive "toward one God" and bind their "souls to him alone."[12] Both thinkers, however, were quite certain that religion embraces the pure inward piety and reverence toward the sacred specially manifested in ritual; piety and awe *(pietas* and *tremens)* were the watchwords.

The pleasant coolness ancient religions promised was encounter with the sacred, fleeting, to be sure, but stable. Like Paul of Tarsus (2 Cor 12:2), Augustine was raised to what seemed to him the third heaven, where he saw that God is Being and that he is non-Being; to achieve stability in the encounter, however, he resumed the catechumenate and sought baptism.[13] For the ancients, the sacred was ensconced in a system that included a communal way of life. Justin, the philosopher, Clement, the student, Lucius, the initiand, Augustine, the catechumen, and Asenath, the proselyte, sought the sacred—Isis, Christ, the One, and Yahweh—within the structured community of initiates, or believers, or covenanted people. The way of entry was through the rites of initiation; the encounter was with the sacred.

At the end of his quest, Lucius ate the roses and sloughed off the skin of an ass; in the end, he was so identified with Isis that he was arrayed like her, even to the point of wearing a crown of gleaming gold palm leaves. At the end of their quest, Epicurus in Rome, Clement in Alexandria, Rhoda in Northeast Syria, Augustine in Milan, and Mygdonia in India stripped off the old self and put on Christ. The newly incorporated member of Qumran drank of the pure wine and partook of the spirit of Yahweh's holiness. The Palestinian proselytes, when they rose from the *mikveh,* were at one with Yahweh and took their rightful place among his covenanted people. Asenath, the princess, became the daughter of the Most High and ate from the honeycomb with the angels of paradise. Iamblichus' Pythagorists and Pythagoreans passed through the veil, sat before the divine teacher face-to-face, and gradually ascended to the One behind the many.

If we can credit Apuleius and Augustine, the sacred was deeply engaged in the process from the very beginning of the quest. Lucius finds that a provident Isis was at work behind fate; it was her will, not the will of a malevolent spirit, that drew him. Augustine confesses that Christ drew him from the moment he was marked with the sign of the cross in infancy. The encounter was the promise of both the crisis and the quest that it generated. No crisis, no quest; no quest, no encounter.

VI. Interaction and Commitment

But the encounter had to start somewhere with someone. For Justin, it begins with the old Jewish Christian during a day at the beach; for Epicurus, with the cranky fanatic; for Rhoda, with Phoebe the deacon; for Gregory and Athenodoros, with Origen the teacher; for Augustine, with Ambrose the catechist. From that point on, as current research shows, conversion is the result of continual interaction between the new religious reality, as advocate, and the potential convert. Interaction takes the form of a combination of education and ritual that at once enables and leads to commitment.[14]

Paganism

For Lucius, the initial encounter is with the priest who carries the roses. The continual interaction begins when he makes his home in the temple with the priests, from whom he learns the obligations of the cult, with whom he tests his capacity for chastity, and among whom he develops virtue, all the while worshiping Isis. Only after nine months is he fully initiated into the community.

At what point he made a clear-cut choice and personal commitment is impossible to say. Is it when he awakes from his sleep on the beach? When he makes his home with the temple priests? When he emerges from his nocturnal journey in the crypt? It bears all the marks of a decision that comes gradually to fruition as he enters the stages and enacts the rites of the Isis mystery.

For the Pythagoreans, once a candidate is admitted as a hearer (akousmatikos), his probation takes eight years, years devoted to study and a communal life laced with rituals, largely unspecified. Interaction starts with extended scrutiny by the master. A five-year silence to acquire self-mastery follows, coupled with attendance at the master's discourses "outside the veil." Although he was initiated as a disciple with "many great cleansings and purifications of the soul," he is still on probation; as a hearer *(akousmatikos),* he hears discourses on practical wisdom, or as a true philosopher *(mathematikos),* discourses on the source and nature of things. Like postulancy, commitment had its stages and took solid root only at initiation.

Why is ritual an essential component of interaction, decision, and commitment? Effective rites solidify and clarify the mysteries of the human heart, especially when radical change is involved.[15] Ritual is performance; it enacts decision and commitment, giving them both private and public existence. As a contemporary performance analyst puts it,

> Someone begins to move to a new place in the social order; this move is accomplished through ritual, or blocked; in either case a crisis arises because any change in status involves a readjustment of the entire scheme; this readjustment is effected ceremonially—that is, by means of theater.[16]

Judaism

We have much less information about the God-fearer than about the Isiacists and Pythagoreans. Nonetheless, literature and inscriptions link God-fearers and synagogues, underscoring the fact that the synagogue was the important initial attraction for God-fearers, particularly in its function as a house of worship and Torah study, where two who sit and exchange words of the Torah between them find that the "*shekinah* [the divine presence] rests between them."[17]

After the exiles returned from Babylon, the word of God increasingly moved from oral tradition to sacred text. The "Torah of the Lord" became "the Book" *(ho biblos),* requiring scholars—copyists, editors, and interpreters.[18]

A. SCRIBES

Enter the *sopherim* (writers), those learned in the law and called scribes. Long a feature of royal bureaucratic service in preexilic Israel, after the exile they began to work as authors, commentators, and transmitters of biblical texts. In the beginning and for a long time, they were priests and Levites. By the second century B.C.E., however, the scribes could also be found in all the forms of Judaism we have encountered; *scribe* became the rough equivalent of "wise man" (Sir 38:34—39:11).

After the destruction of the second temple, the rabbis gradually assumed the scribal role.

Nonetheless, the teaching and interpreting of the Bible was carried out by a variety of teachers in a variety of settings for a variety of students, among them adults, children, and God-fearers. By the first century of our era, the setting is the synagogue—house of worship, place of study, and center of the social safety net—where the Bible and its proper interpretation were integral to prayer, study, and social work. There in the synagogue the God-fearers hear the Bible read, interpreted, prayed, and followed with sincerity of intention, if not with perfection in execution. When this book-centered liturgy and life strikes a spark, the God-fearer goes further and eventually approaches the teacher for instruction about what it takes to become a Jew. At least, this is a reasonable trajectory followed by most Pagan converts to Judaism.

But we know that the interaction between potential converts in the second-temple and rabbinic periods combined teaching and ritual: (1) profession of faith in Yahweh as the one true God; (2) acceptance of the Torah, instruction in it, and obedience to its prescriptions; (3) circumcision for males, the atoning bath, and entry into the community. The conversion of God-fearers was an extended process designed at once to clarify what life as a Jew involved and enable the candidate to make a clear-cut choice and commitment. The community could be sure that a person was a proselyte vested with the full rights and responsibilities of the community only when he or she emerged from the *mikveh*. Conversion was the kind of thorough readjustment that can be effected only ritually, or, as our analyst puts it, "ceremonially."

B. THE DIASPORA

Conversion in the diaspora would not normally have differed much from the process in Palestine. Yet *Joseph and Asenath* cautions against thinking uniformity prevailed. Like the *Confessions*'s account of Augustine's experience in the garden at Milan, the work emphasizes the inner drama of conversion. Joseph is the advocate-teacher. Love and marriage constitute honorable motivation for conversion. Asenath does not simply make up her mind about the gods and the Most High; she enacts her choice and commitment with insightful drama: out the window go the gods and all of her royal insignia for the poor to glean. The scenes of return, repentance, and reconciliation are depicted in terms imbued with the sense of conversion as an awe-inspiring mystery *(mysterium tremendum)*, much like the graphic presentation of initiation at Jerusalem depicted by Cyril and Egeria. Dramatic license obscures the full extent of Asenath's quest and interaction by compressing it into a ritually symbolic eight days. Clearly, the ritual drama is heightened by compression of the events.

C. THE SECTS

Conversion within Judaism meant conversion to the true Israel, exemplified by the Essenes, Pharisees, Johannites, and Christians.

Pharisees

What conversion to Pharisaism entailed is impossible to recover. The identifiable pharisaic sources in rabbinic literature do not address conversion, save to insist on the punctilious observance of the Torah. Nor are any of the celebrated ancient converts much help; Paul of Tarsus says no more than to insist that he was blameless under the Law and that he was "as to the law, a Pharisee" (Phil 3:6). The historian Josephus says that at sixteen he endured "hard training and laborious exercises *[polla ponêtheis]*" with the Pharisees, as well as with the Sadducees and Essenes, and that at nineteen he joined the Pharisees, indicating that they had rule of life, like the Stoic school of philosophers.[19]

We can only speculate about the training and exercises. Study of the oral and written Torah coupled with initiation into the kind of biblical interpretation that later characterized the rabbis seems an important component, together, perhaps, with a trial period of study and observance. A formal commitment to observe the pharisaic way of life seems also to have been in order, very likely in a ritual setting. But beyond the fact of continual interaction between a candidate and the community, nothing is certain.

Johannites

Conversion to the Johannites requires a sojourn into the wilderness and interaction with John and his disciples, including Jesus. The New Testament texts show that instruction about the imminence of final judgment and about what constitutes repentance is part of the interaction, as is the commitment to a penitential way of life characterized by justice and asceticism. At the end comes baptism. The rite symbolizes the candidate's rejection of his old, oppressive way of life and his determination to mend his ways and enables his decision and commitment to a new way. Only then can he anticipate the second baptism of the final and perfect purification at the end of days.

Qumran

The most extensive and demanding interaction with true Israel was conversion to the Essenes, in particular, admission to the covenant of mercy or repentance exemplified in the community at Qumran. The postulants first appear before the Guardian for inquiry into the quality of their character, life, and deeds. Josephus describes a year of solitary desert life with the bare essentials—a loincloth and a hatchet. This constitutes the first stage.

At Pentecost the second stage begins. Those the Guardian approves vow to turn from evil and to the teachings of the community in a ritual setting; they enact the initial decision and commitment to go further for a year.

The third stage brings provisional membership. Admission takes place before the community of full members, who vote to accept or reject. The postulant expresses his decision and commitment in a vow to live strictly by the Law as interpreted by the priest experts. Then follows immersion in a ritual bath of purification, followed by the confession of sins. He then hears a homily about walking in the ways of light guided by the spirit of light. The rites of this second Pentecost advance his decision and commitment; but this decision and commitment do not formally go beyond the coming year.

At the end of the third year, the postulant undergoes another scrutiny of his life and character at Pentecost. The community again votes for or against admission. An affirmative vote admits him, not to full membership, but to preliminary full membership. Within certain restrictions, he lives a full communal life. This third Pentecost advances the approved to hailing distance from full membership.

At Pentecost of the following year, the community again scrutinizes his life and character, voting on admission. With approval, his name is inscribed in the book of members and his property is merged with the community's; he participates fully in the life of the community and possesses the spirit of holiness. In all, the process spanned four years of intense interaction that involved instruction, scrutiny, and progressive response, all within a ritual context.

Christianity

Because Christianity left its Jewish home about the end of the first century to become another (and predominantly, Gentile) religion, I have treated conversion to Christianity apart from the Judaism of the sects. In the beginning, however, Christians were sectarian Jews. Jesus shares John's vision of the last day and the judgment. In time, he modifies John's vision to concentrate on entrance into God's kingdom—at once present and future, now and not yet—the kingdom in which God is at work visiting, healing, and redeeming his people through Jesus and his followers.

A. THE FIRST TWO CENTURIES

Jesus' disciples retain John's process: preaching *(kerygma)* and teaching *(didache),* asceticism, and baptism. The primary goal is repentance, signified by the determination to follow God's will as it is revealed in Christ. Immersion seals the process, incorporating the convert into the community.

Baptism is the hinge on which conversion turns. Three patterns evolve that specify its meaning and effectiveness. The baptism of Jesus in the Jordan is the first. His baptism affirms—at first, implicitly, then, explicitly—that what happens to Jesus in the Jordan happens to the candidate in the baptismal water. The second, the descent of the Holy Spirit—a pattern that predominates in Syria—emphasizes the identity of the agent of what happens in baptism, the Holy Spirit. The third, death and resurrection, which predominates in the third and fourth centuries, focuses attention on the source of the rite's effectiveness: participation in the death and resurrection of Jesus.

But baptism requires systematic preparation combined with the rituals of prayer, fasting, and moral reformation. By the end of the first century, the elements of the process are in place, awaiting the developments of the next three centuries.

As Christians engage the wider Greco-Roman world during the second century, they adapt elements of the Pagan way of conversion to their fundamentally sectarian Jewish way of initiating potential converts.

The *Didache,* Clement of the Pseudo-Clementine *Recognitions,* Justin Martyr, and Clement of Alexandria emphasize the cognitive element. The stages of conversion to Christianity reflect aspects of conversion to a philosophical school.[20] When the Didachist, Justin, and the two Clements accept what they are taught as the truth and undertake to live accordingly, the sectarian Jewish ritual process, with some modifications, takes over: prayer, communal fasting, baptism in the name of the Father, of the Son, and of the Holy Spirit, and entry into the community of Christians, signified by the kiss of welcome (the kiss of peace) and the celebration of their first eucharist.

Clement of Alexandria adds an emphasis we have seen in the Pythagorean way, conversion as an ongoing process. The first stage is faith signified by baptism; the second, moral progress, reflected by extensive instruction and measurable progress; the third, perfection, disclosed by maturity of mind, heart, and life.

B. THE THIRD CENTURY

All during the second century, Christianity encountered increasing hostility from its neighbors and, in the end, from the imperial government. Social and legal hostility left its mark on conversion. With increasing clarity, the process exhibited the characteristics of a rite of passage from the world of Greek and Roman culture, society, and religion to a Christian cultural, social, and religious world.

By the end of the third century, a Roman convert, like the freedman Epicurus, normally spends three years under instruction—both moral and doctrinal—and supervision. He is one of a threshold group called "catechumens," people betwixt and between the world from which they are coming and the world to which they want to go. Liminality is their condition.

When the reformation of Epicurus' life is amply attested and approved, he is admitted to a group of the elect and allowed to advance toward baptismal initiation. He can now hear the gospel read and explained; after instruction, he is exorcised. A solemn episcopal scrutiny in the form of exorcism signifies the arrival of the critical moment, baptismal initiation. He bathes on Thursday for reasons practical and religious. The next two days require a strict fast. On Saturday night he assembles with the rest of the elect for a final episcopal exorcism. At Sunday's first light, he renounces Satan before a priest, who then anoints him. A deacon descends into the water with him and immerses him, as he answers, "I believe," to each of the deacon's three questions about God the Father, the Son, and the Holy Spirit. On emerging from the water, he is anointed again and dresses in a white garment. The bishop anoints him on the forehead and welcomes him to the community with a kiss. Now a full member, he has his first eucharistic meal with the members, the elements signifying his new status and life.

The stages and rites of initiation varied across the Mediterranean world, differing in detail from Hippolytus' Rome to Tertullian's North Africa, Origen's Alexandria and Caesarea, Rhoda's Syria, Philip's eastern Syria, and Thomas' Edessa. But the underlying structure is the same: interaction and commitment, which combined an extended period of instruction and probation with richly articulated rites of initiation that led to incorporation into the community.

C. THE FOURTH CENTURY

Constantine's toleration of Christianity and the eventual establishment of Christianity as the state religion of the Roman empire profoundly alter the process of conversion. Conversion begins with a distinctive rite of enrollment. The newly enrolled are catechumens, whose principal obligation is to attend the instructional part of the eucharist. The purpose is to gradually shape their moral lives and values. Although there were as many reasons why someone wanted to be a catechumen as there were catechumens—marriage; an infant in a Christian home; social, economic, or political preferment; and piety were some—catechumens were, in practice, considered members of the church, albeit not full-fledged. And they might remain catechumens for close to a lifetime.

Some catechumens sought full membership. In Jerusalem or Milan, when they decide to ask for baptism, they submit their names on Epiphany (January 6) for Easter baptism. Enrollment signifies both their intention and the church's acceptance; at that point they become competents.

For the next seven weeks they live a severely ascetic life. The first few weeks are devoted to daily instruction in the liturgy, especially about the moral lessons to be seen in biblical heroes like Abraham. As Easter draws near, instruction changes from biblical to doctrinal. The syllabus is the creed, which they will be called on to profess publicly.

The dramatic pace of their conversion accelerates on the Sunday before Easter, when candidates profess the creed publicly in their own voices. Great Week starts, and each succeeding day intensifies the drama. The turning point arrives the following Saturday night. The central events of the biblical history of salvation from Genesis through Daniel are chanted, explained, contemplated, and prayed.

The awesome moment arrives with cockcrow. Stripped naked, the competents are exorcised and anointed, like athletes headed to the Olympic arena. To make their decisions clear-cut and public, they renounce Satan and profess the creed, breaking an old allegiance and creating a new one. To enact the process of death to the old self and rebirth to the new, they enter the baptismal pool for immersion and emerge to be anointed.

As newly baptized, they are full Christians, and the rites that follow dramatize their new status. They dress in white, receive the welcoming kiss from the community, sing psalms that allude to their new condition, share the eucharist for the first time, and spend the next week as the prized new members of the family. They have been reborn and are risen.

A note of caution: They are just at the beginning, as Clement of Alexandria points out and as their new names signify: novices *(novitioli),* infants *(infantes),* neophytes *(neophytai).*

D. A SUMMARY VIEW

Whether in the first or the fourth century, interaction between potential converts and the community and the development of commitment had a clear pattern in which instruction and ritual were woven inextricably together. The process was cognitive; a new cultural, social, and religious world was built. At the same time the process was performative—that new world was embraced and entered. In Paganism, Judaism, and Christianity, conversion was performed in a deeply symbolic drama, a drama that resists reduction to its psychological, social, or religious components. For the ancients, it was a drama in which the divine and the human intersect.

VII. Transformation

The change at the root of conversion is nothing less than transformation, which, for the ancients, depends on the intersection between the divine and the human. What was transformed? Sometimes one's body, as in the case of the blind woman at the Asclepius sanctuary. But more was at stake than the body. As William James and Arthur Darby Nock saw long ago, conversion results in a reorientation of the "personal center of energy" (James) or "soul" (Nock). The preferred ancient term is *spirit (psyche/spiritus/anima)*.

Contemporary researchers employ a variety of terms for the process of reorientation, among them, *progress, regression, fixation, faith development,* and *the reconstitution of the self*.[21] Dissatisfaction with abstract descriptors, however, has led some to go back to the Greco-Roman metaphors of death and rebirth and enlightenment.[22]

A. DEATH AND REBIRTH

The dominant metaphors for transformation were two sides of the same coin, the passage from death to life and the passage from darkness to light, with the former turning up more frequently than the latter.

In the mystery religions, the candidate for full initiation is considered a person about to die *(homo moriturus)*. Indeed, just before his initiation, Lucius says,

> For the gates of hell and the guarantee of life alike were in the power of the goddess, and the very rite of dedication itself was performed in the manner of a voluntary death and of a life obtained by grace.[23]

Among the Pythagoreans, when a probationer leaves the community he is given twice the value of the resources he brought with him, but from that moment on he is considered one who is dead, even to the point that his fellow probationers build a tomb for him. Those who remain are alive and have the lively hope of living forever, united with the One.

In ancient Judaism, the focus of the metaphor is the Torah; outside its pale there is only alienation and sin. Gentiles are "sinners." When proselytes emerge from the *mikveh,* they are Jews, have a new family, and live a new life in a new world. According to the Talmud, proselytes are like newborn infants.[24] And the one who converts them is counted as one who has created them anew, for he has brought them into the divine presence, spoken of as the wings of the *shekinah*.[25] They are new creations; now they are fully human because they have the possibility of doing the will of God and leading a life that truly reflects the image of God.[26]

Among the sectaries of Qumran, the metaphor of enlightenment turns up more frequently. According the *Community Rule,* the newly initiated are "Sons of Light," whereas those who follow a life of lustful eyes and a sinful heart are "Sons of Darkness" (1). Yet death and rebirth are on the other side of the coin: the Sons of Light are "born of truth" and "spring from a fountain of light," while the Sons of Darkness are "born of falsehood" and "spring from a source of darkness" (3).

Paul reflects something of this Qumran perspective. He writes to the Corinthians, "So if anyone is in Christ, there is a new creation; everything old has passed away; see, everything has become new!" (2 Cor 5:17). His meaning is made more explicit in the First Letter of Peter. Converts have been "born anew, not of perishable but of imperishable seed" (1 Pt 1:22); indeed, they are "like newborn infants, [who] long for the pure, spiritual milk" (1 Pt 2:2).

John the Evangelist's account of Jesus and Nicodemus is equally emphatic: "No one can see the kingdom of God without being born from above," for no one can "enter the kingdom of God without being born of water and Spirit" (Jn 3:3–5).

While John envisions the life of the newborn as a life of seeing and walking in the light, Paul understands their life as walking in the newness of resurrection. Through baptism, converts are united to Christ in his death that they might be united "with him in a resurrection like his" (Rom 6:3–5). Indeed, his interpretation of baptism as participation in the death and resurrection of Christ became one of the models, along with Christ's baptism in the Jordan and the descent of the Holy Spirit at Pentecost, that disclose the meaning of baptism and conversion to early Christians: the life of the reborn is participation in the risen life of the Savior.

Baptism as the passage from death to life gave rise to the image of the baptismal font as tomb and womb.[27] For Cyril of Jerusalem, for instance, the old "self" is buried in the waters just as Christ was buried in the tomb, and two baptismal rites make the point unmistakable. The baptizands are ritually stripped of their clothes, which, by the fourth century, are penitential tunics of sackcloth. According to Ambrose of Milan, they are garments of corruption and death (for Lucius, they were the skins of the ass that he sloughed off).[28] The baptizands are then immersed in the baptismal waters, which Ambrose's contemporary, John Chrysostom (c. 345–407 C.E.), regularly calls a tomb *(taphos),* insisting that the "old self has been crucified with him, in order that the body of sin may be destroyed."[29]

The font as womb emphasizes the passage to life, with rebirth and resurrection used almost interchangeably. The same Chrysostom remarks, "Conception without womb, begetting without bosom, birth without flesh!"[30] Yet he insists that in baptism there are both burial *(taphe)* and resurrection *(anastasis)* at the same time.[31]

This new life is symbolized by a variety of baptismal rites. By emerging from the font naked and glistening, they enact their rebirth. As Christ rose from the tomb, they rise from the water—this is the moment of their conception without womb to which Chrysostom addresses attention. After the anointing, they put on white linen garments. Another contemporary of Ambrose, Gregory of Nyssa (c. 335– 394 C.E.), explains that the white robes are the counterpart of the garments of sin put on in the Fall; they signify their restoration to the original integrity in which Adam was created.[32]

B. ENLIGHTENMENT

As we have already seen in the *Community Rule,* baptism is also a passage from darkness to light. Among the rabbis, the route is a little circuitous. Repeatedly they speak of the proselyte as "brought under the wings of the *shekinah,*" a term the Bible usually symbolizes by fire and light.[33] One need only think of the pillar of fire that leads the Israelites through the wilderness at night or of the devouring fire that surrounds the top of Sinai when God reveals the Torah to Moses (Ex 13:21–22; 24:17). Under the wings of the divine presence, they are in the light and can walk according to God's will, with the Torah as a lamp for their feet.

The theme of light suffuses Luke's account of Paul's conversion; he is blinded and regains his sight at the hands of Ananias just before his baptism (Acts 9:1–19).[34] Sight and light are interchangeable also in the Gospel of John, who, reminiscent of the Qumran sectaries, refers to his community as the "children of light" (Jn 12:35). Indeed, the turning point of the first part of the gospel, generally considered the Book of Signs, is the healing-conversion of the man born blind (Jn 9:1–41): "Jesus said to him, 'You have seen him [the Son of Man], and the one speaking with you is he.' He said, 'Lord, I believe.' And he worshipped him. Jesus said, 'I came into this world for judgment so that those who do not see may see . . .'" (Jn 9:37–39).

Conversion is seeing; seeing is the result of baptism; baptism is enlightenment. It is an equation that the Letter to the Hebrews, in speaking about postbaptismal sin, makes: "For it is impossible to restore again to repentance those who have once been enlightened, and have tasted the heavenly gift, and have shared in the Holy Spirit" (Heb 6:4). Justin Martyr and Clement of Alexandria are simply record- ing a long-standing tradition when they write that baptism, the solemn moment of conversion, is enlightenment *(photisma).*[35]

VIII. Conversion: A Concluding Image

Other metaphors abound in antiquity, especially sanctification and deification. Apuleius, however, has left us the most graphic ancient metaphor, one that at once portrays all the aspects of transformation and embodies the entire process of conversion—from a beast, Lucius had become a god:

> When morning came and the ceremonies *[sollemnibus]* were com- pleted, I came forth wearing twelve robes as a sign of consecration. This is a very holy [religious] attire. . . . Following instructions I stood on a wooden platform set up in the very center of the holy shrine in front of the goddess's [Isis] statue, the focus of attention because of my garment, which was only linen, but elaborately embroidered. An expensive cloak hung down my back from my shoulders all the way to my heels. . . . The initiates call this the Olympian stole [for Mount Olympus, home of the gods]. In my right hand I carried a torch alight with flames, and my head was beautifully bound with a crown made of leaves of shining palm, jut- ting out like rays of light. After I had thus been [adorned] in the likeness of the Sun and set up in the guise of a statue, the curtains were suddenly opened and the people wandered round to [behold] me.[36]

NOTES

1. For discussion, see Lewis R. Rambo, *Understanding Religious Conversion* (New Haven: Yale University Press, 1993) 2–4.

2. Thus, Karl F. Morrison, *Conversion and Text: The Cases of Augustine of Hippo, Herman-Judah, and Constantine Tsatsos* (Charlottesville: University of Virginia Press, 1992) vii–xvii. His fundamental position in this work and in *Understanding Conversion* (Charlottesville: University of Virginia Press, 1992) is to draw a sharp distinction between conversion as supernatural trans- formation completed, if at all, by grace and formal institutional acts like the rit- uals we have studied. For him they are a "hypocritical charade" (3). The

ancients, including Augustine, would agree, but they hold that ritual enactment is normally the indispensable medium.

3. Augustine, *Conf.* 1:1 (James J. O'Donnell, ed., *Augustine: Confessions* [Oxford: Clarendon Press, 1992] 1:3): *tu excitas ut laudare te delectet, quia fecisti nos ad te et inquietum est cor nostrum donec requiescat in te.* Commentators agree that in this statement he sounds a major theme of the work.

4. For discussion, see G. W. Bowersock, *Hellenism in Late Antiquity* (Ann Arbor: University of Michigan Press, 1990) 1–13; and for Syrian Hellenism and the survival of a flourishing Paganism, 29–40.

5. For an analysis of the research, see Rambo, *Understanding Religious Conversion,* 44–55.

6. Augustine, *Conf.* 7:3.5 (O'Donnell, 1:75; for the translation, see Morrison, *Conversion and Text,* 7).

7. Ibid.: *ad illum infernum subducebar erroris.*

8. Peter L. Berger, *The Sacred Canopy: Elements of a Sociological Theory of Religion* (Garden City, N.Y.: Doubleday [Anchor Books], 1969) 1–25. See the earlier and more extensive treatment, Peter L. Berger and Thomas Luckmann, *The Social Construction of Reality: A Treatise in the Sociology of Knowledge* (Garden City, N.Y.: Doubleday, 1966) 169–170, especially 172; and Berger, "Identity as a Problem in the Sociology of Knowledge," in James E. Curtis and John W. Petras, eds., *The Sociology of Knowledge: A Reader* (New York: Praeger Publishers, 1970) 373–84. Rambo brings the research bibliography up to date in *Understanding Religious Conversion,* 186.

9. The hymn is the ancient Latin sequence for Pentecost Sunday, *Veni, Sancte Spiritus,* vv. 3–4: "Come, Father of the poor, come, giver of gifts, come, light of hearts. . . . [You] are our rest in labor, pleasant coolness in the heat, solace in our weeping" (*Veni pater pauperum, veni, dator munerum, veni, lumen cordium. . . . In labore requies, in aestu temperies, in fletu solatium* [*Missale romanum ex decreto sacrosancti concilii Tridentini restitutum* (New York: Benziger Brothers, 1936) 322]).

10. For the modern attempts, see James C. Livingston, *The Anatomy of the Sacred: An Introduction to Religion,* 2nd ed. (New York: Macmillan, 1993) 3–22; and Winston King, "Religion," *ER* 12:282–92. Livingston adopts a working substantive definition: "Religion is that system of activities and beliefs directed toward that which is perceived to be of sacred value and transforming power."

11. Cicero, *De natura deorum academica* 2:28.72 (H. Rackham, ed., *Cicero: De natura deorum academica,* Loeb (1933) 192–93.

12. Augustine, *De diversis quaestionibus* 30:1 (PL 40:19); *De vera religione* 55:111 (PL 34:171); *Retractationes* 13:9 (PL 32:605). Cicero gives the

root as *leg,* as in *legere,* to read; Augustine gives Cicero's derivation and then offers the root as *lig,* as in *ligare,* to bind (*Retract.* 13:9). But see *De civitate dei* 10:3.1, *religere,* as the derivation.

13. Augustine, *Conf.* 7:11.17; 7:17.23 (O'Donnell 1:82–84).

14. See Rambo, *Understanding Religious Conversion,* 102–23.

15. For discussion of contemporary research and experience, see ibid., 127–37.

16. The analyst is Professor of Performance Studies Richard Schechner, cited in Victor Turner, *The Anthropology of Performance* (New York: Performing Arts Journal Publications, 1986) 74. Schechner wrote the preface. Turner takes ceremonial to be a social enactment, and ritual to be a religious one. The difference is depth of engagement. Schechner here uses ceremonial for ritual.

17. *Pirke Aboth* 3:3 (*Pirke Aboth, The Ethics of the Talmud: Sayings of the Fathers,* ed. R. Travers Herford [New York: Schocken Books, 1962] 66). For a recent discussion of the function and architecture, see Eric M. Meyers, "Synagogue," *ABD* 6:251–60. It is important to distinguish private houses and other buildings converted for congregational use from buildings erected as synagogues. The former dominated in the early years; the latter, later. In Palestine, the synagogue building appears toward the end of the second century C.E.

18. For discussion, see Anthony J. Saldarini, *Pharisees, Scribes, and Sadducees in Palestinian Society: A Sociological Approach* (Wilmington: Michael Glazier, 1988) 41–76; his "Scribes," *ABD* 5:1012–16; and James L. Kugel, in Kugel and Rowan A. Greer, *Early Biblical Interpretation* (Philadelphia: Westminster Press [Library of Early Christianity, ed. Wayne A. Meeks], 1986) 52–72.

19. Josephus, *The Life* 1:2 (St. J. Thackeray, Loeb 1 [1926] 6–7).

20. The "two-way" method in the *Didache* radiates the method of teaching in the Hellenistic diaspora, which itself reflects the cognitive emphasis in Greco-Roman conversion, a sort of wisdom discourse.

21. See Rambo, *Understanding Religious Conversion,* 142–58; and Theodore R. Sarbin and Nathan Adler, "Self-Reconstitution Processes: A Preliminary Report," *Psychoanalytic Review* 57 (1970) 599–616.

22. Sarbin and Adler, "Self-Reconstitution Processes," 606–10.

23. Apuleius, *Metamorphoses* 11:21 (J. Gwyn Griffiths, *Apuleius of Madauros: The Isis-Book [Metamorphoses, Book XI]* [Leiden: E. J. Brill, 1975] 94–95).

24. See *Yeb.* 22a (*Bavli,* I. Epstein, ed., *The Babylonian Talmud: Seder Nashim* I, 131).

25. See K. H. Rengstorf, "*gennaô,* The Idea of New Birth by Conversion to the True Religion in Later Judaism," *TDNT* 1:666–68.

26. Ibid.

27. For discussion of the history of the image, see Walter Bedard, *The Symbol of the Baptismal Font in Early Christian Thought* (Washington, D.C.: Catholic University Press [Studies in Christian Theology 45, series 2], 1951).

28. Ambrose, *De Isaac* 6:52 (CSEL 34, 1:676.16–20), cited in Johannes Quasten, "Theodore of Mopsuestia on Exorcism in the Cilicium," *HTR* 35 (1942) 218.

29. Chrysostom, *Baptismal Instruction* 10:8 (text and translation in my *The Liturgy of Baptism in the Baptismal Instructions of St. John Chrysostom,* SCA 15 [1967] 159).

30. Chrysostom, *In principium Actorum* 6 (PG 51:96)—not to be confused with his homilies on the Acts of the Apostles.

31. Chrysostom, *Bapt. Instr.* 10:11 (Finn, *The Liturgy of Baptism in John Chrysostom,* 159).

32. Gregory of Nyssa, *De vita Moysis* (PG 44:409B, cited in Finn, *The Liturgy of Baptism in John Chrysostom,* 192).

33. See *Bavli Shabbat* 31a, above, n. 25; Midrash: *Yalkut Shimoni, Shelah* 14.

34. For discussion, see Ronald D. Witherup, *Conversion in the New Testament* (Collegeville: Liturgical Press [A Michael Glazier Book, Zacchaeus Studies: New Testament, ed. Mary Ann Getty], 1994) 65–68.

35. Justin, *First Apology* 61; Clement, *Paidagogos* 1:6 (PG 8:281a). The numerous patristic references are collected in G. W. H. Lampe, ed., *A Patristic Greek Lexicon* (Oxford: Clarendon Press, 1968) 5:1509–10. For a study, see Thomas Halton, "Baptism as Illumination," *Irish Theological Quarterly* 32 (1965) 28–41.

36. Apuleius, *Metam.* 11:24 (Arthur J. Hanson, ed. and trans., *Apuleius: Metamorphoses,* Loeb [1989] 2:340–42), slightly altered. For detailed commentary, see Griffiths, *The Isis-Book,* 308–20. The twelve stoles signified the twelve hours of the night through which the Sun god traveled; Lucius had discarded his old clothes and was naked in the interim. His cloak is a *chlamys,* decorated with solar and Osirian reminiscences. The torch is typical priestly attire in cult scenes. The crown represents the radiate sun. The entire ambience indicates that he is being treated as a god: initiation divinized him. Griffiths comments that by wearing the clothing of the deity, one becomes the deity (317). The people clearly venerate rather than just admire him. The feast that follows is clearly a birthday feast celebrating his new birth.

BIBLIOGRAPHY

Armstrong, A. Hilary, *Expectations of Immortality in Late Antiquity* (Marquette: Marquette University Press, 1987).

Athanassakis, A. N., ed., *The Orphic Hymns: Text, Translations, and Notes* (Missoula: Scholars Press, 1977).

Aubin, Paul, *Le problème de la 'conversion': Étude sur un terme commun à l'hellenisme et au christianisme des trois premiers siècles* (Paris: Beauchesne, 1962).

Aune, David E., "Oracles," *ER* 11:81–86.

Avery-Peck, Alan, "Judaism Without the Temple," in *Eusebius, Christianity, and Judaism,* ed. Harold W. Attridge and Gohei Hata (Detroit: Wayne State University Press, 1992).

Baigent, Michael, and Richard Leigh, *The Dead Sea Scrolls Deception* (New York: Summit Books, 1991).

Baldovin, John F., *Liturgy in Ancient Jerusalem* (Bramcote, Nottingham: Grove Books [GLS 57], 1989).

Bardy, G., *Eusèbe de Césarée: Histoire Ecclésiastique,* vol. 1 (Paris: Les Éditions du Cerf [SC 31], 1965).

———, ed., *Eusèbe de Césarée: Histoire ecclésiastique, livres I–IV* (Paris: Les Éditions du Cerf [SC 31], 1978).

Barnes, Timothy D., *Tertullian: A Historical and Literary Study* (Oxford: Clarendon Press, 1971).

Barrett-Lennard, R. J. S., trans., *The Sacramentary of Sarapion of Thmuis* (Bramcote, Nottingham: Grove Books [GLS 25], 1993.

Barth, Christoph, "Notes on 'Return' in the Old Testament," *The Ecumenical Review* 19 (1967) 310–12.

Beard, Mary, "Priesthood in the Roman Republic," in Mary Beard and John North, eds., *Pagan Priests: Religion and Power in the Ancient World* (Ithaca: Cornell University Press, 1990).

Bedard, Walter, *The Symbolism of the Baptismal Font in Early Christian Thought* (Washington, D.C.: Catholic University of America Press [Studies in Christian Theology 45, series 2], 1951).

Bell, Clive, *Art* (New York: Capricorn Books, 1958).

Bennett, R., "Pythagoras," *ER* 12:113–15.

Benoit, A., *Le baptême au second siècle* (Paris, 1953).

Berard, V., *L'Odyssée*, vol. 2 (Paris: Les Belles Lettres, 1968).

Berger, Peter L., "Identity as a Problem in the Sociology of Knowledge," in *The Sociology of Knowledge: A Reader,* ed. James C. Curtis and John W. Petras (New York: Praeger Publishers, 1970) 373–83.

———, *The Sacred Canopy: Elements of a Sociological Theory of Religion* (Garden City, N.Y.: Doubleday [Anchor Books], 1969).

———, and Thomas Luckmann, *The Social Construction of Reality: A Treatise in the Sociology of Knowledge* (Garden City, N.Y.: Doubleday, 1966).

Betz, Hans Dieter, *Galatians: A Commentary on Paul's Letter to the Galatians* (Philadelphia: Fortress Press [Hermeneia], 1979).

———, ed., *The Greek Magical Papyri in Translation, Including the Demotic Spells,* 2nd ed. (Chicago: University of Chicago Press, 1986).

Black, Matthew, *The Scrolls and Christian Origins: Studies in the Jewish Background of the New Testament* (New York: Charles Scribner's Sons, 1961).

Blanc, Cécile, "Le baptême d'après Origène," *SP* 11:2 (1972) 113–23.

Borgen, Peder. *Philo, John and Paul: New Perspectives on Judaism and Early Christianity* (Atlanta: Scholars Press [Brown Judaic Studies 131], 1987).

Botte, Bernard, ed., *Ambroise de Milan: des sacramentis, des mysteriis, l'explication du symbole* (Paris: Les Éditions du Cerf [SC 25bis], 1961).

———, *Hippolyte de Rome: La Tradition Apostolique d'après les anciennes versions* (Paris: Les Éditions du Cerf [SC 11bis], 1968.

———, *La Tradition Apostolique de Saint Hippolyte: Essai de Reconstitution* (Münster: Aschendorf Verlag [LQF 39], 1963).

Bowersock, G. W., *Hellenism in Late Antiquity* (Ann Arbor: University of Michigan Press, 1990).

Bradshaw, Paul F., "Baptismal Practice in the Alexandrian Tradition: Eastern or Western," in Bradshaw, ed., *Essays in Early Eastern Initiation* (Bramcote, Nottingham: Grove Books [GLS 56], 1988) 5–17.

———, "Re-dating the *Apostolic Tradition:* Some Preliminary Steps," *Festschrift for Aidan Kavanagh,* ed. J. Baldovin and N. Mitchell (Collegeville: Liturgical Press, forthcoming).

————, *The Search for the Origins of Christian Worship: Sources and Methods for the Study of Early Liturgy* (Oxford: Oxford University Press, 1992).

————, ed., and Carol Bebawi, trans., *The Canons of Hippolytus* (Bramcote, Nottingham: Grove Books [GLS 50], 1987).

Brock, Sebastian, *The Holy Spirit in the Syrian Baptismal Tradition* (Poona, India: Anita Printers [The Syrian Church Series 9, ed. Jacob Vellian], 1979).

————, *The Liturgical Portions of the Didascalia* (Bramcote, Nottingham: Grove Books [GLS 29], 1982).

Brooks, E. W., *Joseph and Asenath: The Confession and Prayer of Asenath, Daughter of Pentephres the Priest* (London: SPCK, 1918).

Brown, Peter, *Augustine of Hippo: A Biography* (Berkeley: University of California Press, 1967).

Brown, Raymond E., *The Epistles of John* (Garden City, N.Y.: Doubleday [Anchor Bible Commentaries], 1982).

Buchanan, George W., "Worship, Feasts, and Ceremonies in the Early Jewish Christian Church," *NTS* 26 (1980).

Buck, M. J. A., trans., *S. Ambrosii: De Helia et Ieiunio* (Washington, D.C.: Catholic University of America [Patristic Studies 19], 1929).

Buckley, Jorunn Jacobsen, "A Cult-Mystery in *The Gospel of Philip*," *JBL* 99 (1980) 569–81.

Burghardt, Walter J., "Catechetics in the Early Church," *The Living Light* 1 (1964) 100–118.

Burkert, Walter, *Ancient Mystery Cults* (Cambridge: Harvard University Press, 1987).

————, *Lore and Science in Ancient Pythagoreanism,* trans. E. Minar (Cambridge: Harvard University Press, 1972).

Burnet, John, ed., *Plato: Politeias, Platonis Opera,* vol. 4 (Oxford: Clarendon Press, 1902).

Busch, Benedictus, "De initiatione christiana secundum sanctum Augustinum," *Ephemerides Liturgicae Analecta* 52 (1938) 159–67 (pre-Augustine North Africa), 385–483 (Augustine's North Africa).

Butterworth, G. W., ed. and trans., *Clement of Alexandria* (London and New York: William Heinemann/ G. P. Putnam's Sons [Loeb], 1919).

Cardman, Francine, "Fourth Century Jerusalem: Religious Geography and Christian Tradition," in *Schools of Thought in the Christian Tradition,* ed. Patrick Henry (Philadelphia: Fortress Press, 1984) 49–64.

Chadwick, Henry, ed. and trans., *Origen: Contra Celsum* (Cambridge: Cambridge University Press, 1965).

————, trans., *St. Augustine: Confessions* (New York: Oxford University Press, 1991).

Charlesworth, James H., ed., *Jesus and the Dead Sea Scrolls* (Garden City, N.Y.: Doubleday [Anchor Bible Reference Library, ed. David Noel Freedman], 1992).

Cohen, Shaye J. D., "Conversion to Judaism in Historical Perspective: From Biblical Israel to Postbiblical Judaism," *Conservative Judaism* (1983) 31–45.

———, "Crossing the Boundary and Becoming a Jew," *HTR* 82 (1989) 13–33.

———, *From the Maccabees to the Mishnah* (Philadelphia: Westminster Press, 1987).

———, "The Rabbinic Conversion Ceremony," *JJS* 41 (1990) 177–203.

Cohn, A., ed., *The Minor Tractates of the Talmud*, vol. 2 (London: Soncino Press, 1965).

Collins, Adela Yarbro, "The Origin of Christian Baptism," *SL* 19 (1989) 28–44.

Collins, John J., "Circumcision and Salvation in the First Century," in Jacob Neusner and Ernest S. Frerichs, eds., *"To See Ourselves as Others See Us": Christians, Jews and Others in Late Antiquity* (Chico: Scholars Press, 1985) 163–86.

———, "Dead Sea Scrolls," *ABD* 2:85–101.

———, "Essenes," *ABD* 2:619–26.

———, "A Symbol of Otherness," in Jacob Neusner and Ernest S. Frerichs, eds., *"To See Ourselves as Others See Us": Christians, Jews and Others in Late Antiquity* (Chico: Scholars Press, 1985) 164–70.

Colson, F. H., and G. H. Whitaker, *Philo* (New York: G. P. Putnam's Sons [Loeb], 1932).

Conn, Walter, *Christian Conversion: A Developmental Interpretation of Autonomy and Surrender* (Mahwah, N.J.: Paulist Press, 1986).

Connolly, R. H., *"Didascalia Apostolorum": The Syriac Version Translated and Accompanied by the Verona Latin Fragments* (Oxford: Clarendon Press, 1929).

———, *Explanatio Symboli ad Initiandos: A Work of St. Ambrose* (Cambridge: Cambridge University Press [Texts and Studies 10], 1952).

———, *The So-Called Egyptian Church Order and Derived Documents* (Cambridge: Cambridge University Press [Texts for Students 8, vol. 4], 1916).

Costa, C., *Seneca: Seventeen Letters* (Warminster, Wilts., U.K.: Ars & Phillips, 1988).

Cramer, Peter, *Baptism and Change in the Early Middle Ages: c. 200–c. 1150* (Cambridge: Cambridge University Press, 1993).

Cross, F. L., *I Peter: A Paschal Liturgy* (London: Mowbray, 1994).

Cumming, Geoffrey J., ed., *Essays on Hippolytus* (Bramcote, Nottingham: Grove Books [GLS 15], 1978).

————, *Hippolytus: A Text for Students* (Bramcote, Nottingham: Grove Books [GLS 8], 1976).

Cumont, Franz, *After Life in Roman Paganism* (1922; reprint, Dover Publications, 1959).

Dahood, Mitchell, *The Anchor Bible: Psalms II, 51–100* (New York: Doubleday, 1968).

Daly, Emily J., trans. *Tertullian: Apology* (Washington, D.C.: Catholic University of America Press [FC 10], 1950).

Daniélou, Jean, *The Bible and the Liturgy* (Notre Dame: University of Notre Dame Press [Liturgical Studies], 1956).

————, *From Shadows to Reality: Studies in Biblical Typology*, trans. Wulstan Hibberd (London: Burns and Oates; Westminster, Md.: Newman Press, 1960).

Davies, Philip R., *The Damascus Covenant: An Interpretation of the "Damascus Document"* (Sheffield: Journal for the Study of the Old Testament Supplement, series 25, 1983).

————, "Damascus Rule (CD)," *ABD* 2:8–10.

De Clerck, Paul, "Pénitence seconde et conversion quotidienne aux IIIème et IVème siècles," *SP* 20 (1989) 352–74.

Deferrari, R. J., trans., *St. Ambrose: Theological and Dogmatic Works* (Washington, D.C.: Catholic University of America Press [FC 44], 1963).

Dillon, John, and Jackson Hershbell, eds., *Iamblichus: On the Pythagorean Way of Life, Text, Translation, and Notes* (Atlanta: Scholars Press, 1991).

Dimant, Devorah, "Pesharim, Qumran," *ABD* 5:244–51.

Dirksen, Aloys H., *The New Testament Concept of Metanoia* (Dissertation, Catholic University of America, 1932).

Dix, Gregory, *The "Apostolic Tradition" of Hippolytus,* rev. ed., ed. Henry Chadwick (London: SPCK, 1968).

Dodd, C. H., *The Apostolic Preaching and Its Developments* (London: Hodder & Stoughton, 1963).

Dodds, E. R., *The Greeks and the Irrational* (Berkeley: University of California Press, 1951).

————, *Pagan and Christian in an Age of Anxiety: Some Aspects of Religious Experience from Marcus Aurelius to Constantine* (1965; reprint, New York: W. W. Norton and Company, 1970).

Dondeyne, A., "La discipline des scrutins dans l'Église latine avant Charlemagne," *Revue d'Histoire Ecclésiastique* 28 (1932) 5–33.

Doval, Alexis J., *The Authorship of the Mystagogic Catecheses Attributed to St. Cyril of Jerusalem* (Dissertation, Oxford University, Faculty of Theology, 1992).

———, "The Location and Structure of the Baptistery in the *Mystagogic Catecheses* of Cyril of Jerusalem," *SP* 26 (1993) 1–13.

Dudden, F. Homes, *The Life and Times of St. Ambrose*, vol. 1 (Oxford: Clarendon Press, 1935).

Duncan, E. J., *Baptism and the Demonstrations of Aphraates, the Persian Sage* (Washington, D.C.: Catholic University of America Press [SCA 8], 1948).

Dupont-Sommer, André, *The Essene Writings from Qumran*, trans. Geza Vermes (Cleveland: World [Meridian], 1962).

Echle, Harry A., "Sacramental Initiation as a Christian Mystery-Initiation according to Clement of Alexandria," in Odo Casel, *Vom Christlichen Mysterium* (Düsseldorf: Patmos-Verlag, 1951).

Edelstein, Emma J., and Ludwig Edelstein, eds., *Asclepius: A Collection and Interpretation of the Testimonies*, 2 vols. (Baltimore: Johns Hopkins University Press, 1945).

Elm, Susanna, "Perceptions of Jerusalem Pilgrimage as Reflected in Two Early Sources on Female Pilgrimage (3d and 4th centuries)," *SP* 20 (1989) 219–23.

Encyclopedia Judaica, "Commandments, the 613," 5:760–83; "Mikveh," 11:1534–44.

Epstein, I., ed., *The Babylonian Talmud, Seder Nashim, Yebamot I* (London: Soncino Press, 1936).

———, *The Babylonian Talmud: Seder Nezikin in Four Volumes,* vol. 4 (London: Soncino Press, 1936).

Erikson, Erik, *Young Man Luther: A Study in Psychoanalysis and History* (New York: Norton, 1958).

Evans, Ernest, ed., *Tertullian's Homily on Baptism* (London: SPCK, 1964).

Farwell, Lyndon I., *Betwixt and Between: The Anthropological Contributions of Mary Douglas and Victor Turner toward a Renewal of Roman Catholic Ritual* (Dissertation, Claremont College, 1976).

Feldman, Louis H., "The Omnipresence of the God-Fearers," *Biblical Archaeology Review* 12.5 (1986) 58–69.

———, ed., *Josephus: Jewish Antiquities VIII–XX* (Cambridge: Harvard University Press [Loeb 9], 1965).

Ferguson, Everett, "Baptistery," in *Encyclopedia of Early Christianity* (New York and London: Garland, 1990) 135–37.

Ferguson, John, *The Religions of the Roman Empire* (Ithaca: Cornell University Press [Aspects of Greek and Roman Life, ed. H. H. Scullard], 1970).

Ferrari, Leo, "Young Augustine: Both Catholic and Manichee," *Augustinian Studies* 26 (1995) 109–28.

Festugière, André-Jean, *Personal Religion Among the Greeks* (Berkeley: University of California Press, 1954).

Fideler, David R., ed., *A Pythagorean Sourcebook and Library: An Anthology of Ancient Writings Which Relate to Pythagoras and Pythagorean Philosophy* (Grand Rapids: Phanes Press, 1987).

Finn, Thomas M., "Baptismal Death and Resurrection: A Study in Fourth Century Eastern Baptismal Theology," *Worship* 43 (1969) 175–89.

———, *Early Christian Baptism and the Catechumenate: West and East Syria* (Collegeville: Liturgical Press [A Michael Glazier Book, The Message of the Fathers 5], 1992).

———, *Early Christian Baptism and the Catechumenate: Italy, North Africa, and Egypt* (Collegeville: Liturgical Press [A Michael Glazier Book, The Message of the Fathers 6], 1992).

———, "The God-fearers Reconsidered," *CBQ* 47 (1985) 75–84.

———, "It Happened One Saturday Night: Ritual and Conversion in Augustine's North Africa," *JAAR* 58 (1990) 589–616.

———, *The Liturgy of Baptism in the Baptismal Instructions of St. John Chrysostom* (Washington, D.C.: Catholic University of America Press [SCA 15], 1967).

———, "Ritual and Conversion: The Case of Augustine," in *Kainà kaì Palaiá: Festschrift in Honor of Thomas L. Halton*, ed. John Pettrucione (Washington, D.C.: Catholic University of America Press, forthcoming 1997).

———, "Ritual Process and the Survival of Early Christianity: A Study of the *Apostolic Tradition* of Hippolytus," *JRS* 3 (1989) 68–89.

———, "Sacraments," in Everett Ferguson et al., eds., *Encyclopedia of Early Christianity* (New York: Garland, 1990).

Fitzmyer, Joseph A., *The Dead Sea Scrolls: Major Publications and Tools for Study*, rev. ed. (Atlanta: Scholars Press, 1990).

———, *The Gospel According to Luke (I–IX): Introduction, Translation, and Notes* (Garden City, N.Y.: Doubleday [AB 28], 1981).

Foley, Helene P., ed., *The Homeric Hymn to Demeter: Translation, Commentary, and Interpretive Essays* (Princeton: Princeton University Press, 1993).

Fox, Robin Lane, *Pagans and Christians* (San Francisco: Harper & Row, 1988).

Freyne, Seán, *Galilee From Alexander the Great to Hadrian, 323 B.C.E.– 135 C.E.: A Study of Second Temple Judaism* (Wilmington: Michael Glazier; Notre Dame: University of Notre Dame Press, 1980).

Gager, John, *Kingdom and Community: The Social World of Early Christianity* (Englewood Cliffs: Prentice-Hall, 1975).

Gallagher, Eugene V., "Conversion and Salvation in the Apocryphal Acts of the Apostles," *The Second Century* 8.1 (1991) 13–29.

———, *Expectation and Experience: Explaining Religious Conversion* (Atlanta: Scholars Press [Ventures in Religion 2, ed. W. Scott Green], 1990).

Gaventa, Beverly R., *From Darkness to Light: Conversion in the New Testament* (Philadelphia: Fortress Press, 1986).

Gingras, George E., ed., *Egeria: Diary of a Pilgrimage* (New York: Paulist Press [ACW 38], 1970).

Goodenough, Erwin R., *Jewish Symbols in the Greco-Roman Period*, 13 vols. (New York: Pantheon Books [Bollingen Series 37], 1953–1968).

Goodman, Martin, *Mission and Conversion: Proselytizing in the Religious History of the Roman Empire* (Oxford: Clarendon Press, 1994).

———, "Proselytizing in Rabbinic Judaism," *JJS* 40 (1989) 176–85.

———, *The Ruling Class of Judaea: The Origins of the Jewish Revolt Against Rome, A.D. 66–70* (Cambridge: Cambridge University Press, 1987).

Gorman, Peter, *Pythagoras: A Life* (London: Routledge & Kegan Paul, 1979).

Grant, R. M., *Early Christianity and Society: Seven Studies* (New York: Harper & Row, 1977).

Grégoire, H., and M. A. Kugener, *Marc le Diacre: Vie de Porphyre* (Paris, 1930).

Griffiths, J. Gwyn, *Apuleius of Madauros: The Isis-Book (Metamorphoses, Book XI)* (Leiden: E. J. Brill, 1975).

Grimes, Ronald L., *Beginnings in Ritual Studies*, rev. ed. (Columbia: University of South Carolina Press, 1995).

———, "Ritual Studies," *ER* 12:422–25.

Grisbrooke, W. Jardine, *The Liturgical Portions of the Apostolic Constitutions* (Bramcote, Nottingham: Grove Books [GLS 61], 1990).

Hall, Stuart G., "Ministry, Worship, and Christian Life," in Ian Hazlett, ed., *Early Christianity: Origins and Evolution to A.D. 600* (Nashville: Abingdon Press, 1991).

———, "Stephen I of Rome and the Baptismal Controversy of 256," in Bernard Vogler, ed., *Miscellanea historiae ecclesiasticae VIII: Colloque de Strasbourg, septembre 1983, sur L'institution et les pouvoirs dans les églises de l'antiquité à nous jours* (Bruxelles: Éditions Nauwelaerts, 1987) 78–82.

Halton, Thomas, "Baptism as Illumination," *Irish Theological Quarterly* 32 (1965) 28–41.

Hanson, J. Arthur, ed. and trans., *Apuleius: Metamorphoses*, 2 vols. (Cambridge: Harvard University Press [Loeb], 1989).

Harkins, Paul, *St. John Chrysostom: Baptismal Instructions* (Westminster, Md: The Newman Press [ACW 51], 1963).

Harmless, William, *Augustine and the Catechumenate* (Collegeville: Liturgical Press [A Pueblo Book], 1995).

Hartman, Lars, "Baptism," *ABD* 1:583–94.

Havener, Ivan, *The Sayings of Jesus: With a Reconstruction of Q [by Athanasius Polag]* (Wilmington: Michael Glazier, 1987).

Heikkinen, J. W., "Notes on 'Epistrepho' and 'Metanoeo'," *Ecumenical Review* 19 (1967) 313–16.

Henry, Patrick, ed., *Schools of Thought in the Christian Tradition* (Philadelphia: Fortress Press, 1984).

Herford, R. Travers, ed., *Pirke Aboth, The Ethics of the Talmud: Sayings of the Fathers* (New York: Schocken Books, 1962).

Higham, T. F., and C. M. Bowra, *The Oxford Book of Greek Verse in Translation* (Oxford: Clarendon Press, 1938).

Hoffmann, R. Joseph, *Celsus on the True Doctrine* (New York: Oxford University Press, 1987).

Holladay, William L., *The Root "Shub" in the Old Testament* (Leiden: E. J. Brill, 1958).

Hollenbach, Paul W., "The Conversion of Jesus: From Baptizer to Healer, ANRW 25.1:197–98.

———, "John the Baptist," *ABD* 3:887–99.

———, "John the Baptizer," ANRW 19.1:851–75.

Holm, Jean, and John Bowker, eds., *Rites of Passage* (London: Pinter Publishers, 1994).

Holte, James Craig, *The Conversion Experience in America: A Sourcebook on Religious Conversion Autobiography* (New York: Greenwood Press, 1992).

Hopkins, Keith, *Death and Renewal* (Cambridge: Cambridge University Press, 1983).

Horsley, Richard A., and John S. Hanson, *Bandits, Prophets, and Messiahs: Popular Movements at the Time of Jesus* (San Francisco: HarperCollins, 1988).

Instituto Francisco Suarez, *La vetus latina hispana, El Salterio,* vol. V, sec. II (Madrid: Consejo superior de investigaciones cientificas, Instituto Francisco Suarez, 1962).

Institutum Patristicum "Augustinianum," *Ricerche su Ippolito* (Rome: Institutum Patristicum "Augustinianum" [*Studia Ephemeridis "Augustinianum"* 13], 1977.

International Commission on English in the Liturgy, *Documents of the Liturgy, 1963–1979: Conciliar, Papal, and Curial Texts* (Collegeville: Liturgical Press, 1979).

Isenberg, Wesley W., "The Gospel According to Philip," in *Nag Hammadi Codex II, 2–7*, vol. 1, ed. Bentley Layton (Leiden: E. J. Brill [Nag Hammadi Studies 20, ed. James M. Robinson], 1989) 142–215.

Jackson, Pamela, *The Holy Spirit in the Catecheses and Mystagogy of Cyril of Jerusalem, Ambrose, and John Chrysostom* (Dissertation, Yale University, 1987).

James, William, *Varieties of Religious Experience* (New York: Longmans, Green, 1902).

Jefford, Clayton N., ed., *The Didache in Context: Essays on Its Text, History, and Transmission* (Leiden and New York: E. J. Brill, 1995).

Johnson, Maxwell E., *Liturgy in Early Christian Egypt*, chap.1 (Bramcote, Nottingham: Grove Books [GLS], forthcoming) MS pp. 7–17.

———, "The Postchrismational Structure of *Apostolic Tradition* 21, The Witness of Ambrose of Milan, and a Tentative Hypothesis Regarding the Current Reform of Confirmation in the Roman Rite," *Worship* 70 (1996) 16–34.

———, *The Prayers of Sarapion of Thmuis* (Dissertation, University of Notre Dame, 1992).

———, "Reconciling Cyril and Egeria on the Catechetical Process in Fourth-Century Jerusalem," in Paul F. Bradshaw, ed., *Essays in Early Eastern Initiation* (Bramcote, Nottingham: Grove Books [GLS 56], 1988) 18–30.

Jones, A. H. M., *Cities of the Eastern Roman Provinces* (Oxford: Oxford University Press, 1937).

Jones, Cheslyn, Geoffrey Wainwright, Edward J. Yarnold, and Paul F. Bradshaw, eds., *The Study of the Liturgy*, rev. ed. (London: SPCK; New York: Oxford University Press, 1992).

Jones, F. Stanley, *An Ancient Jewish Christian Source on the History of Christianity: Pseudo-Clementine Recognitions 1.27–71* (Atlanta: Scholars Press, 1995).

———, "The Pseudo-Clementine *Recognitions*: A History of Research," *The Second Century* 2 (1982) 1–33.

Jungmann, J. A., *The Early Liturgy: To the Time of Gregory the Great*, trans. F. Brunner (South Bend: University of Notre Dame Press [Liturgical Studies 6], 1959).

Kelly, J. N. D., *Early Christian Creeds*, 3rd ed. (New York: David McKay Co., 1972).

Kerényi, Károly, *Asklepios: Archetypal Image of the Physician's Existence* (New York: Pantheon Books [Bollingen 65:3], 1959).

Kimelman, Reuven, "The *Shema* and Its Blessings: The Realization of God's Kingship," in *The Synagogue in Late Antiquity*, ed. Lee I. Levine

(Philadelphia: The American Schools of Oriental Research, 1987) 73–95.

King, Winston, "Religion," *ER* 12:282–92.

Klijn, A. F. J., *The Acts of Thomas: Introduction, Text, and Commentary* (Leiden: E. J. Brill [Supplements to the New Testament, ed. W. C. van Unnik, 5], 1962).

Kloppenberg, John S., *Q Parallels: Synopsis, Critical Notes, and Concordance* (Sonoma, CA: Polebridge Press, 1988).

Kraabel, A. T., "The Disappearance of the God-fearers," *Numen* 28 (1981) 113–26.

Kraemer, David, ed., *The Mind of the Talmud: An Intellectual History of the Bavli* (New York: Oxford University Press, 1990).

Krautheimer, Richard, *Three Capitals: Topography and Politics* (Berkeley: University of California Press, 1983).

Kretschmar, Georg, "Early Christian Liturgy in the Light of Contemporary Historical Research," *SL* 16 (1986/1987) 3–14.

Kugel, James L., "Two Introductions to Midrash," in David Kraemer, ed., *The Mind of the Talmud: An Intellectual History of the Bavli* (New York: Oxford University Press, 1990) 77–103.

———, and Rowan A. Greer, *Early Biblical Interpretation* (Philadelphia: Westminster Press [Library of Early Christianity, ed. Wayne A. Meeks], 1986).

Lampe, G. W. H., ed., *A Patristic Greek Lexicon,* vols. 1–5 (Oxford: Clarendon Press, 1961–1968).

Leaney, A. R. C., *The Rule of Qumran and Its Meaning: Introduction, Translation, and Commentary* (London: SCM Press, 1966).

Leon, Harry J., *The Jews of Ancient Rome* (Philadelphia: Jewish Publication Society of America, 1960).

Levine, Lee I., ed., *The Synagogue in Late Antiquity* (Philadelphia: The American Schools of Oriental Research, 1987).

Lipsius, Richard A., et al., eds., *Acta Apostolorum Apocrypha,* vol. 2, pt. 2 (Hildesheim: Georg Olms, 1959).

Livingston, James C., *The Anatomy of the Sacred: An Introduction to Religion,* 2nd ed. (New York: Macmillan, 1993).

Luck, Georg, *Arcana Mundi: Magic and the Occult in the Greek and Roman Worlds* (Baltimore: Johns Hopkins University Press, 1985).

MacMullen, Ramsay, "Conversion: A Historian's View," *The Second Century* 5 (1985/1986) 67–89.

———, *Paganism in the Roman Empire* (New Haven: Yale University Press, 1981).

Mara, Maria Grazia, "Ambrose of Milan, Ambrosiaster, and Nicetas," in A. Di

Berardino, ed., *Patrology,* vol. 4, trans. Placid Solari (Westminster: Christian Classics, 1986).

Maraval, Pierre, ed., *Égérie: Journal de voyage (Itinéraire) et Valerius du Bierzo: Lettre sur la B^se Égérie* (Paris: Les Éditions du Cerf [SC 296], 1982).

Marrou, Henri-Irénée, and Marguerite Harl, eds., *Clément d'Alexandrie: Le Pédagogue, Livre I* (Paris: Les Éditions du Cerf [SC 70], 1960).

Martin, Joseph, ed., *Cyprian: De lapsis* (Bonn: Peter Hanstein [FP 21], 1930).

Martin, Luther H., *Hellenistic Religions: An Introduction* (New York: Oxford University Press, 1987).

Mazza, Enrico, "Mystagogie: Pensée liturgique d'aujourd'hui et liturgie ancienne," in A. M. Triacca and A. Pistoia, eds., *Conférences Saint-Serge XXXIXe semaine d'études liturgiques* (Rome: Edizioni Liturgiche [Ephemerides Liturgicae Subsidia], 1993).

McDonald, James I. H., *Kerygma and Didache: The Articulation and Structure of the Earliest Christian Message* (Cambridge: Cambridge University Press, 1980).

McDonnell, Kilian, and George T. Montague, *Christian Initiation and Baptism in the Holy Spirit: Evidence from the First Eight Centuries,* 2nd ed. (Collegeville: Liturgical Press [A Michael Glazier Book], 1994).

McEleney, Neil J., "Conversion, Circumcision and the Law," *NTS* 20 (1974) 319–41.

McGehee, Michael David, "Hasmonean Dynasty," *ABD* 3:67–77.

McKnight, Scot, *A Light Among the Gentiles: Jewish Missionary Activity in the Second Temple Period* (Minneapolis: Fortress Press, 1991).

McLynn, Neil B., *Ambrose of Milan: Church and Court in a Christian Capital* (Berkeley: University of California Press, 1994).

Meier, John P., *A Marginal Jew: Rethinking the Historical Jesus,* vol. 2 (Garden City, N.Y.: Doubleday [Anchor Bible Research Library], 1994).

———, in John P. Meier and Raymond E. Brown, eds., *Antioch and Rome: New Testament Cradles of Catholic Christianity* (New York: Paulist Press, 1983).

Meyer, Marvin W., ed., *The Ancient Mysteries: A Sourcebook* (San Francisco: Harper & Row, 1987).

Meyerhoff, Barbara G., Linda A. Camino, and Edith Turner, "Rites of Passage: An Overview," *ER* 12:380–87.

Meyers, Eric M., "Synagogue," *ABD* 6:251–60.

Mingana, A., ed., *Commentary of Theodore of Mopsuestia on the Nicene Creed* (Cambridge: Woodbrooke Studies 5, 1932).

Mitchell, Leonel L., "Ambrosian Baptismal Rites," *SL* 1 (1962) 241–53.

———, "The Development of Catechesis in the Third and Fourth Centuries:

From Hippolytus to Augustine," in J. Westerhoff and O. C. Edwards, eds., *A Faithful Church: Issues in the History of Catechesis* (Wilton: Morehouse-Barlow, 1981) 49–78.

Mitchell, Nathan, "Baptism in the *Didache*," in Clayton N. Jefford, ed., *The Didache in Context: Essays on Its Text, History, and Transmission* (Leiden and New York: E. J. Brill, 1995) 226–55.

Mondésert, Claude, ed., *Clément d'Alexandrie: Le Protreptique: Introduction, Traduction, et Notes* (Paris: Les Éditions du Cerf [SC 2bis], 1949).

―――, and Marcel Caster, eds., *Clément d'Alexandrie: Les Stromates: Stromate I* (Paris: Les Éditions du Cerf [SC 30], 1951).

Moore, Carey A., *Judith: A New Translation with Introduction and Commentary* (Garden City, N.Y.: Doubleday [AB 40], 1964).

Morrison, Karl F., *Conversion and Text: The Cases of Augustine of Hippo, Herman-Judah, and Constantine Tsatsos* (Charlottesville: University of Virginia Press, 1992).

―――, *Understanding Conversion* (Charlottesville: University of Virginia Press, 1992).

Munier, Charles, ed., *Saint Justin: Apologie pour les Chrétiens* (Fribourg: Éditions Universitaires, 1995).

Murphy-O'Connor, Jerome, "Community, Rule of the (1QS)," *ABD* 1:110–12.

―――, "An Essene Missionary Document? CD II, 14–VI, 1," *Revue Biblique* 77 (1970) 201–29.

―――, "John the Baptist: History and Hypothesis," *NTS* 36 (1990) 359–74.

―――, "Qumran, Khirbet," *ABD* 5:590–94.

Murray, Robert, "The Characteristics of Early Syriac Christianity," in Nina Garsoian et al., eds., *East Byzantium: Syria and Armenia in the Formative Period* (Washington, D.C.: Dumbarton Oaks, 1982) 3–16.

―――, *Symbols of Church and Kingdom* (Cambridge: Cambridge University Press, 1975).

Musurillo, Herbert, ed., *The Acts of the Christian Martyrs* (Oxford: Clarendon Press, 1972).

Mylonas, George E., *Eleusis and the Eleusinian Mysteries* (Princeton: Princeton University Press, 1961).

Newsome, James D., *Greeks, Romans, Jews: Contents of Culture and Belief in the New Testament World* (Philadelphia: Trinity International Press, 1992).

Nickelsburg, W. E., and Michael E. Stone, eds., *Faith and Piety in Early Judaism: Texts and Documents* (Philadelphia: Fortress Press, 1983).

Nock, Arthur Darby, "Conversion and Adolescence," in *Essays on Religion in the Ancient World,* ed. Zeph Stewart, vol. 2 (Oxford: Clarendon Press, 1972) 469–80.

————, *Conversion: The Old and the New in Religion from Alexander the Great to Augustine of Hippo* (Oxford: Clarendon Press, 1933).

————, "The Development of Paganism in the Roman Empire," in *The Cambridge Ancient History,* ed. S. A. Cook et al., vol. 12 (Cambridge: Cambridge University Press, 1965) 409–49.

————, "Later Egyptian Piety," in *Essays on Religion in the Ancient World,* ed. Zeph Stewart, vol. 2 (Oxford: Clarendon Press, 1972) 566–74.

————, "A Vision of Mandulis Aion," *HTR* 27 (1934) 53–102.

Nolland, John, "Uncircumcised Proselytes?" *Journal for the Study of Judaism* 12 (1981) 173–94.

North, John, "Diviners and Divination at Rome," in Mary Beard and John North, eds., *Pagan Priests: Religion and Power in the Ancient World* (Ithaca: Cornell University Press, 1990) 51–71.

Novak, David, *The Image of the Non-Jew in Judaism: An Historical and Constructive Study of the Noahide Laws* (New York: E. Mellen, 1983).

O'Connell, Robert J., *St. Augustine's Confessions: The Odyssey of Soul* (Cambridge: Belknap Press, 1969).

O'Donnell, James J., ed., *Augustine: Confessions,* 3 vols. (Oxford: Clarendon Press, 1992).

O'Meara, Dominic J., *Pythagoras Revived: Philosophy and Mathematics in Late Antiquity* (Oxford: Clarendon Press, 1989).

O'Meara, John J., *The Young Augustine: The Growth of St. Augustine's Mind up to His Conversion* (London: Longmans, Green and Co., 1954).

Paredi, Angelo, *Saint Ambrose: His Life and His Times*, trans. M. Joseph Costelloe (South Bend: University of Notre Dame Press, 1964).

Parisot, J., ed., *Aphraatis Sapientis Persae, Patrologia Syriaca,* vols. 1–2 (Paris: Firmin-Didot et Socii, 1907).

Philo, *Questions and Answers on Exodus* II, in Ralph Marcus, ed., *Philo: Supplement* II (Cambridge: Harvard University Press [Loeb], 1953).

————, *Questions on Genesis* III, in Ralph Marcus, ed., *Philo: Supplement* I (Cambridge: Harvard University Press [Loeb], 1953).

Philonenko, Marc, ed., *Joseph et Asenath: Introduction, texte critique, traduction et notes* (Leiden: E. J. Brill, 1968).

Philostratus, *The Life of Apollonius of Tyana,* in F. C. Conybeare, ed., *The Life of Apollonius of Tyana,* vol. 2 (London: Heinemann [Loeb], 1921).

Piédagnel, August, *Cyrille de Jérusalem: Catéchèses mystagogiques* (Paris: Les Éditions du Cerf [SC 126], 1966).

Pokorný, Petr. "Christologie et baptême à l'époque du christianisme primitif," *NTS* 27 (1981) 368–80.

Poque, Suzanne, ed., *Augustin d'Hippone: Sermons pour la Pâque* (Paris: Les Éditions du Cerf [SC 116], 1966).

Porton, Gary G., *Goyim: Gentiles and Israelites in the Mishnah-Tosefta*

(Atlanta: Scholars Press [Brown Judaic Studies, ed. Jacob Neusner], 1988).

———, *The Stranger Within Your Gates: Converts and Conversion in Rabbinic Literature* (Chicago: University of Chicago Press [Chicago Studies in the History of Judaism, ed. William Scott Green], 1994).

———, "Talmud," *ABD* 6:310–15.

Prince, S., *Rituals of Power: The Roman Imperial Cult in Asia Minor* (New York: Cambridge University Press, 1984).

Quasten, Johannes, "Baptismal Creed and Baptismal Act in St. Ambrose's *De mysteriis* and *De sacramentis*," in *Mélanges Joseph de Ghellinck* (Gembloux: Éditions J. Duculot [Museum Lessianum Section Historique 13], 1951) 223–34.

———, "Theodore of Mopsuestia on Exorcism in the Cilicium," *HTR* 35 (1942) 209–19.

Rambo, Lewis, "Conversion," *ER* 4:75–78.

———, "Current Research on Religious Conversion," *RSR* 8 (1982) 146–59.

———, *Understanding Religious Conversion* (New Haven: Yale University Press, 1993).

Rappaport, Uriel, "Maccabean Revolt," *ABD* 4:433–39.

Riggs, John W., "The Sacred Food in *Didache* 9–10," in Clayton N. Jefford, ed., *The Didache in Context: Essays on Its Text, History, and Transmission* (Leiden and New York: E. J. Brill, 1995) 256–83.

Riley, Hugh J., *Christian Initiation: A Comparative Study of the Interpretation of the Baptismal Liturgy in the Mystagogical Writings of Cyril of Jerusalem, John Chrysostom, Theodore of Mopsuestia, and Ambrose of Milan* (Washington, D.C.: Catholic University of America Press [SCA 17], 1974).

Rist, J. M., *Stoic Philosophy* (Cambridge: Cambridge University Press, 1969).

Roetzel, Calvin, *The Letters of Paul: Conversations in Context*, 3rd ed. (Louisville: Westminster/John Knox, 1991).

Rose, H. J., *Handbook of Latin Literature* (London, 1936).

Rouse, W. H. D., ed. and trans., *Lucretius: De rerum natura* (New York: G. P. Putnam's Sons [Loeb], 1931).

Saldarini, Anthony J., "Pharisees," *ABD* 5:289–303.

———, *Pharisees, Scribes, and Sadducees in Palestinian Society: A Sociological Approach* (Wilmington: Michael Glazier, 1988).

Sarbin, Theodore R., and Nathan Adler, "Self-Reconstitution Processes: A Preliminary Report," *Psychoanalytic Review* 57 (1970) 599–616.

Schlam, Carl C., *The Metamorphoses of Apuleius: On Making an Ass of Oneself* (Chapel Hill: University of North Carolina Press, 1992).

Schwarz, E., *Über die pseudoapostolischen Kirchenordnungen* (Strasbourg, 1910).

Scott, Walter, ed., *Corpus Hermeticum: Ancient Greek and Latin Writings Which Contain Religious or Philosophic Teachings Ascribed to Hermes Trismegistus*, vol. 1 (1924; reprint London: Dawsons of Pall Mall, 1968).

Segal, Alan, *Paul the Convert: The Apostolate and Apostasy of Saul the Pharisee* (New Haven: Yale University Press, 1990).

Shanks, Hershel, *Judaism in Stone: The Archaeology of Ancient Synagogues* (New York: Harper & Row; Hagerstown, Md.: Biblical Archaeology Society, 1979).

Shepherd, Massey Hamilton, *The Paschal Mystery and the Apocalypse* (London: Lutterworth [Ecumenical Studies in Worship 6], 1960).

Shinn, Larry D., "Who Gets to Define Religion: The Conversion/ Brainwashing Controversy," *RSR* 19 (1993) 195–207.

Sivan, Hagith, "Holy Land Pilgrimage and Western Audiences: Reflections on Egeria and Her Circle," *Classical Quarterly* 38 (1988) 528–35.

———, "Who Was Egeria? Piety and Pilgrimage in the Age of Gratian," *HTR* 81 (1988) 59–72.

Skarsaune, Oskar, "The Conversion of Justin Martyr," *ST* 30 (1976).

Smith, John Clark, "Conversion in Origen," *Scottish Journal of Theology* 32 (1979) 217–40.

Sperry-White, Grant, *The Testamentum Domini* (Bramcote, Nottingham: Grove Books [GLS 66], 1991).

Starnes, Colin, *Augustine's Conversion: A Guide to the Argument of Confessions I–IX* (Waterloo: Wilfrid Laurier University Press, 1990).

Stauffer, S. Anita, *On Baptismal Fonts: Ancient and Modern* (Bramcote, Nottingham: Grove Books [Grove Renewal of Worship Studies 29–30], 1994).

Stern, Menahem, *Greek and Latin Authors on Jews and Judaism,* 2 vols. (Jerusalem: Israel Academy of Sciences and Humanities, 1976, 1980).

Stone, Michael E., *Scriptures, Sects and Visions: A Profile of Judaism from Ezra to the Jewish Revolts* (Philadelphia: Fortress Press, 1980).

———, ed., *Testament of Abraham* (Missoula: Society of Biblical Literature, 1972).

Story, Cullen I. K., "Justin's Apology I.62–64: Its Importance for the Author's Treatment of Christian Baptism," *VC* 16 (1962).

Tabor, James D., *Things Unutterable: Paul's Ascent to Paradise in Its Greco-Roman, Judaic, and Early Christian Contexts* (Lanham: University Press of America [Studies in Judaism, ed. Jacob Neusner], 1986).

Taft, Robert, "Penance in Contemporary Scholarship," *SL* 18 (1988) 2–21.

Talley, Thomas J., *The Origins of the Liturgical Year* (New York: Pueblo Books, 1986).

Taylor, Lily Ross, *The Divinity of the Roman Emperor* (1931; reprint Chico: Scholars Press, 1981).

Tcherikover, Avigdor (Victor), *Hellenistic Civilization and the Jews*, trans. S. Applebaum (Philadelphia: The Jewish Publication Society of America, 1966).

Telfer, William, ed., *Cyril of Jerusalem and Nemesius of Emesa* (Philadelphia: Westminster Press [Library of Christian Classics 4], 1955).

Thiering, B. E., "Inner and Outer Cleansing at Qumran as a Background to New Testament Baptism," *NTS* 26 (1979/1980) 266–77.

―――, "Qumran Initiation and New Testament Baptism," *NTS* 27 (1980/ 1981) 615–31.

Thomas, Jean, *Le mouvement baptiste en Palestine et Syrie 150 av. J.-C.– 300 ap. J.-C.* (Gembloux, J. Duculot [Dissertation, Louvain], 1965).

Tonneau, R., and R. Devreesse, eds., *Les homélies catéchétiques de Théodore de Mopsueste* (Vatican City: Biblioteca Apostolica Vaticana [Studi e Testi 145], 1949).

Turner, Victor, *The Anthropology of Performance* (New York: Performing Arts Journal Publications, 1986).

―――, *The Ritual Process: Structure and Antistructure* (Chicago: Aldine Press, 1969).

Ulansey, David, *The Origins of the Mithraic Mysteries: Cosmology and Salvation in the Ancient World* (New York: Oxford University Press, 1989).

U.S. Bishop's Conference, *The Rite of Christian Initiation of Adults: Approved for Use in the Dioceses of the United States of America by the National Conference of Catholic Bishops and Confirmed by the Apostolic See* (Washington, D.C.: United States Catholic Conference, 1988).

Van Gennep, Arnold, *The Rites of Passage*, trans. Monika B. Vizedom and Gabrielle L. Caffe (Chicago: University of Chicago Press, 1960).

Vatican, *Ordinis baptismi adultorum,* in *Acta Apostolicae Sedis* 64 (1972).

―――, *The Rite of Christian Initiation of Adults*, 2nd ed. (Vatican City: Vatican Polyglot Press, 1974).

Vellian, Jacob, ed., *Studies on Syrian Baptismal Rites* (Kottayam: C. M. S. Press [Syrian Church Series 6], 1973).

Vermaseren, M. J., *Mithras, The Secret God* (New York: Barnes and Noble, 1963).

Vermes, Geza, *The Dead Sea Scrolls in English*, 3rd. ed. (New York: Viking/Penguin, 1987).

―――, *The Dead Sea Scrolls: Qumran in Perspective* (Cleveland: Collins World, 1978).

Vööbus, Arthur, ed., *The "Didascalia Apostolorum" in Syriac,* 2 vols., (Louvain: Secrétariat du Corpus SCO [CSCO 401, 408], 1979).

Walker, P. W. L., "Eusebius, Cyril, and the Holy Places," *SP* 20 (1989) 306–14.

———, *Fourth Century Christian Attitudes to Jerusalem and the Holy Land: A Comparison of Eusebius of Caesarea and Cyril of Jerusalem* (Dissertation, Cambridge University, 1987).

Walpole, A. S., ed., *Early Latin Hymns* (Hildesheim: Georg Olms, 1966).

Wenger, Antoine, ed., *Jean Chrysostome: Huit catéchèses baptismales* (Paris: Les Éditions du Cerf [SC 50], 1957).

Wheeler, Orrin T., *Baptism According to St. Ambrose* (Dissertation, Woodstock, 1958).

White, L. Michael, "Adolf von Harnack and the 'Expansion' of Early Christianity: A Reappraisal of Social History," *The Second Century* 5.2 (1985/1986) 97–127.

———, *Building God's House in the Roman World: Architectural Adaptation among Pagans, Jews, and Christians* (Baltimore: Johns Hopkins University Press [American Schools of Oriental Research], 1990).

Wilken, Robert L., "Alexandria: A School for Training in Virtue," in Patrick Henry, ed., *Schools of Thought in the Christian Tradition* (Philadelphia: Fortress Press, 1984) 15–30.

———, "Collegia, Philosophical Schools, and Theology," in Stephen Benko and John J. O'Rourke, eds., *The Catacombs and the Colosseum: The Roman Empire as the Setting of Primitive Christianity* (Valley Forge: Judson Press, 1971).

———, *John Chrysostom and the Jews: Rhetoric and Reality in the Late Fourth Century* (Berkeley: University of California Press, 1983).

———, *The Land Called Holy* (New Haven: Yale University Press, 1992).

Wilkinson, John, *Egeria's Travels* (London: SPCK, 1971).

Williams, R. D., *The Aeneid of Virgil, Books 1–6* (New York: St. Martin's Press, 1972).

Willis, G. G., *A History of the Early Roman Liturgy: To the Death of Pope Gregory the Great* (London: The Henry Bradshaw Society, 1994).

Wilmart, A., ed., *Analecta Reginensia* (Vatican City: Biblioteca Apostolica Vaticana [Studi e Testi 59], 1933) 170–79.

Wilson, Monica, "Nyakyusa Ritual and Symbolism," *American Anthropologist* 56 (1954) 228–41.

Wink, Walter, *John the Baptist in the Gospel Tradition* (Cambridge: Cambridge University Press, 1968).

Witherup, Ronald D., *Conversion in the New Testament* (Collegeville: Liturgical Press [A Michael Glazier Book, Zacchaeus Studies: New Testament, ed. Mary Ann Getty], 1994).

Wolfson, Harry Austryn, *Philo: Foundations of Religious Philosophy in Judaism, Christianity, and Islam,* vol. 1 (Cambridge: Harvard University Press, 1948).

Wright, William, ed., *Apocryphal Acts of the Apostles* (London, 1871).

Yarnold, Edward J., *The Awe-Inspiring Rites of Initiation: The Origins of the R.C.I.A.,* 2nd ed. (Collegeville: Liturgical Press, 1994).

————, "Baptism and the Pagan Mysteries in the Fourth Century," *Heythrop Journal* 13 (1972) 247–67.

————, "The Baptism of Constantine," *SP* 26 (1993) 95–101.

————, "The Ceremonies of Initiation in the *De Sacramentis* and the *De Mysteriis* of S. Ambrose," *SP* 10 (1967) 453–63.

————, "Did St. Ambrose Know the *Mystagogic Catecheses* of St. Cyril of Jerusalem?" *SP* 12:1 (1975) 184–89.

SUBJECT INDEX